hotels • riads • villas • maison d'hôtes • kasbahs

moroccochic

For regular updates on our special offers, register at

www.thechiccollection.com

hotels • riads • villas • maison d'hôtes • kasbahs

moroccochic

text françoise kuijper-raymond • brandon lee

thechiccollection

executive editor
melisa teo

editor
laura dozier

assistant editor
josephine pang

french editor
henri julien

french translators
laurence delage • philippa richmond

designers
nelani jinadasa • joanna poh

production manager
sin kam cheong

publishing consultant
isabelle du plessix

editions didier millet pte ltd
121 telok ayer street, #03-01
singapore 068590
telephone : +65.6324 9260
facsimile : +65.6324 9261
enquiries : edm@edmbooks.com.sg
website : www.edmbooks.com
           www.thechiccollection.com

first published 2005 • reprinted 2006
second edition 2009
©2005, 2009 editions didier millet pte ltd

Printed in Singapore.

isbn: 978-981-4217-36-1

COVER CAPTIONS:

1: The pool at Les Jardins de la Koutoubia.

2: Food is an important part of any holiday, and Moroccan cuisine will not disappoint.

3: Djemaa el-Fna Square in Marrakech.

4: The Monoliths of M'Soura on the edge of the Middle Atlas Mountains.

5: Mint tea is served everywhere in Morocco.

6: Medersa Ben Youssef in Marrakech is beautifully decorated, as befits an honoured institute of learning.

7: Babouches make good gifts.

8: The sitting area of one of Les Jardins de la Medina's guestrooms.

9: Oualidia is known for its fresh oysters.

10: A poolside pavilion is a great place to have a chat over light refreshments.

11: Tourism and the film-making industry has caused great change in Ouarzazate.

12: Figs are a common snack.

13: The ornately decorated doors of the Royal Palace in Fez.

14: The walls of Marrakech surround the city, protecting its inhabitants.

15: Jnane Tamsna Country Guesthouse is one of the many luxury accommodations available in the Palmeraie.

16: Henna can be used to create elaborate patterns on the skin.

17: Many riads and hotels feature fountains to help cool the surrounding area.

18: The Portuguese cisterns in El Jadida are still functional today.

19: One of the rooms in Dar Les Cigognes.

20: Hammams are an integral part of Moroccan life.

21: Moroccan hospitality is renowned.

THIS PAGE: Spectacular effects of the play of light and shadow in a beach cave in Legzira.

OPPOSITE: The seagulls' ballet above Essaouira.

PAGE 2: The Ksar Aït Benhaddou, UNESCO World Heritage Site, near Ouarzazate.

PAGE 6: The minaret of Marrakech's beautiful Koutoubia Mosque at sunset.

PAGE 8 AND 9: This is no mirage, more of a miracle in the middle of the desert, where the all too rare sight of water provides a welcome halt for caravans.

contents

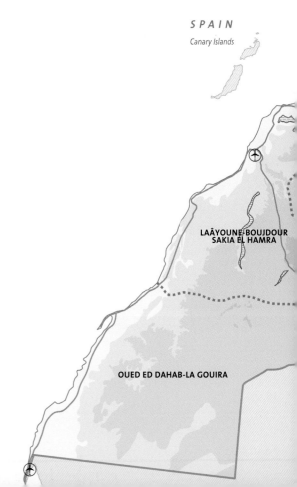

North Atlantic
Ocean

SPAIN

Canary Islands

**LAÂYOUNE-BOUJDOUR
SAKIA EL HAMRA**

OUED ED DAHAB-LA GOUIRA

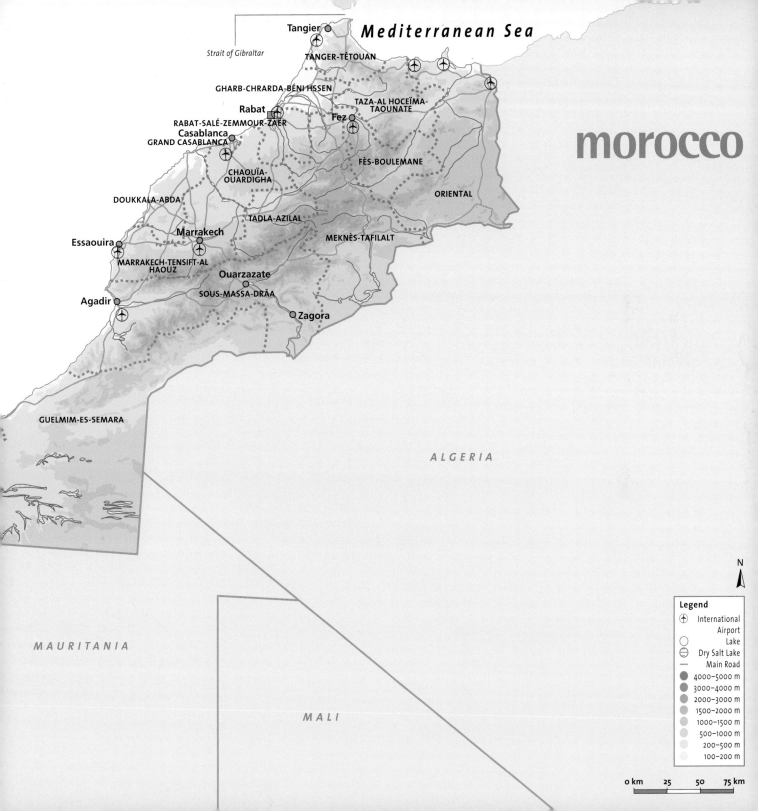

Mediterranean Sea

Strait of Gibraltar

Tangier

TANGER-TÉTOUAN

GHARB-CHRARDA-BÉNI HSSEN

TAZA-AL HOCEÏMA-
TAOUNATE

Rabat

RABAT-SALÉ-ZEMMOUR-ZAER

Fez

Casablanca

GRAND CASABLANCA

FÈS-BOULEMANE

CHAOUÏA-
OUARDIGHA

DOUKKALA-ABDA

ORIENTAL

TADLA-AZILAL

Marrakech

Essaouira

MEKNÈS-TAFILALT

MARRAKECH-TENSIFT-AL
HAOUZ

Ouarzazate

Agadir

SOUS-MASSA-DRÂA

Zagora

GUELMIM-ES-SEMARA

ALGERIA

morocco

MAURITANIA

MALI

N

Legend

⊕ International
   Airport
○ Lake
⊖ Dry Salt Lake
— Main Road
● 4000–5000 m
● 3000–4000 m
● 2000–3000 m
● 1500–2000 m
● 1000–1500 m
● 500–1000 m
● 200–500 m
● 100–200 m

0 km   25   50   75 km

introduction

a thousand years of history

Some say Morocco's history dates back to the 11th century BCE, when the Phoenicians first landed on the Atlantic coast of North Africa, somewhere around present-day Tangier. Palaeontologists push this date back to 200,000 BCE, however, thanks to the remains of human fossils found at Sidi Abderrahman near Casablanca and the skeletons of the cousins of Homo sapiens discovered in the cave at Ouled Bouchikha (formerly used by smugglers) near Rabat.

During prehistoric times, the Berbers were the country's first inhabitants. Nomadic tribes of Semitic, Indo-European and Negroid stock soon crossed each other's paths and intermingled, sharing a common language and customs. Two main groups emerged in two different regions: the Riffians in the north and the Chleuhs in the south. They subsequently became fierce defenders of their lands and cultures, which neither the Phoenicians nor the Carthaginians succeeded in conquering and subjugating. Throughout the Roman occupation—Morocco was annexed in 42 CE—the Riffian mountain tribes maintained constant pressure on the invaders. Then the Arabs arrived in the 7th century, and 'Allah's horsemen' occupied the entire territory, settling down to stay. In the name of the Prophet, they hurried to convert the pagan Berber-tongued population to Islam, while wisely granting certain freedoms.

Until the 8th century, Morocco's history was a succession of Arab and Berber dynasties, alternating periods of greatness and decadence. After that period, a unified Moroccan state started to take shape with the reigns of the Abbasids, then the Idrissids, the dynasty founded by Moulay Idriss. His son, Idriss II, made Fez the new capital, from where he controlled the country's civil and religious interests. However, in-fighting brought down his successors and their dynasty.

The Almoravids (1055–1144), a tribe of formidable veiled warriors cum religious ascetics from the Western Sahara, then proceeded to seize power in the Souss region. They forcibly took possession of the trade route towns and, in 1062, founded their new capital, Marrakech. Led by Youssef ben Tachfine, the Almoravids subdued Fez and gradually conquered the entire country, building an empire that reached all the way into neighbouring Algeria, before crossing the Strait of Gibraltar and invading Andalusian Spain as well, from Seville to Cordoba.

They were succeeded by the Almohad dynasty (1147–1269), who ruled over a vast kingdom which included not only Morocco, but the whole of North Africa, from Algeria through Tunisia right up to Tripoli in Libya. This was the golden age of North Africa, then master of the Mediterranean. However, despite being well organised, the empire was so large that it became almost impossible to govern. The defeat of Al Uqab by Spanish Christians in 1212 completely overthrew the dynasty, leading to the subsequent loss of Andalusia in 1230. North Africa gradually fragmented and the Almohad reign came to an end in 1269.

THIS PAGE: *Under a dramatic evening sky, the ruins of the colonnaded basilica and forum at Volubilis are an inspiring sight.*

OPPOSITE: *Heading south from El Gezira along the Atlantic coast, you pass spectacular ochre cliffs eaten away by the wind and the sea.*

The Merenids, another nomadic tribe from the south, took possession of Fez, then Meknès and finally Marrakech in 1269. In 1374, the Merenid kingdom split into two, the kingdom of Fez and that of Marrakech. For half a century, Morocco underwent several divisions and reunifications, and was aggressed by the Portuguese, the Spaniards and Genoese on the one hand, and the Hafsids and their allies on the other. The Portuguese took possession of the town of Ceuta in 1415, followed by Tangier in 1471. The Catholics finally retook Granada in 1492.

At the beginning of the 16th century, the Saadians, descendants of the Prophet, had the mettle to boot the foreigners out of Morocco. They liberated the coastal towns from their Portuguese overlords and repulsed the Ottomans from the west of the country, allowing it to thrive, thanks to its well-developed agriculture, and display its importance through the construction of magnificent monuments that still exist today, such as the Saadian Tombs and El-Badi Palace in Marrakech. After the death of the illustrious ruler Ahmad el-Mansour, the country was divided between the various local powers.

The rise of the Alaouites (1666 onwards), natives of southern Morocco and also descendants of the Prophet, marked a turning point in the country's history. They looked to the courts of Europe, developed trade and took an active interest in the development of early manufacturing processes. Moulay Ismail, contemporary of Louis XIV, was one of the most remarkable sultans of the Alaouite dynasty. He took control of all the towns along the Saharan axis and continued into Mauritania. From his sumptuous palace in Meknès, he consolidated his power and created an army to wage war against the Turks.

In the 19th century, the French, the English and the Spaniards moved into Morocco, wishing to extend their colonies. The Act of Algeciras, in April 1906, placed the country under international protection. This appropriation provoked popular revolts in the north, leading to France's occupation of Meknès, Fez and Rabat. In 1912, Moulay Hafid signed the Protectorate Treaty, which placed most of Morocco under the protection of the French, with the Rif region under the Spaniards and Tangier and its immediate vicinity under international control. This treaty gave rise to violent riots, as a result of which France nominated Maréchal Lyautey to be Resident-General in Rabat. Having quelled the rebellious tribes, Lyautey set about instituting a new administration. However, the nationalist conflict was by no means over. The war of the Rif, led by Abd el-Krim, was particularly bitter and violent, and raged from 1921 through to 1926, when his Berber warriors were finally defeated by combined Spanish and French forces.

In 1930, the country's intellectuals and elite founded the first Moroccan political party. After the Second World War, the ranks of the nationalists swelled, demanding independence from the colonial powers, and their efforts were encouraged by Sultan Mohammed V. Following the

Sultan's enforced exile, positions became even more entrenched, and France was eventually forced to release him. Morocco's independence was finally proclaimed by the French on 3 March 1956, and by the Spanish on 7 April 1956. The last bastion of colonial rule, Tangier was restored to Morocco in 1958.

After the death of Mohammed V in 1961, his son, Hassan II, took power. Hassan's determination to win back the Western Sahara reinforced national unity, and in November 1975, he organised the 'Green March' with the full backing of his people. After his death, in 1999, his son, Mohammed VI became the 18th king of the Alaouite dynasty. The young king immediately set about the task of tackling the numerous social problems which were undermining the nation, and undertook much-needed social reforms. He surrounded himself with a new generation of advisors, determined to create a firm and transparent regime and win the respect of his citizens in order to transform Morocco into a modern kingdom. From the moment of his accession, Mohammed VI clearly stated his desire to look out for the welfare of the poor, and took a close interest in the largely forsaken Rif region, the issues of illiteracy and education, and the status of women. He also immediately permitted the return from exile of his opponent Abraham Serfaty.

a land of contrasts

Morocco is a vast country, measuring 711,000 sq km (274,519 sq mile) in total, including the Western Sahara which constitutes about a third of its area. From north to south, just about every type of landscape and a variety of climates can be found.

the rif region

The Rif Mountains follow the Mediterranean coast in a 250-km (155-mile) crescent from Tangier to the Algerian border, crossing endlessly varied terrain and culminating in Jbel Tidighine, which stands at 2,450 m (8,038 ft). Sheer cliffs plunge into the sea, and perilous coast roads negotiate jagged coves. Its southern slopes descend gradually to the Sebou Basin, giving way to crops and herds of animals. All around the region are olive trees, lentisks (mastic trees), junipers, heather and hemp. The Caves of Hercules, on Cap Spartel, where the Atlantic Ocean meets the Mediterranean Sea, is a must-see place for spectacular views.

THIS PAGE: A mosaic of blues and ochres, the beautiful town of Chefchaouen lies nestled between two mountains, the crenelated tower of its kasbah looking out over the medina.

OPPOSITE (FROM TOP): The Saadian Tombs are one of the most visited sights in the kasbah district of Marrakech. These three mausoleums back onto the El-Mansour Mosque, their rich architecture illustrating the power of the Saadians; Berber peasants from the Rif region still dress in traditional costume, with a fouta, a square of red and white striped cotton, tied about the waist and a large straw hat decorated with multi-coloured woollen pompons.

the atlas mountains

The Middle Atlas, a transitory climatic and geographical region at the very heart of Morocco, has some of the most staggering natural sites: vast plains, limestone plateaus, springs and numerous waterfalls—it is the country's water reserve, thanks to its former volcanic activity—as well as beautiful forests of cedar, oak and maritime pines. The eastern reaches are wilder and steeper, with peaks of over 3,000 m (9,843 ft) leaning into the beginnings of the High Atlas. Don't miss the Ouzoud Falls, majestic and magical waterfalls crashing down an ochre-coloured cliff-face, one of the most picture-worthy spots in all of Morocco.

The High Atlas Mountains run for 800 km (497 miles), from the Atlantic Ocean to the eastern plateau—an impressive barrier separating the green valleys to the north from their semi-desert counterparts to the south. At 4,167 m (13,671 ft), Jbel Toubkal is one of Africa's highest mountain peaks and is permanently covered in snow. The Dadès and Draâ Valleys, in particular, are beautiful areas worth a visit.

THIS PAGE: Nature is at its grandest in the High Atlas, where the snow-capped mountains alternate with green valleys, terraced hillsides and almond groves.

OPPOSITE: In the Middle Atlas, the Ouzoud Falls, 110 m (361 ft) high, is, without a doubt, one of the most beautiful natural sites in all of Morocco.

Situated to the north of the Saharan platform, the Anti Atlas Mountains stretch from the mouth of the Draâ River, on the Atlantic coast, to Tafilalt in the east, separated from the High Atlas Mountains by a wide rift punctuated by oases, before eventually reaching the Sahara. One of the sights in this region definitely worth seeing is Tafiater—literally 'the place which drains water'—set in a barrier of pink granite.

Just south of Boumalne du Dadès, Jbel Sagho, which is an extension of the Anti Atlas Mountains, signals an abrupt, dramatic change, marking a transition in terrain, the point where mountain becomes desert. The ragged gorges and steep-sided faults fall away into scree which, in turn, breaks down into marl and desert expanses.

people

Morocco's population is estimated to be around 30 million, with more than half under 20 years of age. Traditionally, over 90 per cent of its society was rural, but in recent years, there has been a mass exodus to the towns, with between 400,000 and 500,000 people every year swelling the overcrowded suburbs of the main cities.

The Berbers make up two-thirds of the country's population and have largely maintained their culture, their way of life and their language. The Protectorate tried in vain to divide the Arabs and the Berbers. Concentrated in the Rif region and the High Atlas Mountains, this hierarchical tribal society has managed to retain a sense of family, honour and hospitality, favouring the group over the individual.

from nomad to settler

A multitude of historic events and economic reasons have pushed the nomadic peoples up into the mountains, forcing them to settle on the high plateau. The 'real' nomads, the Blue Men, are now found only in the pre-Saharan south and also in the eastern steppes around Figuig. They either pitch their tents (kaïma) near water sources, or they stay perched on the grassy steppes where they can easily feed their camel herds.

The semi-nomads of the Middle Atlas—the Beni Mguild and Sanhadja Berber tribes—now mostly live a typical transhumant existence, moving with the seasons, transitioning from the low pastures to the mountain pastures before returning to their homes where they store their harvest in the agadir, the communal granary.

The highland people, the Chleuhs, were given plots of cultivatable land and have therefore, for the most part, settled down, as have the inhabitants of the Rif Mountains, living in flat-roofed daub houses or mud ksar (fortified villages).

from trade to tourism

Phosphate has become the 'white gold' of Morocco, now the principal exporter worldwide, with three-quarters of the world's reserve. Top quality citrus fruits and a large variety of vegetables are exported to Europe from the south of Agadir. Fish is plentiful but, in the face of fierce competition from Spain, Portugal and France, Morocco has taken the precaution of fixing fishing quotas and insisting that all foreign catches are handled in Moroccan ports. The textile and leather industries, in particular, are thriving, their output almost entirely exported to the European Union with its seemingly endless demand for quality products at low prices. An abundant supply of labour coupled with low salaries continues to encourage industrialists and foreign investors to establish clothes workshops in Morocco or at least subcontract their production to the Moroccans.

Tourism, however, remains one of the major economic sectors. It is encouraged through a number of measures which favour air transport, communications facilities, hotel capacities and the diversification of already numerous forms of accommodation and activities. In order to do away with the hassle inflicted upon tourists, the souks—particularly that of Marrakech—have been drastically regulated, with, notably, the prohibition of unofficial guides, who acted as intermediaries for the tradesmen. On the main axes across the country, the motorways have been improved and expanded, and driving regulations are increasingly implemented. A major project is under consideration to link Morocco and Spain across the Strait of Gibraltar, either by tunnel or bridge. Either way, it would be a magnificent and historic link between Europe and Africa.

ecology + tourism

'Clean and responsible tourism that takes account of man, nature, the environment and the rules and laws of the region. A responsible approach to tourism supported by public-spirited tourist ventures.' This extract from the message by His Majesty King Mohammed VI at the Assises Internationales de Tourisme (2007) reveals Morocco's commitment to supporting both growth in tourism and environmentally-friendly practices. While tourism is essential to the economy, Morocco has committed to protecting the environment and the country's water resources, to sustainable development, to reducing waste and pollution and to improving the quality of the air and the conservation of the ocean and the coastline. These are just a small selection of the significant remits of the Mohammed VI Foundation for the Environment, created in 2001 during the presidency of Her Royal Highness Princess Lalla Hasnaa. Both the Cleaning Up the Beaches Operation and the Clé Vert Programme, which maintains high standards for tourist accommodation, also fall under its auspices.

vision 2010, increased + diversified tourist facilities

The Azur Plan, which aims to develop tourist facilities, is in the process of creating six new-generation seaside resorts in six priority zones along the Mediterranean and Atlantic coastlines, from Saïdia in the north to Tan-Tan in the south. Specifications relating to the development take into account the environmental impact, overseeing the protection of specific flora and fauna. Developers must abide by strict rules concerning the protection of the environment and the use of water. Golf courses, for example, must be equipped with their own water purification and recycling stations.

The Mada'in Plan, on the other hand, is dedicated to developing and modernising the Kingdom's large towns and cities, aiming to boost the cultural roles of Fez, Casablanca, Agadir, Tangier, Tétouan, Meknès, Rabat and Ouarzazate-Zagora.

Another promising idea, The Land of Welcome for Tourism (Le Pays d'Accueil Touristique) is a new concept in green tourism that also helps to promote rural tourism. The group organises trips into the rural areas, providing accommodation to match travellers' needs, including self-catering, with many itineraries off the beaten track, which will help bring tourists into contact with the local people and allow them to experience the local lifestyles first-hand. Check out some of their latest offerings at www.tourismerural.ma.

Morocco's forgotten regions have recently revealed an ecological niche, that of using natural resources for original sporting and cultural activities such as gliding and snow sports in Dakhla, surfing in Safi and exploring the desert with the desert train that now links Oujda to Bouarf. These activities cleverly combine economy and ecology, a practice on the rise in Morocco.

THIS PAGE: An important export, oranges and citrus fruits of all kinds are also piled high in markets throughout Morocco.

OPPOSITE: Fishing is a significant industry in the country, so make sure to sample some of the fresh-off-the-boat seafood while travelling through Morocco's coastal regions.

the art of building

In addition to the treasures of the natural environment, Morocco has a rich architectural heritage that demands respect and efforts of conservation. The ancient sites of Volubilis and Lixus provide evidence of villas and housing structures dating from antiquity, of almost unbelievable sophistication and luxury. Along the coast, fierce-looking fortified cities date from the Portuguese era. Behind thick walls transpierced by high gateways, the medinas within were built according to elaborate plans. Each dynasty chose its own capital and hurried to build great monuments destined for posterity: mosques and minarets, medersas (Islamic schools), tombs and palaces. The architecture, even when monumental, remained restrained. Hispano-Moorish influence was behind the architectural masterpieces of Fez, Rabat, Marrakech and Meknès. The simplicity of the exteriors contrasts with the sumptuousness of the interiors: walls, floors, ceilings—everything an excuse for abundant decoration with geometric and floral motifs. The riad (individual house) takes its inspiration from this decorative art, albeit in a simplified form.

On the other hand, the simple rural dwellings found in the douars (villages) are principally designed for the practical necessities of protection from sun and rain, and storing the harvest. They are built with whatever material is at hand: daub, wood, branches and thatch. The nomads' huts high up in the mountains are constructed from branches reinforced with dried mud, with the occasional variant, such as those in the Tafraoute region, where the houses are dry-stone cubes covered with ochre or mauve-coloured plaster with whitewashed openings. In the ksar (fortified villages), the houses huddle together, with a communal granary and sometimes an oven and oil press. They are built with clayish earth, straw and gravel, often strengthened with unfired bricks covered in ochre or pinkish-beige cob. The finest examples of this type of building are found in the Draâ and Dadès Valleys—large seigneurial dwellings, veritable fortresses, immensely strong yet fragile. In the Rif, the houses, built of adobe (sun-dried bricks) covered with earth and a layer of lime, are separated by cultivated plots of land and agdals (orchards).

to the rhythm of the muezzin

Islam, the official state religion as proclaimed in the country's constitution, affects every aspect of a Moroccan's life. Five times daily, the muezzin calls the faithful to prayer from high in his minaret, proclaiming, 'Allah Akbar' ('God is great'), in the language of the Koran. Friday is the consecrated day of rest for the Muslims, a day of solemn prayer with readings from the Koran led by the imam (guide). 'Insh'Allah' ('if God wills it') is the pious formula used in all circumstances. In Morocco, the worship of saints is commonplace, as are pilgrimages to a marabout (burial place of a wise man) in order to seek favours, healing or fertility.

THIS PAGE: Rich decoration often adorns Moroccan architecture, such as this intricately-wrought palace door in Fez.

OPPOSITE: Kasbah Amerdihl in the Dadès Valley makes spectacular use of the traditional form of mud architecture, which is found throughout Morocco.

Each dynasty chose its own capital and hurried to build great monuments destined for posterity...

made in morocco

'Beldi' means many things but most importantly it represents the best in traditional Moroccan craftsmanship, and it is omnipresent in a number of unique goods which make perfect souvenirs: carpets, furniture made from thuya wood, precious fabrics, pottery, copper lanterns, babouches (slippers) and Berber jewellery.

tangier

Morocco's antique shops are real Ali Baba caverns. **Majid**'s shop (66 Rue les Almouhads) is no different, a reliable address where everyone in Tangier goes to find precious or unusual objects for furnishing their riads. He has a fabulous choice of carpets as well as a superb collection of old jewellery.

Two other recommended shops are the **Galerie Tindouf** and the **Bazar Tindouf** (72 Rue de la Liberté), owned by two brothers, a stone's throw from each other, opposite the El Minzah Hotel. The Bazar is the perfect place to scour for a treasure, watched all the while by the beady eye of Soussi; the Galerie, on the other hand, is altogether larger, more of a place for displaying fine pieces that have already been through an initial selection, which naturally makes this shop more pricey.

As for Tangier's most famous perfumers, **Parfumerie Madini** (14 Rue Sébou and 5 Boulevard Pasteur): it is a rite of passage. The Madini dynasty has been distilling essential oils and concocting exquisite aromas since the dawn of time, adored by the likes of Barbara Hutton and Elisabeth Taylor, and its perfumes continue to work their magic today.

fez

Fez's craftsmen are numerous and talented. It is the undisputed capital of these ancient skills, the place where they have been kept alive and allowed to evolve with the times, and a visit to the **Nejjarine Museum of Wood and Carpentry** (Place Nejjarine) is a must. You'll learn all about wood and its associated crafts, both past and present. Also, the tourist office has flagged a circuit around town to help you discover the full range of Fassi craftsmanship.

Finding some of the best treasures sometimes requires a bit of wandering. Side streets up and down **Talaâ Kbira**, the town's main thoroughfare, lead through to small squares filled with the stalls of shoe-makers, wood-turners and basket makers. Cobblers and tanners are grouped around a courtyard in the **Kaât Smen Fondouk**. In the **Aïn Allou Souk** there are 60 or so shops entirely given over to working leather.

The **Henna Souk** in Ghassoul concentrates on beauty treatments, black soap, rosewater and the like. In the **Attarine Souk**, grocery shops vie for space with souvenir boutiques, while **Derb Touil** is reserved for the weaving industry.

Somewhat easier to find are a number of recommended addresses in the new town and on the edge of the medina. **Le Trésor Berbère** (66 Bis, Zqaq Lahjar, Talaâ Sghira), housed in a former medersa, is piled high with jewellery, objects and furniture from all around the world. There's a lot to sift through, but you're bound to find the unique treasure that you're looking for eventually.

Carpets are also piled high at the **Palais de Fès** (15 Mokhfia, R'cif), where Azzedine can immediately lay his hands on those dyed with saffron or roses and woven by women in the High Atlas Mountains, or those from Rabat, Chichaoua or Tazenakht.

Also, don't miss the **Centre Artisanal de Fès** (31 Avenue Alla ben Abdellah, Ville Nouvelle), workshops grouped around gardens where you can watch the craftspeople at work.

Another well-known address is **Maison de Broderie** (2 Bis, Derb Blida), where the famous Fez embroidery work continues to be stitched meticulously by hand.

The metalworkers are mainly found in one area of the **Seffarine medina** (as are the laceworkers) where they skilfully chase and pierce copper into graceful lanterns.

If you would like your own dinner service, complete with monogram or personalised design, **La Cocema** (Aïn Kadous) is the place to visit; it provides beautiful porcelain with original designs for all of Morocco's grand households.

Four kilometres (2.5 miles) out of town on the road to Taza lies **Aïn Noqbi**, the potters' and ceramists' district, with the most incredible range of pottery in all styles.

rabat + the coast

In Essaouira, the medina is highly organised, perfect for calmly dedicating oneself to shopping without worrying about getting lost, and one spot not to be missed is within an 18th-century riad, once an important trading post. **Galerie la Kasbah** (4 Rue de Tétouan, Essaouira),

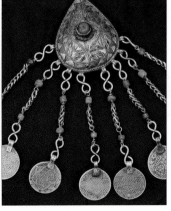

THIS PAGE (FROM TOP): Berber women weave the much-admired rugs in southern Morocco by hand; beaded brooches and heavy necklaces are the traditional finery of the Berber people.
OPPOSITE: A visit to the bustling bazaars in the Marrakech medina, packed with treasures such as colourful lanterns, is a must.

has magnificent carved wooden doors, ceramics and all manner of precious objects from another age, which await you in the various rooms opening out onto a central courtyard where you are invited to take time to sip mint tea, to choose and, who knows, even to buy.

In his narrow shop named **Galerie Aïda** (2 Rue de la Skala, Essaouira), Joseph successfully combines the roles of bookseller and antiquarian. Up front he has an excellent selection of books and works on Morocco, while further back you find unusual objects, antiques and jewellery displayed in glass cabinets—a collector's haven.

Near the wall of the skala (fortress), the **Galerie Jama** (22 Rue Ibnou Rochd, Essaouira) is no ordinary boutique—it's full of old textiles, carpets, caftans, jewellery, priceless pottery and real antiques.

Omar Samat's yellow-fronted shop, **Tazra** (45 Rue Attarine, Essaouira), sells a great selection of ethnic and Berber jewellery, as well as his one-off, highly original designs.

Unusual Berber jewellery can also be found in the middle of the souk at Hassan Haissoune's **Bijouterie Ethnique** (5 El Konouse, Essaouira), a booth quite different from those of the traditional jewellers there.

From the jewellers souk to the fish market, it is but a pace, and this is the home to the weaving workshop **Elahri** (181 Souk el Gouz, Essaouira). The loom stands proudly in the middle of the room, surrounded by an extensive choice of haïks (the large white veils worn by the women of Essaouira), striped sabra (a Moroccan

silk made from aloe plants) in sharp colours—the latest trend—and beautiful thin, woolen bedcovers of the highest quality.

It is difficult to know where to begin with all the different workshops working thuya wood, Essaouira's speciality. **Coopérative Artisanale des Marqueteurs** (6 Rue Khalid ben Oualid, Essaouira), based near the port in a narrow lane, represents a selection of true craftsmen, all totally dedicated to their profession.

In the same vein, **Le Bois de Thuya** (Centre Artisanal d'Essaouira, 118 Rue Sidi Med ben Abdellah) sells well-made thuya-wood furniture, together with smaller objects and boxes, created by craftsmen in situ.

Amentet (Rue el Khabbazine, Essaouira) is a jewellery workshop inspired by Berber and Tuareg designs. The stylised pendants with silver motifs applied to thuya wood—part of its latest collection—are especially popular.

The **Mega Mall** (Km 4, 2 Avenue Imam Malik, Route des Zaërs, Souissi, Rabat) is something of a pleasant surprise. It's here that all the embassy and foreign delegation staff flock to shop, for every luxury brand name can be found, along with beldi from Morocco and the Middle East.

In the mall, a few shops should not be missed. **Al Naffis** has a wide choice of exquisite brocaded fabrics, silks and chiffons fit for princesses, while **IB**'s exotic, heady Oriental perfumes sold in elegant bottles are every woman's dream! **Mounir's** sells beautiful table linen which can be embroidered to order. Their black linen tablecloths embroidered with red dahlias are superb. **Chama**, next door, specialises in traditional caftans.

marrakech

The choice is overwhelming in Marrakech's medina. If the piled-high stalls in the souk start to get you down, why not enjoy a little chic minimalism? In **Brigitte Perkins' Fondouk** (Medina, near Djemaa el-Fna Square; call for an appointment), she creates the most remarkable textiles and linen in conjunction with women-embroiderers from the village of Tamesloht.

Another good address is the antiquarian **Mustapha Blaoui**'s warehouse (142 Rue de Bab Doukkala, Medina) who receives his clients and friends with the utmost courtesy, as if in a salon. People come here from the world over to find that rare piece. For those who fail to find exactly what they are looking for, he will happily continue the search elsewhere and have it forwarded.

In the Guéliz district, new shops are gradually replacing the old ones that specialised in traditional ware. There are, however, some old retailers still in business, including **Amazonite** (94 Boulevard el Mansour Eddahbi, Guéliz), owned by the Idrissi family. You can have absolute faith in what you are buying in their shop—a series of rooms piled high with carpets, antiquities, old jewellery and more.

Ben Rahal (28 Rue de la Liberté, Avenue Mohammed V, Guéliz) specialises in carpets and is a reputable address where you may well find the silk kilim (traditional Moroccan carpet) of your dreams.

THIS PAGE (CLOCKWISE FROM TOP LEFT): Kilims blend in well with western décor; ornate perfume bottles and precious fragrances are available at the well-known Parfumerie Madini; Majid in Tangier offers a fine selection of jewellery.

OPPOSITE (FROM TOP): The Galerie Tindouf sells traditional pottery; interior designers are crazy about zellij tile work.

dining

tangier

To appreciate the atmosphere and hospitality of a Moroccan home, try **Dar Nour** (20 Rue Gourna, Kasbah). The quince tajines and date tarts are divine, and in summer, grilled dishes are served outdoors on the terraces.

Saveurs de Poissons (Rue du Portugal) is a good find. Inside, hidden from the outside world but well-known to regulars, in a small room with just a few tables, is a local, inexpensive eatery.

At **Darna, la Maison Communautaire des Femmes** (Place du Grand Socco) you lunch on the patio and can enjoy a fixed menu at a reasonable price. It's good, and your money helps finance this women's collective which also includes a hammam, shop and library.

Having lunch at the restaurant of the **Hôtel Club le Mirage** (BP 2198, Les Grottes d'Hercule) on its terrace facing the sea is a must. The site itself, on Cap Spartel, is magnificent. The menu has seafood, with sea bream cooked in a salt crust as its speciality, and typical dishes such as briouats (minced-meat pastries) and keftas (minced-meat kebabs).

Pastries are everywhere in Morocco. **Pâtisserie La Espagñola** (97 Rue de la Liberté), beside the El Minzah Hotel, is an institution, and **La Giralda** (5 Boulevard Pasteur, Ville Nouvelle), a boudoir-like setting with a bay view, bustles at tea time.

fez

In a palace straight out of an updated version of *One Thousand and One Nights*, dinner in the restaurant of the **Riad Fes** (Derb Ben

Slimane, Zerbtana) is a moment of pure delight. If you cannot stay here, dinner is the perfect opportunity for discovering an elegant Fassi home. A traditional menu is served: little vegetable hors d'oeuvres, preserved tomatoes, pigeon pastilla and a meltingly succulent rack of lamb, not forgetting the lighter-than-light sweet milk pastillas.

The cuisine of Dada Abbadi is the pride of **La Maison Bleue** (2 Place de L'Istiqlal, Batha). This large riad is the perfect place to sample those like-my-grandmother-used-to-make-them dishes. The mouth-watering quail pastilla, the Safi-style chicken tajine and the Andalusian-style couscous (a recipe dating back to the 13th century) with couscous grains or vermicelli garnished with icing sugar, cinnamon and almonds are all little bites of history.

Le Kiotori (12 Rue Ahmed Chaouki), in front of the hotel Jnane Palace, is possibly the best Japanese restaurant in Morocco. In a very Zen setting, an astonishing array of sushi, sashimi, maki, prawn tempura and traditional kushiyaki (skewered grilled food) are served with green tea.

Near the Jnan Sbil Garden, behind a row of century-old palm trees, lies **Mezzanine** (17 Kasbat Chams, Ville Nouvelle), where, from 11 in the morning until midnight, you can sample a variety of Moroccan-style tapas accompanied by wines sold by the glass.

rabat + the coast
In a resolutely Moroccan setting with covered benches, poufs and alcoves, Ménad Berkani, chef at the Sofitel

Essaouira Medina Beach & Spa's **Aïlen** (Avenue Mohammed V, Essaouira), conjures up Moroccan cuisine that is both homey and elaborate. Nothing but local produce for his tajines and couscous, which are served by the plate with wines from Mogador and Val d'Argan.

Meanwhile, fish is king at **Le Patio** (28 Bis, Rue Moulay Rachid, Essaouira), where Marie and Antoine have created a delightfully romantic setting with deep red walls, candles and small intimate dining spaces draped with curtains, perfect for you to regale in their exquisite talent for fresh fish dishes.

Dining at **L'Elézir** (1 Rue d'Agadir, Essaouira) is like stepping back into the sixties. Orange perspex lamps, glass chandeliers, a fluorescent radio, Knoll-style tables and armchairs—everything in this Italian restaurant is a collector's item. It is a whimsical setting for sampling delectable ravioli and homemade gnocchi.

If one could recommend only one place in Agadir, it would undoubtedly be **La Scala** (Rue de l'Oued Souss, Complexe Tamlelt, Agadir), well-known to gourmets. Its specialities include lobster, sea bream cooked in a salt crust or wild sea bass grilled with herbs from the Atlas Mountains, full of flavour and freshness. At night, in a candlelit setting, La Scala is totally magical.

Sheltered within a large garden filled with datura plants and orange trees, the restaurant of **Villa Mandarine** (19 Rue Ouled Bousbaa, Souissi, Rabat) is the smart place to be seen dining, alongside Rabat's ministers, diplomats and foodies.

THIS PAGE (FROM TOP): Amanjena, located just outside Marrakech's city centre, has dreamlike settings for its dining establishments, The Thai Restaurant and The Restaurant (pictured); Oualidia is famous for its oysters.
OPPOSITE: The inviting atmosphere of the lounge bar at Le Comptoir Paris Marrakech is one of the trendiest places for having dinner and drinks.

Poached foie gras with ceps, pan-fried soupions with tagliatelle, griddled John Dory—Wolfgang Grobauer's menu has won over the palettes of even the most demanding of the capital's gourmets.

Rabat also has its own brasserie in the middle of town. **Le Grand Comptoir** (279 Boulevard Mohammed V, Rabat)—and the owners, the Lecharpentier family, even call themselves 'grand comptoiristes'—is an elegant establishment restored to its original 1920s glory. The creative menu includes choucroute, herring with potatoes, foie gras, Dakhla oysters and superbly fresh fish. Open seven days a week, it is particularly busy in the evening, with guest musicians and singers providing a lively, jazzy atmosphere.

If Morocco had Michelin stars, **La Maison du Gourmet** (159 Rue Taha Houcine, Gauthier, Casablanca) would most certainly qualify. While the cuisine is essentially French, it has many subtle Moroccan flavours and ingredients. The confit de canard and foie gras pastillas (filo pastry pies with fillings) are simply perfect. The harira (a traditional soup), is sublime. The zaalouk (grilled aubergine mashed with tomatoes, coriander leaves and garlic) and taktouka (sautéed grilled peppers and tomatoes) ravioli are both amazing.

Sens (27th floor, Kenzi Tower Hotel, Twin Center, Boulevard Zerktouni, Casablanca), Casablanca's new in-place, is well worth checking out, if you can get in. You dine in alcoves facing vast bay windows looking out onto the grand mosque and a 360° view of the city. Here, the Pourcel brothers, Jacques and Laurent, have created a menu which combines flavours from all around the Mediterranean region.

To capture the taste of the ocean, stop in at **Ostréa II** (Parc à Huîtres N°007, Oualidia) for some famous Oualidia oysters as well as for some crab, spider crab or other seasonal shellfish, no sooner delivered than devoured.

marrakech

Le Restaurant Gastronomique of Es Saadi Gardens & Resort (Rue Ibrahim el Mazini, Hivernage), untouched by passing trends, remains the best in Marrakech. With consistency, care and attention to quality, Chef Arnaud Boissier has maintained a faithful clientele to whom he offers an extensive menu. It includes ravioli and rock fish, foie gras briouates with caramelised apples, fish tajine and other fine things.

Also in the resort, on the top floor of the Palace, in a large white room adorned with stuccowork and stone tracery, **La Cour des Lions** (Rue Ibrahim el Mazini, Hivernage) is Marrakech's top Franco-Moroccan gourmet establishment. The cuisine is both creative and traditional, each dish subtly combining French know-how and Moroccan culture. Thus the zaalouk is accompanied by prawns or a lentil salsa, while iced watermelon is served with caramelised marrow and pan-fried foie gras.

Marrakech has a special magic, and the gardens of **Dar Rhizlane** (Rue Jnane el Harti, Hivernage) form part of this enchantment. At night, the orange trees and candles placed around the garden are reflected a thousand times in the still waters of the ornamental pond. Zakia, the chef, has composed a 'tasting menu' full of local flavours, with small Moroccan starters, a chicken or lamb tajine and a dessert, a light, delicious beldi.

Le Comptoir Paris Marrakech (Avenue Ecchouada, Hivernage) is a lively spot for dinner, served outdoors or in the opulently decorated lounge bar, which is a great spot for after-dinner drinks and entertainment.

Ever since Christine opened her exquisite little restaurant, **Le Tobsil** (22 Derb Moulay Abdallah ben Hessaien, R'mila, Bab Ksour, Medina), housed in a riad, it has been full. Her secret is quality, welcome, and Moroccan cuisine that has remained consistently flavoursome and delicate, served in a friendly atmosphere with live music.

Hôtel & Ryads Naoura Barrière Marrakech (Rue Djebel Alakhdar, Bab Doukkala), on the other hand, has Le Fouquet in the middle of the medina! The famous Champs-Elysées restaurant has brought its know-how to Marrakech, adding a very French touch to the dining scene.

Grand Café de la Poste (Angle de Avenue Mohammed V, Boulevard el Mansour, Guéliz) is the place to sit and admire passersby. Open until midnight, everybody calls in here for a drink at some point or other. Housed in a superbly restored building constructed during the Protectorate, it has been converted into a stylish, neo-colonial brasserie.

Your nose will soon lead you to **Adamo** (44 Bis, Rue Tarik idn Ziad, Guéliz), where the smell of warm bread, pastries and other delicacies baking in the oven waft throughout the entire Guéliz district.

In the palatial **Ksar Char-Bagh** (BP 2449, La Palmeraie) the dining room is all refinement and elegance. Each dish is a mélange of herbs and vegetables fresh from the garden. The scallop carpaccio is served with beetroot and apples, the tomato pastilla with a coriander carrot sorbet, the caramel-coated turbot with broad beans.

Dar Inès (Les Jardins d'Inès, BP 1488, Circuit de la Palmeraie) is in a cool pavilion beside a pool. Its chef, Jean Marie Gueraishe, creates his menu from the day's market: light dishes with a Mediterranean touch.

Arriving at the hotel Amanjena, in its sublime setting, is all part of the experience of eating at **The Thai Restaurant** (Km 12, Route de Ouarzazate). You are led with great ceremony along alleyways lit with lanterns leading to vast ponds. All three chefs are straight from Bangkok, as are all the ingredients essential to their cuisine.

Crystal Lounge (Boulevard Mohammed VI, Quartier de l'Agdal) within the vast Pacha Marrakech complex, faces the pool. The setting is very lively, and the food aromatic, inspired by classic Italian cuisine. Whether you choose the delicately-flavoured arborio risotto or the thinly sliced octopus, everything is perfect.

Don't wait too long to discover **Le Touggana** (Km 9, Route de l'Ourika). It has a fine and varied menu of carpaccios, tartares, pasta, meat and fish, all prepared with the best Moroccan ingredients.

THIS PAGE (FROM TOP): Make sure to try a few Moroccan classics, such as a heavenly vegetable tajine; Villa Mandarine's patio, lush with greenery, is an ideal environment for enjoying gourmet cuisine.
OPPOSITE: Savour Mediterranean fare at the elegant poolside pavilion of Marrakech's Dar Inès.

nightlife

Moroccan nights are as beautiful as its days, full of lively, hip venues, exclusive hotel bars, night clubs, famous DJs and cafés.

tangier

Les Fils du Détroit (Place de la Kasbah) is a minute café, an authentic, intimate place, a Mecca of Arabo-Andalusian and Gnaoui music. Around 5 pm and until late into the night, people gather here, religiously listening to the sounds of the gambri (lute) and derbouga (drum), sipping tea all the while.

Le Relais Lounge (Complexe Dawliz, 42 Rue de Hollande) is the bar of Relais de Paris. In its cool theatre-like interior, the lounge has extremely popular Latino evenings with mojito cocktails and DJs.

The 1950s décor of **Café du Cinema Rif** (Place du 9 Avril, Grand Socco) is the meeting place for the town's film-lovers. A wireless Internet area is available to guests.

On a perch overhanging the cliffs, **Café Hafa** (La Falaise) has existed since 1921. Every literary figure and hippy visting Tangier has passed through here, sipping mint tea whilst admiring the sunset, the Strait of Gibraltar and the Andalusian coast just opposite. Sadly this magic has been somewhat tarnished by the construction of a two-lane bypass below, right along the seafront.

Caid's Piano Bar in Hotel El Minzah (85 Rue de la Liberté) is not what it once was, but it's still a popular haunt for night owls nostalgic for the glamorous past, and for the hotel's famous parties, which were once all the rage.

Tangerin's (1 Rue Magellan) is a small nightclub with a bar, a piano in the corner and techno music.

Morocco Palace (Rue du Prince Moulay Abdallah) is a fun, kitschly-decorated Moroccan venue with a dance floor on which a belly dancer, accompanied by music, performs her hip-wriggling magic.

555 (Boulevard Mohammed VI) is located right on the beach and is the young in-crowd's favourite discotheque. Have a drink by the pool, while facing the sea, and then party late into the night.

fez

Café Clock (7 Derb el Magana, Talaâ Kbira) lies hidden in a narrow lane within the medina. It is a literary café run by Mike Richardson, an Australian—a place where you settle down in the library or out on the terrace with a coffee or a snack. Friendly and lively, it's a location that's bound to attract artists.

rabat + coast

It's one mad crush to get into **So** (Hotel Sofitel Agadir, Baie des Palmiers, Commune de Bensergao, Agadir), where it's full-on fun all weekend long. There's the vast dance area with laser beams, giant screens and live music; the gentle lights and tasty cocktails in the Nice Bar; and the decidedly classy atmosphere paired with champagne in So Zen.

Le Bistrot du Pietri (4 Rue Tobrouk, Rabat), ensconced in Le Pietri Urban Hotel, has an elegant vibe and is full of music. The owner, Driss, welcomes jazz musicians and any new talent passing by.

Situated in the Hotel Hyatt Regency, Casablanca (Place des Nations Unies, Casablanca) which, at lunchtime, is the reserve of businessmen, **Café M** transforms itself at night into the trendy dining place for the urban chic. After dinner, you don't even need to quit the building, just glide into **SixPM** where the town's young mingle with tourists to the DJ's chill lounge compilation, the rhythms gradually accelerating as the evening progresses and the crowd swells.

THIS PAGE (FROM TOP): Cocktails in Morocco benefit from an abundance of fresh fruit; Murano Resort, one of the most recent of Marrakech's fashionable nightspots, in the Palmeraie.

OPPOSITE: Set in Es Saadi Gardens & Resort, the colourful Le ThéâtrO lives up to its name, making it a good spot for people watching.

nightlife

THIS PAGE *(FROM TOP): Le Blokk, another totally extravagant new venue, for wild evenings à la Blues Brothers; Saturday night fever full tilt: flashing lights, blaring disco music and a packed dance floor.*
OPPOSITE: *The sumptuous courtyards of riads, such as this lovely alcove in the Riad Fes, can create the stylish sanctuary that practically begs for you to stop, relax and have a drink.*

marrakech

An in-place frequented by the rich and young, **Le ThéâtrO** (Es Saadi Gardens & Resort, Rue Ibrahim el Mazini, Hivernage) resembles a small theatre clad in red and velvet, with artists and DJs up on stage and the youthful audience dancing below to techno and house music.

Le Comptoir Paris Marrakech (Avenue Ecchouada, Hivernage) remains an institution, with in-house entertainment, dinner and live music. Marcel Chiche's venue is the place to go to be seen having a good time among showbiz figures.

Couleur Pourpre (7 Rue Ibn Zeidoune, Guéliz) is a tapas bar where the house cocktails are seved in transparent shakers to the accompaniment of a different band every night, except Sunday, which is reserved for karaoke!

Marrakech badly needed a place where you could go and sit quietly at any time of day. A year ago, Sandra had the excellent idea of opening just such a place, **Café du Livre** (44 Rue Tarik Ibn Ziad, Guéliz)—a spot where you can enjoy light refreshment, salads or sandwiches or drinks, whilst browsing lazily through the newspapers and magazines.

Le Palace (Palmeraie Golf Palace, Circuit de la Palmeraie) is a club with in-house entertainment run by Fabrice Altefrohne. Every Friday night, diners are treated to an air-borne spectacle of graceful acrobats on trapezes of billowing fabric, followed by an Oriental scene with dancers.

Dar Soukkar (Km 3, 8 Route de l'Ourika), formerly a sugar factory, has been transformed into a magical, festive place with ponds, palm trees, alleyways, terraces and a profusion of lanterns spread throughout the 2-hectare (5-acre) site. Venetian chandeliers, Orientalist paintings, deep sofas and Buddhas form the bizarre universe where Jean-Pierre, the master of ceremonies, endlessly transforms the evening's ambience. The restaurant, Les Jardins de l'Orientale, offers Thai, Italian and Moroccan food.

Murano Resort (BP 13172, Douar Abbiad, La Palmeraie) is another very Parisian hotel, with the same offbeat style as its Parisian big brother of the same name. Its special evenings and Sunday brunches are all the rage.

Le Blokk (Route de Casablanca, Circuit de la Palmeraie), a recently-opened 1970s Surrealist-looking nightclub owned by Jamal, is pure David Lynch in Marrakech. People flock here to listen to Moroccan singers in suits performing pre-1960s songs in Blues Brothers' fashion.

Pacha Marrakech (Boulevard Mohammed VI, Quartier de l'Agdal) is the place to be seen, the trendy heart of Marrakech nightlife, and the continent's largest night club cum discotheque, volume guaranteed. The music, compiled by top DJs from around the world, draws hip clubbers from afar—as many as 2,000 can hang out in this kasbah-like venue.

The rendezvous point of the trendy young things from here and elsewhere, **Bô-Zin** (3, 5 Route de l'Ourika, Douar Lahna) is a place for drinking, eating and dancing until early in the morning, with a chauffeur at your disposition, should you so wish.

hammam + spa

The beauty ritual, an ancient Oriental art centred around hammams and baths, is a tradition in North Africa. Spas, on the other hand, are a popular novelty imported from the West. Every hotel, riad and resort is keen to include a spa as part of their luxury facilities while retaining their hammams and traditional products, such as black soap, rosewater and argan oil—a happy compromise between East and West.

tangier

Serenity Day Spa (Rue Adolpho Fessere, California) is an institute entirely dedicated to women's beauty, well-being and serenity— 3,000 sq m (32,292 sq ft) of the latest technology spread over four floors: bodybuilding rooms, a jacuzzi, an ozone pool, and an Oriental hammam which utilises a chromotherapy technique that caters to fitness buffs. The establishment also offers a selection of massages such as Amazonian hot chocolate massages and balneotherapy with mineral salts and essential oils.

The renowned El Minzah Hotel hosts the **El Minzah Wellness Health Club** (85 Rue de la Liberté), where every treatment for the body and mind is available, along with specialist advice from personal trainers. In striking contrast with the elegant 1930s architecture of the hotel, the spa is housed in a building constructed in local style, which is more in keeping with the tastes of today's clientele.

Bedecked with Chefchaouen carpets and old paintings, the **Hotel Rif & Spa Tangier** (152 Avenue Mohammed VI) has an intimate atmosphere, perched on the rooftop. Guests can enjoy a splendid view over the Bay of Tangier while exercising, relaxing in the hammam or indulging in a massage.

fez

Luxuriously restored and modernised, **SPA** (Bab Guissa), housed in Sofitel Palais Jamaï, brings to the table treatments that are almost rituals, conducted in an Oriental setting with star-studded ceilings, water gently gurgling in ornamental ponds, and sweet scents all around.

The spa in **Riad Maison Bleue** (33 Derb el Mitter, Talaâ Kbira) is on the terrace and is absolutely divine. From the relaxation room one can look out on the Borj Skala (fortress) and the surrounding hills. It is a haven of privacy for giving oneself over to relaxing, indulging in a cinnamon or sesame-seed massage or a private hammam session, with a little toning-up in between.

rabat + the coast

The spa at **L'Heure Bleue Palais & Spa** (2 Rue Ibn Battouta, Bab Marrakech, Essaouira) is based on the notion of ethnic chic, with a mix of holistic and traditional beauty treatments on its spa menu. Black soap, argan and nigella sativa oil, flower petals and clay are some of the components in the products used. After a vigorous therapy session, a quick dip in the rooftop pool right outside the spa's doorstep is pure heaven.

The spa at the **Sofitel Essaouira Medina Beach & Spa** (Avenue Mohammed V, Essaouira), is located beside the ocean, and draws upon all the beneficial properties of the sea. It's an ultra-modern institute which offers a whole programme of treatments for fitness, self-revitalisation and rediscovering your serenity. The treatments often utilise local products, such as argan oil.

The small **Hammam Lalla Mira** (14 Rue d'Algérie, Essaouira) is the first of its kind to be heated by solar panels and make use of recycled water. The hotel that houses it is Morocco's first eco-establishment.

To purchase some of Morocco's precious argan oil, **Coopérative Tamounte** (Village d'Imi'Tlit, Route d'Adagir, Essaouira) or **Coopérative Tiguemine** (Km 15, Route de Marrakech, Essaouira) are the places to visit. Run by women, they hand down the recipe for making argan oil from mother to daughter.

Cinq Mondes (18 Rue Ibrahim Ennakhai, Maârif, Casablanca) provides a plethora of original and exclusive treatments, such as Japanese aroma and flower baths, spice scrubs and Taoist face treatments, among others.

marrakech

Es Saadi Gardens & Resort (Rue Ibrahim el Mazini, Hivernage) has one of the most impressive spas in Morocco. It boasts 3,000 sq m (32,292 sq ft) of space surrounded by a park and has its own indoor pool. The director, Caroline Bouchet Boulhal, has hand-picked the spa's menu of activities, and techniques from both East and West make an appearance: pilates, the latest Power Plate, music therapy, yoga and qigong are all

available. The programme is constantly evolving but the excellent quality remains unchanged.

At Palmeraie Golf Palace, **Palmeraie Spa** (BP 1488, Circuit de la Palmeraie) occupies a vast 4,000 sq m (43,056 sq ft) and an American specialist, Susan Stein, is always on hand for advice. There are 16 massage rooms and even a few suites with private hammams and personalised care programmes offering Oriental-style techniques combined with American efficiency.

U Spa (Rue Djebel Alakhdar, Bab Doukkala), Hôtel & Ryads Naoura Barrière Marrakech's gem of a spa, has eight separate areas for dispensing beauty treatments, two hammams and even an aquatic circuit! Its various treatments are based on essential oils and locally-made natural products.

Sens de Marrakech's (18 Zone Industriel Sidi Ghanem) range of beauty products is as beautiful as it is pleasing, with distinctive bottles and decorative braids containing oils, Barbary fig cream, desert sand scrub and southern spice exfoliants. After years of research, Fèrouz Jalal has created a totally natural line of products made from brown seaweed and essential oils that can be used for both the face and body.

La Roseraie Health Centre (Km 60, Route de Taroudant, Val d'Ouirgane Valley) is nestled in the midst of roses, wild flowers and lemon trees. With such an idyllic setting on offer, everyone should accept the invitation to relax and indulge in a treatment with products based on oils and wild herbs.

THIS PAGE (CLOCKWISE FROM TOP LEFT): Try reserving a hammam for a private session—the ultimate way to relax; precious argan oil with added floral essence, used for body massages; spas in Morocco are worlds of softly-lit well-being, and many establishments use natural products made in-house.
OPPOSITE: Splendour and opulence are calling cards of Morocco's best spas.

golf

With 17 golf courses and over 200 holes, and many more planned for 2012, Morocco is a golf kingdom. In these oases of green, the backdrop varies from the snow-capped Atlas Mountains to the ramparts of imperial cities, the blue line of the ocean or the lush vegetation of cedar forests. Playing golf in Morocco has become a way of living, combining nature and culture with sport.

tangier

The first club in Morocco, **Royal Club de Tanger** (Route de Boubana), was inaugurated by Sultan Moulay Abdelaziz in 1917—an 18-hole course in the middle of a forest of pine, cypress and eucalyptus trees. Modernised by the British architects Cotton and Pennink, it retains its British charm. The fifth green calls for an obligatory pause for a stunning view of Tangier.

    Royal Golf de Cabo Negro (BP 696 G, Tétouan) is an 18-hole course nestled against the foothills of the Rif Mountains. A wild and rather rustic course, it follows the line of the dunes amid bushes, agave plants and mimosa trees.

fez

With fairways among the olive groves, **Royal Golf de Fès** (Km 17, Route d'Imouzzer) is an 18-hole course from the hand of the master, Cabell B Robinson, in the midst of a vast olive grove 700 m (2,297 ft) above sea level. The fairways follow the natural layout of the site, undulating and rather steep, which makes it suitable for players with quite a high level of play; the very long hole 11, with a pond, is particularly difficult.

    Royal Golf de Meknès (J'nane al Bahraouia, Ville Ancienne, Meknès), a nine-hole course, is enclosed within lush gardens at the heart of the city. A flat course, impeccably maintained both on and off the fairway, it is totally magical when floodlit at night. It's the perfect place to enjoy a little history while playing a round.

rabat + the coast

Back in 1951, Mr Wilson, an eccentric Scottish golfer, dug a single hole in the middle of some wasteland. In the 1960s, Colonel Major Kamili created a nine-hole golf course on the same site. Now, playing at **Royal Golf d'Agadir** (Km 12, Route d'Aït Melloul, Agadir) beneath the permanently blue sky, accompanied by the fragrance of eucalyptus mixed with the salty sea breeze, is a most enjoyable, rather British and very fortifying experience.

Three courses in one, **Club Méditerranée Dunes Golf Course** (Chemin Oued Souss, Agadir) has three loops and 27 holes, offering something for golfers of all levels. Hole seven and eight have fantastic views over the Wadi Souss and the site of Inezgane, respectively.

Dazzled by the lushness of the vegetation along the Atlantic coast, Muela and Courbin conceived **Golf du Soleil** (Chemin des Dunes, Agadir) as a Garden of Eden. The entire circuit is very long—two nine-hole courses and an 18-hole one—and varied, winding its way between the many large trees, lakes, water hazards and the rolling lines of the dunes.

One of the most elegant, prestigious clubs in Morocco, **Royal Golf Dar Es Salam** (Km 9, Avenue Imam Malik, Souissi, Rabat) has 45 holes, created in 1971 by Robert Trent Jones. Flanked by eucalyptus and mimosa trees, papyrus plants and Roman columns, its undulating greens are greatly appreciated by professionals; it is home to the Hassan II Trophy every year.

A fine course for good golfers, **Royal Golf d'Afna**, (Hippodrome d'Anfa, Casablanca) is a nine-hole course within the racecourse complex. This very chic golf club, on the edge of the city, has a restaurant, pool, sauna and clubhouse, which has a magnificent view across the gardens towards the minaret of the Hassan II Mosque.

Royal Golf d'El Jadida (Km 7, Route de Casablanca, El Jadida), an 18-hole course that opened in 1993, is a varied circuit full of surprises. The course winds between a forest of eucalyptus, pine and acacia and runs alongside the beach for the last three holes. Watch out for crosswinds.

marrakech

Palmeraie Golf Club (Les Jardins de la Palmeraie, Circuit de la Palmeraie), an 18-hole course, was designed in 1992 by Robert Trent Jones who appears to have relished creating as many challenges for would-be golfers as possible. Facing the Atlas Mountains, this is an exceptional course, with water hazards and palms trees, narrow greens and large bunkers.

Royal Golf Club de Marrakech (Ancienne Route de Ouarzazate), created in the 1920s for the Pacha of Marrakech by Arnaud Massy, still feels remarkably modern. It was one of King Hassan II's favourite golf courses. An old-style course, it has a bevy of gardeners who maintain the fairways and greens with the care of an English nanny. The nine holes, designed by architects Gerry Watine and Thierry Sprecher, are in keeping with the style of this most royal of clubs, while making use of modern construction techniques.

Royal Golf d'Amelkis (Km 12, Route de Ouarzazate) was named after the queen of a Berber tribe from the Atlas region. This highly technical 18-hole course was inaugurated in 1995. After negotiating the undulations, small reddish hills and seven lakes, further pitfalls await you; hole 15 is particularly difficult.

THIS PAGE (FROM TOP): Playing golf amid sand dunes is an extraordinary experience on offer in the south of the country where sand takes the place of perfectly mown grass; the impeccably maintained greens in Marrakech's Palmeraie are the perfect terrain for golf lovers.

OPPOSITE (FROM TOP): Agadir's Golf du Soliel is a paradise for those who like to catch up on a little sunbathing while playing a round; with the snow-capped peaks of the Atlas as a backdrop, the Palmeraie Golf Club, designed by Trent Jones, is one of the most beautiful and prestigious clubs in Morocco.

boutiques + galleries

Morocco has style; it is a hive of creativity. From Tangier to Fez to Essaouira to Marrakech, boutiques, workshops and galleries are busy creating and copying the latest trends, forging a path between tradition and modernity.

tangier

El Tapisero (61 Boulevard Yacoub el Mansour, Charf) has been the reference for contemporary carpets since the 1970s, and so it remains today. Whether plain or with geometric patterns, the carpets are woven and hand-knotted by women using an ancient technique, which gives them a special quality.

A new cultural centre, the **Galerie Dar D'Art** (6 Rue Khalil Matrane) is dedicated to contemporary and Orientalist paintings, presenting the work of up-and-coming, talented artists.

The **Galerie Mohammed Drissi** (52 Rue d'Angleterre) is another contemporary art gallery which holds thematic exhibitions of the work of new Moroccan and foreign painters and photographers.

The bookshop **Librairie des Colonnes** (54 Boulevard Pasteur, Ville Nouvelle) remains a mythical place, one that was run for decades by Rachel Mouyal. Readings were held here with Paul Morand, Jean Genet and Samuel Beckett.

Cinema Rif (Place du 9 Avril, Grand Socco) has been revived as a venue for independent films. Drawing inspiration from the Tangier of the 1950s very, the building contains two projection rooms, an editing room, a library and a café.

fez

Orientalist Art Gallery (35 Rue Abdelaziz Boutaleb, Ville Nouvelle) is the town's most contemporary venue. It exhibits the work of young Moroccan painters and organises cultural encounters.

Back in the medina, if you enter through the Bab Boujiloud, you cannot miss **Made in M** (246 Talaâ Kbira, Medina), a boutique selling a selection of candles, beauty products, ceramics and bags.

Youbi Design (66 Avenue Ibnou Houryia, Rue Liberia, Zouhour) specialises in selling babouches. Youbi continues to work leather in the traditional way, without chemical products, but he has updated his designs for babouches, bags and belts to today's tastes.

rabat + the coast

The work of self-taught local artists was taken up by Danish art-lover and talent-hunter Frédérik Damgaard in his **Galerie d'Art Damgaard** (Avenue Oqba Nafiaa, Essaouira) a long while back, with names such as Mohammed Tabal, Sanana, Mountir, Ali Maimoune and Asmah. The brightly-coloured, powerful works are deeply rooted in the Gnaoua culture.

Le Taros (Place Moulay Hassan, Essaouira) is a restaurant, bar, art gallery and shop rolled into one. Its owner, Alain Fillaud, another talent-hunter, exhibits fearlessly, lending the space to unbridled creativity, crazed musicians and techno evenings. Meanwhile, you can have a drink in the company of seagulls, dine beside the fireplace or pamper yourself with a luxurious cashmere shawl.

In the small Oudaias Kasbah in Rabat, you cannot miss the bookshop cum gallery, **Librairie d'Art Miloudi Nouiga** (Kasbah des Oudaias, Rue Jemaa, Rabat). Here you'll find an excellent selection of postcards, posters and books on Morocco.

In the centre of town, **Villa des Arts de Rabat** (10 Rue Beni Mellal, Angle Avenue Mohamed V, Hassan, Rabat), built in 1929, underwent a restoration to re-open its doors as a contemporary arts venue, a forum for events and encounters. With exhibition rooms, galleries, a forum, workshops and a Virtual Museum (the first of its kind), the Villa des Arts is an entire cultural experience, and a poetic one at that.

Urban Living (Rond-Point des Sports, Rue du Point du Jour, Casablanca) is a boutique for decorative objects where you find very contemporary, Italian-inspired furniture in black wood, functional objects, mirrors, lamp stands, and small sculptures in cast aluminium, works by contemporary Moroccan artists such as Karim Alaoui.

Housed in a magnificent cube-shaped white villa, **Galerie Venise Cadre** (25 Boulevard Moulay Rachid, Casablanca) exhibits the work of established Moroccan artists, like the painter Medhi Gotbi.

The original **Villa des Arts de Casablanca** (30 Boulevard Brahim Roudani, Casablanca) is set in a white villa dating from the early 1900s. Pure Art Deco, the entrance hall is overtly modern with a black iron stairwell and a black crystal chandelier. The rooms exhibit works at the cutting edge of creativity.

THIS PAGE (FROM TOP): An abundance of hand-woven fabrics means boutiques are often treasure troves of one-of-a-kind clothing and bags; silk cushions with intricate embroidery demonstrate the skill of Moroccan craftspeople.

OPPOSITE: Akbar Delights is a boutique cum salon in Marrakech inspired by the palaces of Rajasthan, filled with precious objects and the very lightest of silken clothes.

marrakech

Matisse Art Gallery (61 Rue de Yougoslavie, N° 43 Passage Ghandouri, Guéliz) is one of the best galleries, exhibiting contemporary established Moroccan painters such as Assani and Farid Belkahia.

Galerie Noir sur Blanc (48 Rue de Yougoslavie, Guéliz) has made a name for itself exhibiting the work of talented young artists, painter-sculptors and photographers from Morocco and elsewhere.

Light Gallery (2 Derb Chtouka, Kasbah), a highly 'architectural', white venue, is not what you might expect to come across in a narrow lane in the medina. Equally surprising is its

great selection of avant-garde works, which include photographs by Patrick Tourneboeuf and Olivier Culmann, pictorial works by Holger Jacobs and mineral sculptures by Aucha.

Galerie Photo 127 (127 Avenue Mohammed V, Guéliz) is devoted to photography, and dealer Nathalie Locatelli is focusing on this little-developed art in Morocco, showcasing powerful works by big names like Carole Ballaïche, Gérard Rondeau, Bernard Faucon and Marie Laure de Decker.

For the past 12 years, Frédérique Birkemeyer's shop, **Intensité Nomade** (139 Avenue Mohammed V, Guéliz), has sold the very best of the 'made in

Morocco' trend, as well as her own collection, a line of haute couture caftans and evening dresses, and another more casual, hippy-chic line.

Galerie Rê (Résidence Al Andalous III, Angle Rue de la Mosquée at Rue Ibn Toumert, N° 3, Guéliz) is a multi-functional space for art. Well-known Moroccan painters like Kacimi, Bouchchichi and Tibari Kantour, as well as foreigners such as Sébastien Pignon and Titus Carmel, have exhibited here.

On the Rue de la Liberté, the exquisite boutique **Scènes de Lin** (70 Rue de la Liberté, Guéliz) is entirely given over to furnishings and interior decoration. In its workshop, owner

Anne Marie Chaoui, one of the pioneers of the reinterpretation of traditional Moroccan crafts, dreams up the most divine bed and table linen in white cotton, honeycomb cloth and embroidered linen and equally stunning cushions and assorted bedspreads made of mlifa (the traditional flannel used for djellabas). Lighting, sofas and poufs in soft leathers and simple shapes make it the clear favourite of both stylists and magazines.

At **Akbar Delights** (45 Place Bab Fteuh, Medina and Amanjena, Km 12, Route de Ouarzazate) you might well think you were in a palace in Rajasthan. Isabelle receives her clients in her shops as if they were maharanees. Offering a fabulous choice of tunics and dresses in light fabrics, the goods are embroidered, florid, inserted with chiffon, silk, cotton and linen—all hip with a Moroccan feel.

Michèle Baconnier (6 Rue du Vieux Marrackhi, Guéliz) is a haven of freshness, displaying objects collected from all over the world, such as embroidered or finely pleated tunics in white or coloured Egyptian cotton; exquisite gold and silver ballerina shoes; babouches made of suzani (an Ouzbek material); and old jewellery reworked with semi-precious stones—all evoking the charms of the Middle East.

Even the most exacting clients are fascinated by the work of the metalworker at **Yahya Création** (61 Rue de Yougoslavie, Magazin 49–50, Passage Ghandouri, Guéliz). 'Embroidering' copper as if it were delicate lace, he chisels, shapes, cuts away and transforms the simplest of lamps into a magical lantern. Some of his pieces, in the form of engraved discs, are exhibited like pictures. This young craftsman has become, in the space of a few years, the master metalworker of the moment.

In the garden of her palace cum guesthouse, **Ksar Char-Bagh** (BP 2449, La Palmeraie), Nicole has converted several houses into four boutiques full of things you simply cannot do without: designer clothes, tables and trays in tooled metal and a choice of fabrics.

The souks are full of objects made of nickel silver, but in his workshop at **TM Design** (Rue el Arrak, QI Menara), Thierry Matalon is one of the few to use it for making valuable objects: chandeliers, flasks, ornamental bowls, vases and boxes.

Akkal (322 Zone Industriel Sidi Ghanem) is where Charlotte Barrkowski reinvents Moroccan pottery, using the same clay as her predecessors to produce a beautiful range of matt and glazed ceramics and decorative objects for the table. Her latest creations are globe shapes and the mini-maxi collection.

Angie (391 Zone Industriel Sidi Ghanem) sells a selection of irresistible linen made exclusively from natural fibres, with discreet embroidered patterns, such as the attractive red poppy motif.

Amira Bougies (277 Zone Industriel Sidi Ghanem) is a gallery of candles and night lights, in every shape and size, all the rage in Marrakech. Whatever the atmosphere—Zen, nomad or romantic—flame is the thing.

THIS PAGE (FROM TOP): Years of experience are required to punch out metal by hand with skill; Ksar Char-Bagh in the Palmeraie stocks the very finest contemporary Moroccan designs and products.

OPPOSITE (FROM TOP): The vast, modern, white interior of the Light Gallery is all the more unexpected for being situated in the middle of Marrakech's medina; many of Morocco's most talented designers take inspiration from traditional crafts, such as this delicately emblazoned piece of thuya wood from Essaouira.

national parks

Morocco has a wide variety of bioclimates and an equally wide range of natural milieux with 4,500 different plant species and over a hundred animal species. But such rich and diverse flora and fauna does not exist without problems, and many of its species, such as the cedar forests, the Audoin seagull and the oryx are considerably weakened or threatened with extinction.

Aware of the importance of this outstanding biodiversity on a global level, Morocco has created a number of impressive national parks and sites, and designated several Protected Areas.

Protected Areas are sanctuaries which can only be observed from a distance; they are no-go zones reserved for seals, gazelles, migrating birds and argan trees.

The reserves of Sidi Bou Ghaba, Merja Zerga, Khnifiss and Afennourir have been created to preserve the habitats of thousands of migrating birds. Several other important reserves have been founded to protect the Barbary sheep as well as to preserve the gazelle population and the fir plantations.

National parks are wonderful places to visit in Morocco. They represent the best of each biotope, with endemic plants and extremely rare animal species, encompassing the most stunning landscapes. As yet, they are relatively unknown to tourists, requiring the utmost respect when being explored.

tangier

Talassemtane National Park represents 60,000 hectares (148,263 acres) along the limestone backbone of the Rif Mountains, and can be visited easily from the town of Chefchaouen, some 120 km (75 miles) south of Tangier. The landscape is exceptionally varied and beautiful, ranging from dome-shaped peaks to cliffs and deep gorges, and the biodiversity is no less impressive, with over a thousand different plant species, many of them endemic. The park is also refuge to a number of threatened species such as Barbary macaques and otters.

The **Al-Hoceima National Park** covers the coastal area of the central Rif region, with spectacular cliffs that

drop vertically into the clear waters of the creeks below. The park is home to an extremely rich selection of marine life, including dolphins, monk seals and colonies of osprey, as well as the nearly extinct Audoin seagull.

fez

Tazekka National Park, near Taza in the Middle Atlas, which is about 90 km (56 miles) from Fez, contains the most beautiful forests of cedar and oak trees. Both sides of the mountain range, one steep and one more gently sloping, are now an excellent home to the Barbary deer which was introduced here in 1993.

Ifrane National Park covers almost all of the eastern part of the Middle Atlas, 53,000 hectares (130, 966 acres), mainly forested. It is the region's main 'water tower' and its principle sheep-rearing area. The park also houses a large population of Barbary macaques.

The **Eastern High Atlas National Park** is situated between the Imilchi region and Jbel Aberdouz and is divided into three zones: the plateau of lakes, the mountainous zone and the backbone of the Jbel. The forests of cedars and juniper and the far-reaching steppes are the home of the Barbary sheep, the park's symbol.

rabat + the coast

Over 154 areas with outstanding ecosystems—sites of biological and ecological interest (SIBE)—are listed in the **Argan Forest Biosphere Reserve** created by UNESCO in 1998. It covers the entire potential area of the argan forest, stretching from Essaouira to Talouine. The town of

Taroudant is a good base camp from which to get a glimpse of the natural splendour of this precious forest.

Souss-Massa National Park, near Agadir, covers long stretches of dunes along the coast between the Souss and Tiznite Wadis. Its fragile relief is largely composed of maritime dunes which are planted with argania spinosa, and this picturesque landscape is home to gazelles, jackals and migrating birds.

The **Bas Draâ National Park** to the east of Tan Tan is virtual desert, where little other than the occasional acacia tree and Saharan bush grow. Large fauna such as gazelles and leopards love it however. The **Iriqui Park** in the Haut Draâ is more humid with vast steppes where gazelles, hyenas, varans and snakes abound.

Dakhla National Park is a 1.9 million-hectare (4.7 million-acre) territory in the very south of the country. The area along the coast is a highly-protected zone for monk seals and dorcas gazelles. The remainder of the park is given over to the preservation of Saharan ecosystems and to the creation of a much-needed sanctuary for some increasingly rare large fauna, such as oryx, damas gazelles and ostriches.

Classified as part of Morocco's natural heritage, the **Sidi Bou Ghaba Nature Reserve** is situated near the immensely popular seaside resort of Mehdiya, just north of Rabat. It is one of the last remaining havens of peace available for preservation in this area.

marrakech

Toubkal National Park, only 65 km (40 miles) from Marrakech, occupies the central part of the High Atlas Mountains, between the valleys of the N' Fiss and the Ourika. The going is steep and one has to overcome some of Morocco's highest peaks. This wild and harsh countryside is the hideout of the lynx, among many other species. There is an immense biodiversity here, where many rare species survive.

views

These special places are not to be missed; they are perfect spots to stop for just long enough to admire a sunset, or to rest up for a few days.

tangier

If you've always dreamt of staying in Tangier's kasbah, now's your chance, in **Dar Nour** (20 Rue Gourna, Kasbah), an exquisite guesthouse perched on the surrounding defensive wall. From the terrace you have a splendid 360° view over the city.

The tip of **Cap Spartel** is the dividing point between the Mediterranean Sea and the Atlantic Ocean, with the Spanish coast far off in the distance. It is a magical place, to be admired from the cliffs.

In the Rif region, the beautiful little **Chefchaouen medina** still has a wood-fired hammam and other marvels, such as views of the white and blue houses on the hillside.

From Al-Hoceima, take the road that leads to the fishing village of **Torrës al Kala**. It is a very charming place with a pebble beach, small cafés, fishing boats and the sheer cliffs of the Bokkoyas Mountains plunging dramatically into the sea.

Spending a few days in Asilah is absolute heaven! **Maison d'Hôtes Monique Chevassus** (35 Ben Marzouk, Medina, Asilah) is a fine place to stop for a little contemplation, staying in one of the five rooms looking out over the ramparts and the sea.

Twenty-five km (16 miles) southeast of Asilah lies the **Monoliths of M'Soura**, a unique stone circle dating from the Neolithic era, composed of more than 200 menhirs surrounding a tumulus.

fez

It's from the terrace of the Vizir's superb chamber in the **Sofitel Palais Jamaï** (Bab Guissa) that you have the most secretive and magical view over the medina in Fez.

rabat + the coast

Don't miss the **Ouzoud Falls** (Tanaghmeilt, Azilal) near Agadir. Water crashes down from a height of 100 m (328 ft) into a sea of green. There's a giddying view from the restaurant Havre de Paix at the top.

Also near Agadir, the **Souss-Massa National Park** is an ornithological sanctuary of great richness. There is a beach and a troglodyte village nearby, and the **Ksar Massa** (BP 222, Sidi, R'bat 80450, Massa) is a good base from which to do a little birdwatching. You can see a plentiful number of ducks, pink flamingos, herons and more.

On the road to Taroudant, the **Domaine de la Roseraie** (Km 60, Route de Taroudant, Val d'Ouirgane) lies in a 25-hectare (62-acre) nature park at the gates of the High Atlas.

The **Valley of Tafraoute** in the Anti Atlas is an outstanding geological site. The best time to visit it is in January and February, the few special months when the almond trees are in full blossom.

When you come to Tan Tan, you'll be at the mouth of the **Wadi Draâ**, where it widens to flow into the sea; it is traversed by spectacular fords, only practicable at low tide.

Further south, heading towards Layoune, the **Naila Laguna** is an unexpected series of blue lagoons framed by a line of white dunes.

Ostréa II (Parc à Huîtres N°007) is an ideally situated hotel and seafood restaurant in Oualidia, on the Atlantic coast, with superb views over the oyster beds, laguna and the sea stretching as far as the eye can see.

North of Rabat, the **Sidi Bourhaba Lake** (BP 133, Réserve de Sidi Bou Ghaba), in the nature reserve near Mehdiya Plage, is a protected resting place for birds and the habitat of the marsh owls, a rare sight nowadays. It is a peaceful landscape ideal for hiking and lake views.

marrakech

The **Majorelle Gardens** (Avenue Yacoub el Mansour, Ville Nouvelle) is the most exquisite place in Marrakech. Stroll through the alleyways in an array of greens, in perfect contrast to the intense blue of the villa which once belonged to the painter Majorelle.

The gardens of the **French Consulate, Morocco** in Marrakech (1 Rue Ibn Khaldoun, Dar Moulay Ali) have fantastic views of the minaret of the Koutoubia Mosque.

THIS PAGE (FROM TOP): On the road from Marrakech to Ouarzazate, make sure to stop and visit the ruins of the majestic Telouet Kasbah; views of the ocean from over one of the many white rooftops in Asilah; the unexpected sight of a concentric circle of stones on a hilltop, surrounded by the peaks of the Middle Atlas Mountains.

OPPOSITE: On the rugged coastline fringed by steep cliffs, Cap Spartel, near Tangier, marks the dividing point between the Mediterranean Sea and the Atlantic Ocean.

Djemaa el-Fna Square is the most lively place in Marrakech, a living theatre with storytellers, merchants and jugglers. Climb up to the terrace of the **Café de France** (Djemaa el-Fna Square, near Derb Zaari), where you can look down on the entire colourful scene.

En route to the **Oukaimeden Ski Resort** about 75 km (47 miles) from Marrakech in Ourika, you will pass through villages still inhabited by Berber tribes. The views along this route are utterly majestic.

One of the most beautiful in Morocco, the road (the N9) from Marrakech to Ouarzazate through the **Tizi n'Tichka Pass** cuts through the High Atlas and is absolutely stunning: long, winding and steep, through landscape that is constantly changing colour. It is worth every minute of the journey.

Turn a few kilometres beyond the pass off of the Marrakech-Ouarzazate Road, and stop awhile to visit the ruins of the **Telouet Kasbah**, one of the Glaoui palaces.

Kasbah du Toubkal (BP 31, Imlil, Asni, Marrakech) sits high on a rock in the Toubkal National Park. To reach it you have to follow the path that winds its way up the rock face, preferably astride a mule. Once at the top, you can enjoy the unique thrill of being in a wild, secluded and beautiful spot, while appreciating the comforts of this lovely hotel.

To further explore the land of the Berbers, treat yourself to a walk in the picturesque **Aït Bougmez Valley**, 200 km (124 miles) east of Marrakech. You will see terraced cultivation, adobe houses and unique fortified grain stores, all of which are typical of the Berber civilisation.

The geological folds in the **Imilchil Valley** are strange and vast, and the most interesting and spectacular are those beside the road between the village of Imilchil and the Place du Moussem.

As you leave Ouarzazate, the ksar and the village of **Aït Benhaddou** rise up ahead of you like the backdrop in a film. Indeed numerous films have been shot here including *The Jewel of the Nile* and *Lawrence of Arabia*. You have to ford the wadi in order to visit both the village and the ksar.

Spring is the best time to see the **Valley of the Roses** (enter the Valley at Imassine), when water from the seguias (irrigation channels), swollen by the melted snow, flows abundantly through the cultivated areas. A good place to stop and absorb the scenery and fragrance, the small town of **El Kela** is the centre of the area's Damask rose cultivation.

If you've never experienced the desert or an oasis, you can seize the opportunity by staying in one of **Les Camps Nomades**' luxury tents, either at the Palmeraie de Skoura in the Dadès Valley, or in the Sahara on the edge of the Merzouga Dunes.

The **Palmeraie de Tineghir** with its Glaoui kasbah is another superb sight, one which can be peacefully contemplated from the **Hotel Kenzi Saghro** (BP 46–45, 800, Tineghir).

THIS PAGE (FROM TOP): Almond trees are in full bloom during January and February—an ideal time to visit; the tents of Les Camps Nomades, a luxurious way to see the desert; soak in the sun and sea views on the deck of Ksar Massa.

OPPOSITE (FROM TOP): Kasbah du Toubkal has an unrivalled perch for taking in the splendour of the High Atlas; the medina in Chefchaouen is one of the most charming in the Rif.

unesco heritage sites

Morocco has eight areas of cultural interest, which now form part of UNESCO's list of World Heritage Sites.

tangier

About 60 km (37 miles) southeast of Tangier, the **Tétouan medina** runs from the Place Hassan II to the walls of the royal palace, its entrance so discreet it's almost secretive. There's a very special atmosphere here, and every step of the way reveals beautiful architectural details within a labyrinth of covered alleyways.

fez

The **Fez medina**, an age-old, walled-off enclave of unrivalled splendour, has grown up over the years around the 14th-century **Qaraouiyyine** Mosque (Place Seffarine). Fourteen babs (gateways) lead through to a labyrinth of narrow lanes and interlocking districts.

The **Meknès medina** looks as impressive and powerful as ever, with kilometres of ramparts and monumental gateways. Once inside, there's a souk and a number of beautiful kissaria (covered markets), the **Dar Jamaï Museum** (Sahat el Hadim) in a former palace complete with harem, and the **Medersa Bou Inania** (Sahat el Hadim), where you can climb on the roof for views of the nearby mosque.

The Roman site of **Volubilis** is an open-air museum. Toward the end of the 1st century BCE, it was an important trading post and a prosperous city. In 1874, archeological exploration unearthed 20 or so monuments dating from the 2nd and 3rd centuries CE, including the House of Hercules and that of Dionysius.

rabat + the coast

Essaouira's medina is small and charming, huddled behind ramparts which protect it from the swell of the ocean. It is made up of various districts, mellah, grain and fish markets, on either side of a long avenue running from the Bab el-Menzah on the ocean side to Bab Doukkala inland.

The Portuguese city of **El Jadida** is made up of ramparts flanked by four bastions and a medina enclosing a magnificent cistern which, in the 16th century, formed part of the castle. The cistern is an underground chamber supported by 25 pillars capable of holding over 2 million litres (4 million pints) of rainwater.

marrakech

Marrakech's medina is the largest and most vibrant of its kind in North Africa, with 250,000 inhabitants in just over 600 hectares (1,483 acres). It also happens to contain many remarkable monuments: the **Saadian Tombs** (Rue de la Kasbah), the **Koutoubia Mosque** (Avenue Mohammed V), **El-Badi Palace** (Place des Ferblantiers) and the **Bahia Palace** (Rue de la Bahia, Zitoun el-Jadid).

Since 2001, the **Djemaa el-Fna Square**, a unique and vast square which is a permanent stage for storytellers, has been designated by UNESCO as a masterpiece of Oral and Intangible Heritage of Humanity.

THIS PAGE (CLOCKWISE FROM TOP): Colourful fishing boats bob in front of the Portuguese fortress in El Jadida; the green roof of the Qaraouiyyine Mosque in Fez, a signature element of the city's skyline; a palm tree emerging above the ramparts in Essaouira; vendors prepare food in Djemaa el-Fna Square, filling the air with mouth-watering aromas.
OPPOSITE: The formidable entrance to the Meknès medina.

tangier

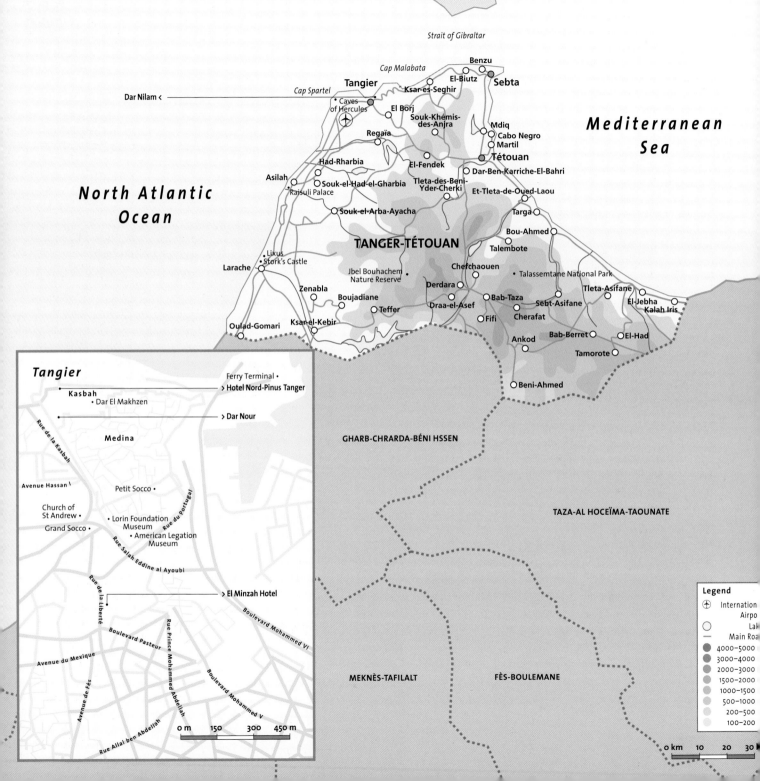

SPAIN

Strait of Gibraltar

Cap Malabata

Cap Spartel

Benzu
El-Biutz
Sebta
Ksar-es-Seghir

Tangier

Dar Nilam ‹

• Caves
  of Hercules
El Borj
Souk-Khémis-
des-Anjra

Regaïa

Mdiq
Cabo Negro
Martil

*Mediterranean
Sea*

El-Fendek
Tétouan

*North Atlantic
Ocean*

Hád-Rharbia

Asilah
Souk-el-Had-el-Gharbia
Rajsuli Palace

Dar-Ben-Karriche-El-Bahri
Tleta-des-Beni-
Yder-Cherki
Et-Tleta-de-Oued-Laou

Souk-el-Arba-Ayacha

Targa

Bou-Ahmed

TANGER-TÉTOUAN

Talembote

Chefchaouen
• Talassemtane National Park

Lixus
• Stork's Castle

Larache

Jbel Bouhachem
Nature Reserve

Derdara

Zenabla
Boujadiane

Teffer

Draa-el-Asef

Bab-Taza

Fifi

Cherafat

Sebt-Asifane

Tleta-Asifane

Él-Jebha
Kalah Iris

Oulad-Gomari

Ksar-el-Kebir

Ankod

Bab-Berret

El-Had

Tamorote

Beni-Ahmed

GHARB-CHRARDA-BÉNI HSSEN

TAZA-AL HOCEÏMA-TAOUNATE

MEKNÈS-TAFILALT

FÈS-BOULEMANE

Tangier

Ferry Terminal •
› **Hotel Nord-Pinus Tanger**

Kasbah
• Dar El Makhzen

› **Dar Nour**

Medina

Petit Socco •

Church of
St Andrew •

• Lorin Foundation
  Museum

Grand Socco •

• American Legation
  Museum

Rue de la Kasbah

Avenue Hassan \

Rue du Portugal

Rue Salah Eddine al Ayoubi

Rue de la Liberté

› **El Minzah Hotel**

Boulevard Mohammed VI

Boulevard Pasteur

Rue Prince Mohammed Abdellah

Boulevard Mohammed V

Avenue du Mexique

Avenue de Fès

Rue Allal ben Abdellah

0 m   150   300   450 m

Legend

⊕   Internation
    Airpo

◯   Lak

—   Main Roa

4000–5000
3000–4000
2000–3000
1500–2000
1000–1500
500–1000
200–500
100–200

0 km   10   20   30

tangier

cosmopolitan tangier, first port of call

Between Andalusia and the tip of Morocco, between Gibraltar and the Caves of Hercules, there is the merest channel. Here, just a 15-minute hop by plane (or a 2-hour boat ride) from Continental Europe, lies Tangier, a place where many a dream of exotic travel, fuelled by the enigmatic poetry of Africa, starts and ends. Here is where the Atlantic mingles with the Mediterranean, a heady mix of East and West.

born of legend

'Antaeus, son of Neptune and of the goddess Earth, founded the city. He called it Tingis, after the name of his wife—a love story from the outset! Later it became Tangia, the much-desired mistress of nine giants, all of whom loved her passionately.' This was how the writer Mohammed Choukri referred to the mythical origins of the city, which have seduced so many generations.

past, present

Tangier—certainly Moroccan, perhaps unloved, definitely cosmopolitan. Generations of different nationalities have flocked to this Tower of Babel, feeding off its myth. The town is so giddy with everybody else's culture that it has difficulty defining its own identity. Many versions abound, some kinder than others. Both traditional and modern at heart, Tangier was a relatively liberal place under colonial rule and throughout the 1960s, accommodating all manner of adventurers, artists and outcasts seeking temporary exile and excitement. It was also an immensely creative place, inspiring much bohemian literature and dramatic painting. Charf Hill, the golden rockface, provided Tangier's transplants with elegant homes and sea views, and its unusual light filled the dazzling palettes of many Orientalist and Impressionist painters, from Delacroix to Matisse.

Attracted by this 'coloratura', foreign writers, including Daniel Rondeau, Jean Genet, Paul Morand, Paul Bowles and Dominique Pons, flocked to Tangier. They all sharpened their pens on the 'Rocher', but the descriptions they gave of Tangier are of cinematographic nights viewed from an unmoving lens. Could it have been the easterly wind which turned people's heads, or was it the unbearable lightness of the air that was responsible for the extraordinary migration of celebrities to this permissive, bohemian society? Francis Bacon, Pier Paolo Pasolini, Allen Ginsberg, Samuel Beckett, Orson Welles and Bernardo Bertolucci all found their artistic inspiration here, borrowing its décor and making ample use of its hospitality.

Turned in so many directions by so many hands, be they loving, awkward or rough, Tangier would soon have burnt itself out were it not for the easterly wind (the Chergui) that blows continuously, sometimes up to seven days a week, cleansing and reviving it.

THIS PAGE: *Life has hardly changed for centuries in the narrow lanes of the Kasbah.*

PAGE 50: *From the port there is a fine view of old Tangier backing up the hillside, the occasional daub of colour amid such whiteness echoing the tone of the deep blue waters below.*

famous children

Rue d'Italie, Avenue d'Espagne, Rue de Hollande or the former Rue Tolstoy—names evocative of a not-so-distant past. Tangier clings to its former glory. The early 20th-century façades with their ornate balconies still appear to be waiting for infantas and chaperones from a Goya painting. Further up the Rue du Prince Moulay Abdallah, the extraordinary Art Deco façade of the Cervantes Grand Theatre conjures up its heyday when Caruso performed to great acclaim. The Fuentes boarding house in the Petit Socco (Little Square) was the favourite of foreign artists and journalists. In the adjacent square, once a business centre with banks and European-style hotels, other trades have taken root, along with small dealers and 'kif' smokers.

Strolling through Tangier can become a walking tour of artistic landmarks. The writer Jean Genet's daily round included the Place de France and the Café de Paris. He lived at El Minzah, No. 136, Rue de la Liberté, the former residence of Lord Bute, which is still one of the town's mythical hotels. At No. 86, the Galerie Delacroix in the French Cultural Centre still exhibits works of promising young local artists. Delacroix stayed in Tangier as early as 1832. Inspired by the light, he made hundreds of sketches of people and horses which he later used to create his great Orientalist paintings such as 'Une Cour à Tanger', now hanging in the Louvre Museum. Matisse came to Tangier in 1911. He lived for two years in the former Villa de France Hotel at No. 143, Rue de Hollande. From his bedroom, he painted many remarkable pictures, including 'Une Chambre Avec Vue' and 'Le Café Maure', now exhibited in the Musée Pouchkine and the Hermitage.

Another remnant of Tangier's artistic past, the Colonnes bookshop at No. 54, Boulevard Pasteur, was the former literary salon of Rachel Mouyal, and it became the meeting place for writers passing through town. At the back of her shop, as in Sylvia Beach's famous 'Blue Oyster Room' in Paris, Rachel endlessly discussed the world of Tangier with such illustrious visitors as Dominique Pons, Tahar ben Jelloun, Paul Bowles, Mohammed Choukri and others.

The Grand Socco, the vast square renamed 'Place du 9 Avril 1947', forms the link between the medina and the new town. From here, the souk extends along Rue d'Angleterre where, every Thursday and Sunday, there is a big market to which the peasants from the Rif flock in their striped fouta and large straw hats bedecked with pompons, to sell chickens, fruit and vegetables.

No. 8, Rue d'Amérique has been occupied by the American Legation since 1821, when it was given the palace by Sultan Moulay Slimane. An exquisite museum on Tangier in the 16th and 18th centuries is in the former harem, along with works by the portraitist James McBeay.

Tangier's main museum is in the Place de la Kasbah. Housed in a former sultan's palace, it is a masterpiece of 18th-century architecture, with a large arcaded courtyard with zellij-tile décor and capitals sculpted with acanthus leaves. Next to it is the Café Maure, overlooked by the white

THIS PAGE (FROM TOP): *Tangier was a source of inspiration for Henri Matisse, and this view was painted from his window in the former Villa de France; the Cervantes Grande Theatre is a beautiful remnant of Tangier's artistic heyday.*

OPPOSITE: *The port of Tangier forms an important link between Spain and Africa, and between the Atlantic Ocean and the Mediterranean Sea.*

...their ornate balconies still appear to be waiting for infantas and chaperones from a Goya painting.

THIS PAGE: In Chefchaouen, the Rif's proud capital, the walls and doors are traditionally painted cobalt blue.

OPPOSITE (FROM TOP): Powdered dyes are used to repaint the façades of houses; Chefchaouen is nestled in between the peaks of Jbel Kelaa and Jbel Meggou.

domes and glazed roof tiles of the home of Adolfo de Velasco. This well-known Moroccan figure and art-lover lived in the sultan's former harem, which he turned into a magnificent house full of beautiful and precious objects.

The seething Rue de la Kasbah connects back to the Petit Socco, which still remembers such personages as Barbara Hulton, the rich and extravagant heiress to the Woolworth fortune, who stayed in a white palace in the small Rue Amgha for 20 years. She liked to inhale the heady fragrance of tuberose flowers, amber and roses—a secret mixture specially prepared for her by the perfumer Madini, based at No. 14, Rue Sébou.

In yet another exotic palace in the upper reaches of the Marshan district, the American multimillionaire, Malcolm Forbes, hosted occasional extravagant parties, sometimes in the company of actress Liz Taylor, which provided plenty of gossip for the world's media columns. From the Petit Socco to the Grand Socco, from the medina by the port to the new town, the city of Tangier is full of reminders of those crazy years.

getting away in the rif: tétouan

Some 60 km (37 miles) southeast of Tangier, Tétouan lives in the shadow of the great metropolis. Situated on a fertile plateau in the foothills of the Rif Mountains, it is a charming place, the white and green houses of the medina poking up above the crenellated ramparts.

This Arab-Andalusian town, former capital of the Spanish Protectorate during the early 20th century, dates back to the Merenid dynasty, when it was a popular hideout for pirates, which Henri III of Castile destroyed, massacring its entire population while he was about it. It was not until the 16th century that people settled here again—mainly Muslims and Jews fleeing Spain—and that its pirating activities got underway once more. The town expanded considerably at the time of Moulay Ismail in the 17th century.

Everything about Tétouan reminds one of Andalusia. The inhabitants still go for their evening stroll, the paseo, in the Place Hassan II and along Boulevard Mohammed V, between the medina and the new town. In the middle of the old town, small shady squares like those of the El Fouki and the Ousaa souks, are filled with stalls selling spices and pancakes. Wherever one looks, water flows from fountains, pools of freshness. A nose is as good a guide as any as one finds the way among the maze of narrow streets and passages: the bitter odour emanating from the leather in Rue el-Jarrazine, where the tanners have their workshops; the enticing fragrances of spices and unctions; or the mouth-watering smells of wood-smoke and grilling kebabs. Place el-Kebira is home to antique dealers and their eccentric collections of goods. The architecture and layout of the old Jewish quarter, the mellah or 'little Jerusalem', are essentially the same as at the time of its creation in 1807. Balconies and grille-fronted windows adorn the houses, creating a look that is quite different from that of the medina.

chefchaouen (or chaouen), the blue town

Some 120 km (75 miles) south of Tangier, Chefchaouen, fiefdom of the Jebala Berber tribe, is one of the prettiest towns in the Rif region, and although often excluded from tour circuits because of its remoteness, it is well worth taking the time to visit. Its name, Chefchaouen (which means 'look at the horns of the mountain'), is invitation enough to go look at it! Set between Jbel Kelaa and Jbel Meggou, at the foot of the source of Ras el-Ma, this Mediterranean town has remained more or less untouched over the years, its houses and shops clinging to the hillside, small white buildings with pale blue windows and doorsteps.

As at Tétouan, successive waves of Andalusian refugees, Muslims and Jews settled here in the protective shadow of the city walls—a cultural mix which included the refined and comfortable lifestyle of Granada. What better place to while away the time than in one of the numerous cafés lining the Plaza Uta el-Hammam in the shadow of the grand mosque—a favourite meeting place of the locals. The kasbah was built at the time of the founding of the city in the 15th century and hides peaceful Andalusian-style gardens behind its high walls. The medina, all twists and turns, milky whites and blues, with its interlocking houses, is, in itself, remarkably charming.

the mediterranean coast

Just a stone's throw from Spain, the Rif coastline is pristine and easily accessible for quick getaway. There are several seaside resorts stretched out along this coastline, including Cabo Negro, Martil, Al-Hoceima and Achakar, near Tangier, which has been awarded the Blue Flag eco-label for the cleanliness of its beaches and water. There is also still plenty of what has always made this coastline so charming: fishing ports (such as Mdiq) with multicoloured fishing boats and beachside cafés, traditional fishing villages on the banks of the Wadi Laou, wild shores, pine forests, cliffs, creeks, miles of dunes and Arabo-Andalusian medinas. Seven km (4 miles) of beach stretch out from the beautiful kasbah of Saïdia, and for nature-lovers, the hinterland contains many treasures such as the sight of the Moulouya River, the Valley of Zegzel and the forest of Tafoghalt.

The only things missing from this idyllic picture, until recently, were a few flagship resorts. The Azur Plan has filled this gap, creating two seaside resorts that are committed to respecting the environment whilst meeting the exacting requirements of today's clientele. The first, Tamuda Bay, occupies a 300-hectare (741-acre) site and is an exclusive, peaceful getaway, a luxury seaside resort composed of eight hotels, four golf courses, a lakeside city and a marina. Just 15 km (9 miles) from the Tétouan medina, with golden sandy beaches, freshwater bathing and water sport facilities, Tamuda Bay is the perfect place for taking advantage of being beside the sea, while indulging one's cultural curiosity. The second, Mediterrania Saïdia, is a recently completed luxury complex just 40 minutes from the airport of Oujda, with prestigious hotels and residences lining the sea front, surrounded by three golf courses. An 800-berth yacht harbour is yet to come, together with a sailing school and a sea museum.

THIS PAGE: *A camel ride along Tangier's beach at sunset is an absolute must.*

OPPOSITE: *The Rif's rugged coast is breathtaking, sheer cliffs plunging straight down into the sea, with the occasional sandy cove in between.*

...a stone's throw from Spain, the Rif coastline is pristine and easily accessible for a quick getaway.

dar nilam

Located just off the Bay of Tangier, Dar Nilam is a serenely beautiful guesthouse just 500 m (1,640 ft) from the beach, up a winding path through a small forest. The 'House of the Blue Diamond' (as its name is translated), presents itself very much like a precious jewel, nestled in a bed of resplendent greenery and brilliant blossoms. A cornucopia of exotic fruit trees, subtropical plants and indigenous birds can be found all around the property, with shady rest areas interspersed among it all. Visitors arriving from the nearby town centre will find themselves almost worlds away from the activity of modern Moroccan life, and yet Dar Nilam lies only 2 km (1.24 miles) from the heart of Tangier—making it doubly attractive as a holiday haven.

An impressive staircase leads up to the first floor of the house, which displays the same affection for wide open spaces as the exterior landscape design. Bright and airy, the reception hallway branches out to three living rooms. A reading area with a fireplace lies just around the corner, offering guests a chance to socialise while admiring a lovely view of the sea. Everywhere, fine details and tiling of traditionally inspired Moroccan architecture draw visitors' attention. Bringing together the influences of Africa and the Orient, the décor signifies Dar Nilam's core philosophy of style, harmony and comfort—traits present in all aspects of the hotel experience.

Five well-appointed accommodations embrace a fusion of regional furnishings and continental conveniences; each is a unique amalgamation of colour, fine materials and large windows. Two rooms and three suites are available, with the former coming in both twin and king-sized bed configurations. One room features a rich red colour scheme, while the other boasts sunnier shades of beige and

THIS PAGE (FROM TOP): A traditional Moroccan meal is served in the elegant dining room; one of the cosy salons, where guests can gather to socialise.

OPPOSITE (FROM TOP): Suite Leila is swathed in opulent golds and mellow honey tones; the hotel's lush landscaped gardens welcome all visitors.

blue to go with its view of the garden. All the suites come with en suite bathrooms and the usual amenities such as a minibar, satellite television and wireless Internet access.

Two of the suites are junior class suites, at around 26 sq m (280 sq ft) each. Suite Alia has a superb view of the sea, and its interiors marry burgundy with copper for a vibrant end result. Its companion, Suite Leila, is a striking assembly of rich gold and warm honey that is most inviting during the hours of sunrise and sunset, when the view of nearby mountains is clearest. Suite Lalla Naima is the largest suite, with a separate living area and large terrace overlooking the sea. Fittingly, this sumptuous suite is decorated in marine hues.

A large pool is perfect for some light exercise, while a Moorish bath and hammam promise to ease weary bodies into blissful submission. Making use of Eastern Oriental techniques, the hammam is billed as a space for total well-being, offering a range of shiatsu, reflexology and stone therapies. Likewise, Moroccan cuisine is composed of many diverse influences, and the restaurant serves authentic fare made with recipes passed down over several generations. The entire property can be booked for the ultimate in exclusivity, and this may be the best way to enjoy its many pleasures. Here at Dar Nilam, travellers enjoy the rare privilege of being made to feel completely at home.

rooms
2 rooms • 3 suites

food
traditional Moroccan

drink
beverage list

features
Zen spa with treatment rooms • hammam • airport transfers • childcare services • pool • Internet access • solarium

nearby
Tangier city centre • beach

contact
BP 1262, 28 Lotissement Tingis, Baie de Tanger 90000 Tangier •
telephone: +212.39.301 146 •
facsimile: +212.39.325 595 •
email: info@darnilam.com •
website: www.darnilam.com

dar nour

Tangier has a longstanding association with artists and writers which stems from the freewheeling, cosmopolitan makeup that followed the creation of its international zone in 1923. Such esteemed talents as Tennessee Williams, Jack Kerouac, Jean Genet and Mohamed Choukri are incontrovertibly linked to the northern capital, and it in turn has been immortalised in their stories and art.

Dar Nour, or the 'House of Light', has the distinction of being the very first guesthouse to open in Tangier. While the revival of riads, mainly in Marrakech, has been a success story of explosive growth, Tangier is a different, more enigmatic sort of city, and as a result its hotels take a slower route that emphasises their character and authenticity. Opened in 1999, Dar Nour occupies a large historic house in the centre of the kasbah, found at the end of a little street where the writer Paul Bowles once lived, amidst the twisting lanes of the labyrinthian medina. It was also home to Mohamed Choukri, and one can only imagine that this was where the two literary giants collaborated on the latter's *For Bread Alone*.

Its current owners are an archaeologist, a journalist and an architect brought together by their common appreciation for the city and its stories. Through their work, the property has over the years gathered strands of local and regional culture in the form of antique furniture, art pieces, ceramics and books from across the Arab lands and beyond to present a living tapestry that defines the Moroccan experience in a way that allows guests to live it fully for themselves.

Each of Dar Nour's 10 rooms and junior suites are an extension of this philosophy, individually designed with features that are themselves clues about the ways of the land and its people. The Faris Room, for instance, references Marrakech with its unique clay-red walls and large store of Oriental mystique. Decorated with a delicate blend of traditional and modern influences, it displays fine cedar wood panelling and two elegant arches that can't help but catch the eye.

rooms
3 rooms • 7 suites • 1 private house

food
traditional and modern Moroccan

drink
beverage list

features
rooftop terraces • guided tours • laundry • library lounge • parking

nearby
hammam • gym • medina • shops • library • Bay of Tangier • massage

contact
20 Rue Gourna, Kasbah
90000 Tangier •
telephone: +212.62.112 724 •
email: contactdarnour@yahoo.fr •
website: www.darnour.com

True to the hotel's name, the Fayza Junior Suite is blessed with an abundance of natural light. It also enjoys direct access to two sun-kissed terraces outside, making it the perfect choice for guests who wish to sunbathe and soak up the Moroccan climate.

Families may prefer to reserve one of the larger suites such as the Jassim, which is a duplex apartment that can house three guests comfortably. Its earth-toned walls are draped with colourful rugs, and a selection of handsome, simple contemporary furniture has been carefully arranged to help create a relaxed environment. The upstairs lounge opens out onto further terraces, from which guests may appreciate a light breeze or look out over the new town area, the Bay of Tangier, and the medina below.

For an even more exclusive stay, Dar Nour offers guests the 'Little House', a three-storey residence near the main building. It includes a kitchen, a bedroom and two bathrooms. Its sitting room leads onto one of two terraces with a panoramic view of the city and the sea. In the mornings, its residents are only a short stroll away from Dar Nour's lavish breakfasts, which are served until every guest has eaten his or her fill. Should any prospective guest have any queries, the owners, Catherine, Jean-Olivier and Philippe are available via telephone.

el minzah hotel

Built by John Crichton-Stuart, the Marquis of Bute, the El Minzah Hotel has been a symbol of great British elegance and traditional Moroccan charm in the city of Tangier for almost 80 years. A rare deluxe five-star establishment, the hotel offers its guests world-class standards of luxury that can hardly be found anywhere else. Rising to fame during the years of Tangier's international governance, El Minzah Hotel was widely recognised as the finest hotel in North Africa and as an important social hub for diplomats, aristocrats and celebrities. During the war, its Caid's Piano Bar was a popular destination for the Allied forces, and would eventually serve as the real life inspiration for the 'Cafe Americain' featured in Humphrey Bogart's landmark motion picture, *Casablanca*.

Today, the newly refurbished 140-room property is still the place to be in Tangier, as all of the romantic attributes and picturesque charms patrons enjoyed in its heyday have remained the same. Situated in the middle of the city, on the edge of the Strait of Gibraltar, El Minzah Hotel is blessed with a remarkable view that encompasses Europe and Africa at once. In addition, the hotel is conveniently located a short distance from the beach and other such popular attractions as the superb shopping and entertainment areas of downtown Tangier and the medina.

The hotel's styling and interior designs are a combination of Spanish and Moorish influences, echoed in all great Moroccan architecture, surrounded by an abundance of trees and greenery on the grounds. The heart of the El Minzah Hotel is a sunken Andalusian patio bordered by Corinthian-style pillars, and walls mosaicked with hand-cut Moroccan tiles. Dining by the peaceful fountain is a particularly welcome indulgence during the hotter days of summer.

All accommodations, from the standard single rooms to the Royal Suite, also benefit from the Hispano-Moorish design. Antique carved wood furnishings, high ceilings and patterned arches transmit a story of the region's rich history and sincere hospitality. Most of the guestrooms face the southeast and enjoy panoramic views of the Bay of Tangier and Rif Mountains—a number of them even come with private terraces. Each climate-controlled room features an array of modern amenities such as cable television channels, safes, minibars and complimentary high-speed Internet access.

THIS PAGE (FROM TOP): Almost eight decades of history stand behind El Minzah Hotel; take in breathtaking views from the rooftop for hours, watching sunset turn to night.

OPPOSITE (FROM TOP): Neutral colours help create a restful environment in the rooms; guests may want to head to the Wellness Health Club after indulging in the delicious food from the hotel's kitchens.

rooms
123 rooms • 17 suites

food
El Korsan: traditional Moroccan •
El Erz: international

drink
Wine Bar • Caid's Piano Bar • Misbah Club

features
Wellness Health Club • spa • hammam •
gift shop • high-speed Internet access •
2 pools • 3 meeting rooms

nearby
Kasbah Museum • Caves of Hercules • beach •
medina • golf courses • horse riding • shops •
tennis courts • galleries

contact
85 Rue de la Liberté •
90000 Tangier •
telephone: +212.39.333 444 •
facsimile: +212.39.333 999 •
email: infos@elminzah.com •
website: www.elminzah.com

With the provision of two gourmet restaurants and spa facilities, the El Minzah Hotel is a fully featured destination in its own right. El Erz serves international cuisine in a setting that has both contemporary and traditional elements, with crisp white table settings under an original beamed ceiling. The menu is one of Tangier's largest, featuring fresh seafood and perfectly grilled steaks. The El Korsan restaurant, on the other hand, is entirely dedicated to presenting an authentic Moroccan experience. A kitchen staffed by strictly female chefs produces traditional food that is often joined in the 120-seat dining hall by live music and dance entertainment.

The Wellness Health Club is an impressive 2,000-sq m (21,528-sq ft) spa dedicated to stress relief, fitness and beauty. The complex houses 20 treatment rooms, two pools, a gymnasium, sauna, traditional hammam, boutique and health food restaurant. Other activities are offered nearby, including tennis courts, a golf course and a horse riding club.

Over the years, the El Minzah Hotel has been a favourite of such personalities as Gina Lollobrigida, Sir Winston Churchill and Sir Rex Harrison. By virtue of its incredible location, richly appointed, highly comfortable rooms and beautiful construction, it's not at all difficult to guess their reasons.

hotel nord-pinus tanger

THIS PAGE: *The hotel's salon has large windows that showcase lovely views of the sea and sky.*

OPPOSITE (FROM TOP): *Look out onto the Strait of Gibraltar while relaxing on a private balcony; the outdoor terrace offers guests an alternative dining spot where they can enjoy a meal under bright sunshine in the day and a clear sky full of twinkling stars at night.*

This is a notion that those in the know have been repeating for years, at first in hushed, wishful tones, then with increasing authority: the city of Tangier is long overdue for a return to the glory of its former days at the centre of international interests. Slowly, piece by piece, a picture of Tangier's revival has been coming together with the development of large-scale building projects and a renewed focus on tourism infrastructure. These days the Old Town is more alive than ever, with scores of exotic handicrafts and textiles to be found lining its maze of winding alleys.

The owner of the Grand Hotel Nord-Pinus in Provence has been a part of that early prescient crowd, deciding to create a new luxury destination in Tangier that would bring the exclusive charms of the French property to a uniquely Moroccan setting. The result is Hotel Nord-Pinus Tanger, which can be found within the city's kasbah. Towering above the rooftops below from its favourable position along the sea-facing edge of the historic fortress' Portuguese ramparts, the hotel enjoys clear views out over the Strait of Gibraltar to as far as the Spanish coast. The kasbah's 17th-century palaces and museums filled with artefacts and artwork are located nearby, alongside many impressive examples of local architecture that remain in use.

The intimate five-room Hotel Nord-Pinus Tanger takes the form of a traditional riad, and was once the lavish, palatial residence of an 18th-century pasha. Great care has been taken to preserve the idiosyncrasies of the building's original design, evident from the moment one first lays eyes on the front door—an immense construction framed by an intricately carved stone pediment that overflows with character. At the centre of the building is an open-air patio area defined by loping Portuguese-style arches and exquisite hand-cut tiles. Restoration work took 16 long months to complete, while interiors proudly remain in a state of flux to this day.

Possibly because the building already excels at establishing a sense of place, the interior design has been given free rein in creating a sumptuous living environment. In some corners, one senses a larger overarching

rooms
1 room • 4 suites

food
traditional Moroccan and fresh seafood

drink
terrace bar

features
body and hair care • airport transfers • wireless Internet access • hammam next door • massages • access to Le Mirage's private beach

nearby
kasbah • shops • museums

contact
11 Rue du Riad Sultan, Kasbah 90000 Tangier • telephone: +212.61.228 140 • facsimile: +212.39.336 363 • email: info@nord-pinus-tanger.com • website: www.nord-pinus-tanger.com

plan that encompasses all of the region's history, while other details suggest the opulent luxury of the property's French sibling. Period furnishings, like a chandelier transplanted from a mosque in Syria, are as likely to make an appearance as ultramodern tangerine loungers and modernist Jacques Adnet leather armchairs.

This audacious sense of style extends to the accommodations, which comprise a double room and four suites dressed in fine silks and rugs, artful zellij tile work, gold-leaf designs and a collection of original photographic work. Some rooms have walls and ceilings that are carved from cedar, while other spaces are more contemporary, but still feature a hint of the traditional. Despite this

love of the traditional, all rooms are equipped with such modern amenities as televisions, air-conditioning and wireless Internet access.

While the eclectic, elegant interiors instill a sense of wonder, it is comforting to learn that the hotel restaurant's cuisine is strictly from the old books. And with an abundance of fresh-caught seafood and excellent market produce, why wouldn't it be? Crisp salads, tajines, grilled fish and candied lemons are only a few examples of the dinner company one can expect to keep out on the spectacular outdoor terrace. Standing by the terrace's balustrade with a drink in hand, watching the distant lights, it would seem entirely possible that Tangier's much-discussed revival is already in full swing.

fez

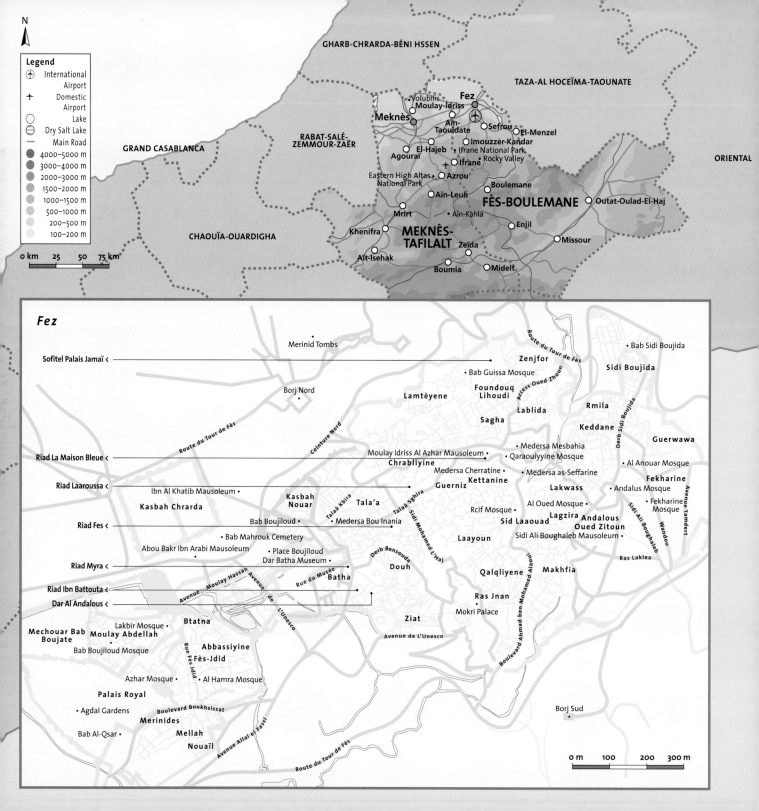

fez

a city of the written word

Wandering around the old town of Fez is like stepping back in time, a voyage into the past, surrounded by holy scriptures inscribed in stone: in calligraphy, on stucco mouldings, carved, drawn in rigid Kufic script or in flowery cursive writing on arches, etched into the pediments of palaces. Moulded by a religion which forbids all images, Fez has devoted itself to the written word.

Carillo, a Spanish writer who lived here in the 1920s, described Fez in his Andalusian Reflections as 'enlivened by the strange scent of Islamic flora'. Mohammed Alaoui Belrhiti, the Fassi poet, states that 'the Orient and Islam, to which Fez belongs, are still an opaque mirror on which skims a folkloric appeal'. This charmingly archaic image, far from rebuffing the visitor, satisfies one in search of a foreign experience.

an organised labyrinth

Fez is exclusive and distant, and, unlike Marrakech, is not an easy place to get to know quickly. Its double layout, including the two medinas of Fez el-Bali (a UNESCO World Heritage site) and Fez el-Jdid, is part of a sociocultural code unchanged since the Middle Ages. Nestling behind the ramparts, each district fits neatly into a jigsaw puzzle of shops, workshops, cafés, fondouks (inns) and countless abandoned palaces belonging to former viziers, pashas and sultans—scattered remnants of a glorious past.

Within this apparent anarchy, however, there is a consistent and seemingly inflexible structure based on the presence of a medersa (Islamic school) and a mosque—peaceful places for study and prayer—along with a drinking fountain, a bread oven, and a hammam—places for social contact and exchange. Witness here a blend of the sacred and the profane.

fez from the outside

The town spreads out before one in an almost biblical setting, on a promontory running from the Borj Nord to the Borj Sud, resembling a Paul Klee painting with a precariously balanced pile of houses. In a halo of dusty light, one can make out the whitewashed terraces splashed with the vivid colours of washing flapping in the breeze. Here and there, a minaret rises up, and then there are great holes of nothingness, overgrown open spaces and enclosed gardens, peaceful swathes of green which allow one to breathe.

THIS PAGE : The Bab Boujiloud is the entrance to the maze-like medina of Fez el-Bali.

PAGE 68: Looking out over Fez from the terrace of a private house at sunset—a very special moment.

fez from within

Come down through the olive groves through the Bab Boujiloud and plunge into the colourful bowels of Fez, the most beautiful medina in the world.

On one of her journeys, the novelist Anaïs Nin observed that Fez was an image of her inner self, 'Wearing a veil, full and inexhaustible, labyrinthian, so rich and variable I myself get lost'. That is how it is, for the town has a mystique: first one hears distant murmurs, then the tumult arising from the souks; one catches glimpses of it at the end of narrow lanes, stunned by the bitter, sensual odours; one is sucked in by the passing crowd, expanding like a river in flood. Beneath overhangings, amid light and shadow, one enters the souks, the world of henna, spices, haberdashers and metalworkers, constantly dodging donkeys heavily laden with everything under the sun, accompanied by their masters' cries of 'balek, balek' ('watch out, watch out').

restoration + rehabilitation

Fez, the imperial city, is undergoing a suitably royal facelift! The programme includes the restoration and rehabilitation of the town's historic monuments, which are particularly remarkable and numerous, especially in the medina, starting with its 14th-century surrounding walls. Magnificent pale stone walls wind their way around the medina like a golden belt. The restoration of these ramparts, 6 km (4 miles) in length, is being undertaken in sections. Fez is also placing its immortal works of art under the protective wing of the UNESCO World Heritage list.

These numerous historic sites include 9,600 listed workshops, nearly 10,000 houses, 300 fondouks, former inns and caravanserai, as well as sumptuous but dilapidated palaces, in dire need of restoration, such as the Dar Glaoui or that of the former vizier.

The 23 hectares (57 acres) of the Aïn Azliten district within the medina are also undergoing a positive renaissance, with engineers and architects working alongside a multi-disciplinary team of cultural experts to renovate this urban space, badly in need of improved lighting and restored façades and shop fronts. Also on the list is the restoration of the Aïn Alkhaïl Mosque, a project strongly backed by the European Union.

Two other major projects within this golden triangle of treasures formed within the borders of the Fez el-Bali are the restoration of the Qaraouiyyine Mosque, founded in the 9th century by a woman and formerly one of Islam's largest universities, and the Mausoleum of Moulay Idriss, the city's founder and patron saint.

THIS PAGE (FROM TOP): Fassi cuisine is said to be the best in Morocco, and it is particularly famous for its pigeon pastillas; the narrow lanes of the haberdashery market, one of the favourite haunts of Muslim women.

OPPOSITE: Despite their smell, the Chouara tanneries are one of the most memorable and colourful sights in Morocco.

The medina also contains numerous palaces, magnificent mansions hidden away behind heavy portals, many of them in a state of near ruin. It is envisaged that the town itself will purchase two of the most beautiful of these palaces, Dar Ba-Mohammed and Dar Glaoui, in concert with their heirs—a much hoped for salvage operation.

Some of the fondouks, like those of Achiyech, El Berka and Sagha, which once served as lodgings and shops, are about to receive a new lease of life. These vast, architecturally-rich, traditional buildings will be transformed into hotels, cultural centres, literary cafés and venues for viewing, understanding and purchasing local crafts.

Lastly, a competition has been launched to redesign the layout and revitalise the Place Boujiloud, one of the Fassi's favourite haunts. The intent is to make it a window for tourism, with information kiosks, where cultural events, demonstrations of regional gastronomy and so on could be hosted.

restore, renovate + welcome

Fez is already part of the traditional tourist circuit of imperial cities. In order to become a separate destination for short stays and city-breaks, it needs to be able to receive guests more royally. To this end, it aims to increase the number of beds available from 5,800 to 10,000 or more, developing the luxury end of the market, as well as encouraging private accommodation, which is a newly developing concept in Morocco.

ecology + good living

Two prime sites, one in a park and the other overlooking the medina, have both been selected to provide luxury accommodation that is in perfect harmony with the idea of sustainable development.

The first is an innovative development on a highly symbolic site, Wadi Fez. Within an urban park at the entrance to the new town, the project aims to give the impression of a 'clear forest' centred around water and the wadi's humid zones, a sort of 'inhabited garden' with hotels and residences in total harmony with their setting. Seventy hectares (173 acres) will be reserved for an 18-hole golf course and an activity area that will include a variety of facilities such as a Fassi crafts centre.

The second project consists of six hotel units, 300 residential units and a convention centre overlooking the medina, in the Ouislane Sector near Borj Sud. The hotels and residential units will have the most splendid view over the historic town and the hills, and at just a stone's throw from the medina itself and near the town centre, the project is perfectly situated for tourists' weekend breaks with a dose of culture.

the 'ziyarates' private accommodation project

This intelligent approach to tourism links tourist accommodation with humane development, a mix of culture, spirituality and mutual support. Thirty households have been carefully chosen to welcome tourists into the bosom of Fassi families within the medina, to enable them to share their everyday lives and values in the very best tradition of Moroccan hospitality. A fine exchange is in store, leading to an authentic and respectful form of tourism.

a town of craftsmen

The craftsmen of Fez seem to defy time continuing to ply their trades in much the same way since the Middle Ages. Look through any doorway into the minuscule, dark workshops in the medina and one will see them busy at work, the metalworkers, potters, weavers, leatherworkers, and embroiderers all. Their humble creations, which are entirely worked by hand, soon become works of art. Rejuvenating these traditional crafts is quite a slow process because, under the domination of the maalem, the master-dispenser of all knowledge, the apprentices in the guild schools are taught to have great veneration for the techniques, practices and motifs that have been passed down for generations. However, unfortunately rote repetition does not always give rise to creativity and inspiration.

ornamentation

Ornamentation is the principal goal of these crafts: stucco, zellij tile and zouac cover everything from floor to ceiling, including columns, pillars and galleries. Basic structures, be they rough brick, concrete, lime or plain mud are given delicate coatings, sometimes sparkling and colourful, sometimes more sober.

Chiselled with a gouge, cold-hammered, stencilled, embroidered... the techniques are many, as are the materials. Plaster, cedarwood, copper, golden-coloured tiles and leather—everything can be transformed into lace.

The motifs are abstract, geometric, epigraphic, floral or a mixture of all of these. The walls of living rooms are decorated to about halfway up with arabesques cut directly into freshly applied plaster. Carved monochrome stucco is also used on the walls in conjunction with zellij tile decoration, mosaic-like multicoloured glazed ceramic squares. The windows are hung with black screens pierced with foliated scrolls in archaic, mantilla-like friezes. The moucharabiehs, stone railings and sculpted wooden screens, made to look through without being seen from the other side, become 'cedar-stitch' canvases through which shards of light fall onto the floor. The engraved and pierced copper lanterns fragment and filter the light, creating magical shadows on the walls. Necklaces, bracelets and hands of Fatima, carefully worked in gold filigree and perforated, become light and delicate ornaments.

crafts in the medina: embroidery

The Moroccan technique of embroidery is the work of women, mostly done from the home. On a background cloth of cotton or white linen, the women deftly apply the famous reversible Fez stitch, a technique introduced by Franciscan nuns. Their patterns are invariably either geometric or floral, done with indelibly coloured threads, and the work is incredibly time-consuming. A tablecloth requires three months of work.

woven brocade

Bright multicoloured shuttles and silk threads in resplendent gold and silver are the weavers' basic tools for creating their wonderful 60 cm (24 in) wide strips of brocaded material on ancient wooden looms. The most complex patterns consist of pleats of different colours, surrounded by strips in relief, a technique learned from the Ottomans. There are now only a handful of craftsmen who still create such work, including Abdelkader Ouazzan in Oued Zhoun el-Blida.

THIS PAGE (FROM TOP): The tomb of Sidi Ahmad al-Tijaniun in Fez el-Bali is a fine example of Moorish architecture, with intricately carved woodwork, stucco décor and mosaic-like glazed ceramic tiles; detail of a colonnade covered with traditional blue and white zellij tile work.

OPPOSITE: Peaceful gardens, some with elegant ornamental ponds, lie hidden behind heavily sculpted palace doors.

pottery

The deservedly famous pottery of Fez—coloured a rich cobalt blue on a white background—owes its renown not only to the quality of its grey clay, its water and its glazes, but also to the elegance of its decorative genius. Work in a contemporary style is best seen in Aïn Noqbi, the potters' district, on the edge of town, while a visit to the Dar Batha Museum (in the Place de L'Istiqlal), formerly a Hispano-Moorish palace, will reveal some of the finest ceramics made in Fez, Safi and Salé from the 15th to the 18th centuries. Z'lafa (large bowls), tabsil (plates), cora (vases), all blue on white backgrounds, are decorated with detailed geometric and floral patterns in remarkably fine, assured strokes.

woodwork

Zouac is the generic Moroccan term for woodwork. Doors, ceilings and panels fashioned in fragrant cedarwood, are painstakingly carved with a gouge and wooden mallet. A restored fondouk and former caravanserai, the Nejjarine Museum of Wood and Carpentry (Place Nejjarine), has been converted into a museum of arts and woodcrafts, displaying the best work of carpenters, sculptors and painters. Furniture makers, it should be noted, were only required for making chests and shelves, the sole items of furniture in a traditional Arab household.

gebs (plasterwork)

The interior courtyard of the Medersa el-Attarine (located in the El-Attarine Souk), currently under restoration, contains excellent examples of gebs, traditional stucco work (a mixture of plaster, ground marble and egg white). Drawing on the beautiful richness of swirling Arabic script, the gebs here are like an abstract poem, a profusion of exquisitely delicate lace-like friezes, in varying shades of grey and white.

the road from fez to rabat

There are two places along this route which must be visited, both of them classed as UNESCO World Heritage Sites: Meknès, the imperial city, and Volubilis, the city of antiquity. Their ruins and remains still clearly evoke the splendour of the Roman and Alaouite civilisations.

meknès, morocco's versailles

The history of this former imperial city is inextricably linked to Moulay Ismail, the second of the Alaouite sultans. In 1672, he quit Marrakech and chose to settle in Meknès instead. A contemporary of Louis XIV, Moulay Ismail suffered similar delusions of grandeur, and he was

determined to make his new capital the equal of Versailles. He certainly succeeded in terms of size and splendour. Moulay Ismail also undertook pharaonic building projects. He thought nothing of pilfering some of his predecessors' monuments, depriving Volubilis, for example, of some of its most beautiful decorative elements and pillaging from the Bahia Palace in Marrakech. He recruited armies of masons and workers from neighbouring tribes and forcibly enrolled vast numbers of black slaves, prisoners and Christian captives.

The town is surrounded by ramparts pierced by vast gateways. The most famous of these gateways, Bab el-Mansour, is considered to be the most beautiful in Morocco. Flanked by two square towers, the doors are remarkably elegant and delicate, despite their imposing size. They are the work of Mansour el-Aleuj—hence the gate's name—a Christian architect who converted to Islam, otherwise known as 'the victorious renegade'. The golden stone on the façade shows up the delicate relief decoration—geometric tracery breaking loose from the green ceramic background. Opposite the gateway, El-Hedime Square (literally 'demolition square'), once a depot for building materials and stone, now forms a link between the medina and the imperial city—a lively place towards the end of the day.

THIS PAGE: Majestic and perfectly proportioned, the Bab el-Mansour in Meknès, also known as the Gateway of the Renegade, leads through to the small medina and symbolises the absolute power of the Sultan.

OPPOSITE (FROM TOP): Detail of a gebs, contouring a wall like a poem written in cursive script; babouches are all the rage: made with embroidered sabra or coloured leather.

The Dar Kebira district, now a working class area, is where the palace of the same name was built in 1697. Wandering among the rooms and reading the various dazzling descriptions, one can just about picture the 'Versailles' that once stood here.

The visible remains of the palace include the Dar el-Ma and Agdal Ponds, the royal pavilion and the walls of the prison. The palace, protected by three circles of walls, consisted of 20 or so pavilions and two mosques, linked by long avenues adorned with ponds which irrigated the gardens. Warehouses, granaries, stables, arsenals and a prison, constructed below ground, made up the rest of the complex—a town within a town.

volubilis, the mosaic museum

Volubilis is an exceptionally well-preserved large Roman colonial town, situated on the edge of the Empire, hence its inclusion as a UNESCO World Heritage Site. Set in 40 hectares (100 acres) of rural landscape, surrounded by orchards and olive oil presses, over half of the original settlement has yet to be excavated.

This vast area, scattered with villas, triumphal arches, capitals, temples and thermae, was surrounded by 2.5 km (1.6 miles) of thick ramparts, one section of which remains from the time of Marcus Aurelius. This ancient city was founded in the 3rd century BCE, the Carthaginian era. During the 2nd century BCE, it was absorbed into the Mauretanian kingdom and later became one of the capitals of Juba II (52 BCE–23 CE), King of Mauretania and ally of Rome. At the beginning of the Roman conquest, around 40 CE, Volubilis was one of the main cities in the province of Tingitana. By the end of the 3rd century, it was in the hands of the Christianised Berbers, who built a wall to divide the city. The town was severely damaged by the Lisbon earthquake of 1755 and never recovered.

It is the Roman period of Volubilis, during the reign of the emperor Caracalla, that brought about the especially notable mosaics which still decorate the ruins today. All the houses had the same basic layout, with reception rooms, private lodgings and terraces. Some of them are virtually carpeted with very well-preserved mosaic, made up of hundreds of small pieces of marble and limestone in subtly shaded colours.

These mosaics are a mine of information on the social mores of this ancient time, as well as a tutorial on Greek mythology. The name of each house is taken from the theme of its mosaic. Thus, the mosaic in the House of Dionysius is a eulogy to the god of wine; that of the Four Seasons, is an allegory with nymphs frolicking in a leafy setting. Some pieces from Volubilis are now in the museum in Rabat, but most of the mosaics have been left in situ and are in an excellent state of preservation, which makes Volubilis well worth a visit.

THIS PAGE: Detail of a Roman mosaic unearthed at Volubilis, its colours as bright as the day it was made.

OPPOSITE: A visit to Volubilis, Morocco's most important site dating from antiquity, should not be missed: the well-preserved remains of Roman houses are truly remarkable.

...a mine of information on the social mores of this ancient time...

dar al andalous

The story of old Fez is a proud one, renowned for centuries as home to one of the most dignified and advanced civilisations—a multicultural city of wealth, refined arts and academia. Despite this, traditions have always been central to the Fassi way of life. When it came to the building of family homes, years of work and preparation were required on the part of the owners, collaborating individually with a wide range of craftsmen to develop them entirely from the ground up. As a result, these residences were often remarkable examples of the region's architectural techniques, having been built by many hands.

The Dar Al Andalous hotel in the Medina El-Bali is the product of joining two riads built at the beginning of the last century. They belonged to one of Fez's most prominent families and are accordingly large and grand in the scope of their execution. Their design is typical of most riads, with central courtyard patios and many signs of Arab-Andalusian influence. Renovated in 2002, the entire property has now been updated to become a guesthouse suited to the needs of modern visitors, while still immersed in the city's rich visual and cultural history.

Possessing two courtyard patios, Dar Al Andalous provides a glimpse of the privileged lifestyles once led by Fez's rich home owners. Isolated from the heat and noise outside by solid walls measuring over two storeys high, the patios are relaxing spaces furnished with comfortable seats and leafy plants. Small

marble fountains lend an air of serenity to lazy afternoons spent reading or candlelight dinners in the evenings. Original details like towering cedar doors, intricate mosaics and decorative patterned windows enhance the Moroccan feel of these public spaces.

Putting the emphasis on luxury on show, the riad has twice as many suites as it does standard double rooms. A total of eight suites are available, while the four rooms are not to be underestimated by any means: each room still enjoys the high standard of modern conveniences maintained throughout the hotel. All rooms are air-conditioned and come

THIS PAGE (FROM TOP): The courtyard is an informal yet intimate setting for conversation; stained-glass windows add a cacophony of hues to the rooms and suites.

OPPOSITE (FROM TOP): Rich colours bring warmth to the rooms; the terrace is ideal for a romantic candlelight dinner.

rooms
4 rooms • 8 suites

food
Al Fassia: traditional Moroccan

drink
beverage list

features
hammam • rooftop terrace • solarium • traditional music performances • wireless Internet access

nearby
Dar Batha Museum • Medina El-Bali • tennis • thermal spas • golf

contact
14 Derb Bennani, Douh-Batha, Medina 30000 Fez •
telephone: +212.35.740 700 or +212.35.741 082 •
facsimile: +212.35.740 712 •
email: dar.alandalous@menara.ma •
website: www.dar-alandalous.com

with minibars, safes, televisions with satellite channel access and the ever-important wireless Internet access. Room sizes vary from 16 sq m (172 sq ft), as in the case of the Medina Room which can be booked as a single, to the Diafa Room's generous 24 sq m (258 sq ft) of space, which houses a king-sized bed, lounge and en suite bathroom. The remaining two rooms—somewhere in the middle in size—have private terraces with amazing views of Zalagh Mountain.

Many of the suites have four-poster king-sized beds and more spacious compositions. The Mezzanine Suite on the second level is particularly large at 32 sq m (344 sq ft) and overlooks the courtyard from its position. For

the ultimate indulgence, three deluxe suites are equipped with Moroccan-style lounges and in-room jacuzzis. Antique stained-glass windows in some of the guestrooms add to the unique look and feel created by the mix of designer furniture and classic elements.

In addition to its beautiful patios and first-class accommodations, Dar Al Andalous also offers guests an expansive terrace with views of the medina, a hammam which offers an array of body treatments and the Al Fassia restaurant: a local institution of traditional cuisine. With so much to offer from a central location in Fez's medina, near the Dar Batha Museum and other sites of interest, this hotel is an attraction in its own right.

sofitel palais jamaï

THIS PAGE: *Dine by candlelight on the pool terrace, with its amazing view of the medina.*

OPPOSITE (FROM LEFT): *The hotel is decorated in traditional Moorish style and opulence; a quick dip in the pool can rejuvenate you after a day's excitement in the medina.*

Located just behind the old ramparts of Fez, the Sofitel Palais Jamaï is the only hotel inside the medina of Fez. Built in 1879 for Jamaï, the Grand Vizier of Sultan Moulay El-Hassan I, this beautiful palace remained the Jamaï family home until the 1930s. Its ornamental Moorish style is an aesthetic wonder, and its features include painted walls and ceilings, fine woodwork, Moroccan ceramic mosaics and stucco embroideries. Around the niches and vaults a sense of history permeates and the regal air is palpable. When the Jamaï family left, a hotel seemed the palace's obvious destiny, and with Sofitel's careful restoration it remains a celebrated accommodation in Morocco's spiritual and cultural capital.

Guests have included no less than royalty itself—His Majesty Mohammed VI stayed here when he was a young prince. And the palace has continued to impress. In 2006, readers of *Condé Nast Traveler* voted the Palais Jamaï the Best Hotel in Africa. With 123 rooms and 19 suites, there are varying degrees of opulence available, but it is guaranteed in each room, where every inch is decorated with intricate Moorish detail. The flooring, the bedding, the chandeliers, everything that can be decorated is done so tastefully yet decadently. Yet, if the inside of the building is an eyeful, there's even more to be had through the windows.

The rooms offer amazing views; the hotel's Andalusian gardens—complete with tangerine and lemon trees—form the foreground, the sprawling medina the background. If your room does not face the medina then the L'Oliveraie restaurant serves breakfast and, at lunch, a buffet and barbecue on the pool terrace that faces this magnificent view, so no one misses out. Other dining options include Al Jounaïna, with an international, but predominantly French, menu. To continue the Moroccan experience, go to Al Fassia. It serves refined Moroccan cuisine in a traditional setting—it even has its own Andalusian band and belly dancer.

For daytime pursuits, the SPA offers the best of Moroccan therapy. In the beautiful hammam the staff can take you through the paces of a traditional bathing ritual, an experience not to be missed. The décor is again authentic: brick-red tadelkat plaster covers the walls, white marble benches provide resting places and the spa rooms feature blue enamel inlays. The jacuzzi is stylish and comfortable and the massage menu should cover any particular need.

Everywhere, you'll be greeted by friendly and helpful staff who are ever ready to attend to you. The concierge can organise a guide to show you around the medina, a good idea as—this being the largest medina in the world—it can get a little overwhelming. With all this wrapped up in what the Sofitel Group names as one of its legendary hotels, Sofitel is justified in being proud of the Palais. For a sense of history, for its grandeur and for its stylish decadence, it can't be beaten.

For a sense of history, for its grandeur and for its stylish decadence, it can't be beaten.

rooms
123 rooms • 19 suites

food
Al Jounaïna: international •
Al Fassia: Moroccan •
L'Oliveraie: buffet and barbecue

drink
Al Mandar

features
hammam • fitness centre • relaxation pool •
sauna • tennis court • excursions •
heated outdoor pool • wireless Internet access

nearby
Bab Guissa • Medersa el-Attarine • Bab Ftouh •
Bab Segma • Medersa Bou Inania •
Bab Smarine • Qaraouiyyine Mosque •
Moulay Idriss Mosque

contact
Bab Guissa, 30000 Fez •
telephone: +212.35.634 331 •
facsimile: +212.35.635 096 •
email: H2141@accor.com •
website: www.sofitel.com

riad fes

A 30-minute drive from Fez's international airport, the Riad Fes is a boutique hotel with 21 rooms. One of the most talked about converted riads in the city, this hotel boasts uncompromisingly high standards of luxury and service whilst offering the convenience of a central location. Museums and historical sites are located nearby, and Moroccan handicrafts and souvenirs are available from the many convenient souks and shops.

Composed of two standalone properties, Riad Fes is the largest of its kind in the city. Both houses have their own design schemes, which offer the benefit of two very different experiences in one hotel stay. The differences are the most readily evident in their inner courtyard patios. One is a reflection of the region's past, with Islamic patterns, intricate mosaics, antique wood doors and stucco walls lit by a large Fassi lamp overhead. The other, in the Andalous Pavilion, resonates with a more subdued calm inspired by the Alhambra, and features fine marble work, colonnades and a pool at the centre of it all. Its clean lines simultaneously embrace modern aesthetics and the property's Moroccan heritage.

Both houses carry their distinctive styles right through to the rooms, which are unique creations in themselves. Guests may elect to stay in standard or deluxe rooms, while suites range from the smaller junior suites to the sumptuous Ambassador and Royal Suites. All rooms come with modern amenities like air-conditioning and satellite television channels.

Standard rooms are spacious and some even come with a private terrace. Bathrobes and slippers are provided for all guests, who may also avail themselves of complimentary Internet access and Moroccan tea throughout the day. Deluxe rooms, with their exquisite furnishings and lavish en suite bathrooms, overlook the Andalous Pavilion's courtyard.

Housed in the original building, junior suites overlook the classic 19th-century patio and gardens, spread out over as much as 40 sq m (431 sq ft) of lush fabrics and antiques. For rooms with space to stretch out in style, there are the 50-sq-m- (538-sq-ft-) large Ambassador Suites, decorated with objets d'art. Key features include access to a terrace with views of the interior gardens and spectacular marble and tadelakt plaster bathrooms. The Royal Suite is Riad Fes' finest room, featuring a new living room and private terrace, detailed stucco work and a carved ceiling. Although it is very large and spacious, the suite has an air of intimacy, and is thus recommended for honeymooning couples.

Even with the overwhelming abundance of good food in Fez, the hotel's restaurant stands as some of the best dining available. Savour authentic Moroccan cuisine in one of three themed dining rooms, or up on a roof terrace with views of the entire medina. High above the unbroken maze of winding footpaths and ancient buildings, the elegant Riad Fes puts guests on top of a world that could not exist anywhere else.

THIS PAGE: *The opulent interior of one of the Ambassador Suites.*

OPPOSITE (FROM LEFT): *The patio's décor was inspired by Moorish art and architecture; from the terrace, you can view the entirety of the medina while savouring authentic Moroccan cuisine.*

rooms
21 rooms • 5 suites

food
traditional Moroccan

drink
L' Alcazar Bar

features
hammam • rooftop terrace • 3 dining rooms • wireless Internet access • complimentary tea

nearby
golf • shops • hot springs • horse riding • Volubilis • Bahlil Caves • medina

contact
Derb Ben Slimane, Zerbtana
30000 Fez •
telephone: +212.35.947 610 or +212.35.741 206 •
facsimile: +212.35.741 143 •
email: contact@riadfes.com •
website: www.riadfes.com

riad ibn battouta

Nestled between the bustling medina of Fez and Dar Batha Museum, Riad Ibn Battouta is a hideaway for the weary traveller. It is here that history thrives on alongside modernity. Painstakingly restored by hand, the hotel showcases traditional Moroccan architecture. Named after the celebrated Arab explorer, this thematic boutique hotel promises to be more than just a place to rest for the night.

Rooms at Riad Ibn Battouta are a luxurious affair. Individually decorated, each of the seven suites showcases parts of the life of the Son of Morocco and his travels. Guests are able to explore exotic destinations such as

THIS PAGE (FROM TOP): Lounges offer quiet settings for intimate conversations with friends; guests who prefer to be under an open sky can relax on plush couches in the courtyard.

OPPOSITE (FROM TOP): Intricate tiling decorates much of the hotel; as its name implies, north Moroccan influences hold sway in the Nord Maroc Room.

Sanaa or Ispahan as seen through Ibn Battouta's eyes, as the suites are decorated according to the theme of his destinations. Reversible air-conditioning in all rooms ensures a comfortable stay, no matter which season it is. For even greater luxury, guests can choose to stay in either of the two suites that come with their own private terrace. These terraces provide breathtaking views of the medina and the hills of the Middle Atlas.

If relaxation is among your top priorities, worry not! Adhering to Moroccan tradition, a well-equipped hammam is at the disposal of guests. Here, well-trained therapists provide beauty and health treatments. Argan oil massages are also available to soothe away the stresses of everyday life.

For some adventure, guests can head to the nearby medina. Reputed to be one of the largest and most interesting medinas of the Arabic world, you can definitely experience Fez at its best. If that is too much excitement for you, the roof terrace of the hotel is

Riad Ibn Battouta has never failed to celebrate the cultural diversity of Morocco.

available for guests to take in some fresh air and appreciate the splendour of the hills of the Middle Atlas. Guests can also relax in the comfortable library, where the wide selection of books will not disappoint.

Moroccan cuisine is considered to be one of the most refined, for its subtle flavours can only result from the unique blend of several cultural backgrounds. The hotel's restaurant provides delicious Moroccan fare, where recipes from the 14th century are blended with modern tastes.

Culinary classes allow guests to take a piece of Moroccan tradition home with them in the form of Moroccan cooking. Participants are fully immersed in the Moroccan cooking experience—they are brought to the nearby markets to buy their own raw ingredients for the classes before being instructed by master chefs in the afternoon. After the lesson, guests can tuck into their culinary creations. Arabic calligraphy classes are also available for those who are handier with a pen rather than a pan. No matter their level of proficiency, participants are safe in the skilled hands of renowned masters who will guide them through the exploration of the art.

Riad Ibn Battouta has never failed to celebrate the cultural diversity of Morocco. With great style and elegance, this hotel provides a unique and memorable experience for the discerning traveller.

rooms
7 suites, 2 with private terraces

food
traditional Moroccan, organic and vegetarian available upon request

drink
bar

features
terrace • patio • library • fountain • hammam • salon of music • spa • in-room massage

nearby
medina • Dar Batha Museum

contact
9 Derb Lalla Mina, Avenue Allal el Fassi, Batha, 30000 Fez •
telephone: +212.35.637 191 or +212.71.654 217 •
facsimile: +212.35.637 190 •
email: contact@riadibnbattouta.com •
website: www.riadibnbattouta.com

riad la maison bleue

THIS PAGE: *The suites at La Maison Bleue are furnished in a distinctly Moroccan manner.*

OPPOSITE (FROM TOP): *Relax with a drink at the bar after a day of adventure in the medina; many traditional treatments, including body scrubs and masks, are available at the spa shared by the two properties.*

Two sister properties in the heart of Fez's medina, La Maison Bleue and the Riad Maison Bleue are exclusive private hotels established in buildings of extraordinary grandeur and historical value. Both are splendid choices for travellers seeking a central location from which to explore the labyrinthine depths of the medina. They also share a superb spa and serve fine Moroccan cuisine from their respective restaurants.

The main house, La Maison Bleue, was built as a large family home in 1915 for a renowned judge and astrologer. It continues to be operated today by his grandchildren, who have retained the original charm of the palatial mansion and resisted the urge to create more rooms. Instead, just six rooms occupy the wealth of space within the house, each one an authentically decorated living space of blue zellij mosaics, antique carved doors and original stucco work. Five are deluxe rooms with king-sized beds, some of them magnificent four-poster affairs, while the last is a cosy single room. Despite their traditional aspects, all are equipped with modern conveniences like Internet access, air-conditioning and in-room safes.

At the centre of the property is a large courtyard which serves as a hub for visitor activity. Three public lounge areas surround it, furnished in the style of Moroccan salons. These are ideal places to savour mint tea or meals. Alternatively, guests may be served in the courtyard, where breakfast is customarily presented, or on a rooftop terrace with an unbroken view of Fez's rooftops below. The cuisine is unmistakably Moroccan with a menu of highlights including cooked salads, lamb tajines and pastillas. There is also a quiet library with a large collection of books, handwritten letters and original oil paintings.

The Riad Maison Bleue is much more than an extension to the original hotel, it is a remarkable hotel in its own right. This 19th-

rooms
La Maison Bleue: 6 rooms •
Riad Maison Bleue: 13 rooms

food
traditional Moroccan

drink
beverage list

features
hammam • spa treatments • pool • library •
rooftop terraces • Internet access

nearby
medina • museums • shops • palaces

contact
La Maison Bleue: 2 Place de L'Istiqlal, Batha
30000 Fez •
telephone: +212.35.741 843 •
facsimile: +212.35.740 686 •

Riad Maison Bleue: 33 Derb el Mitter, Talaâ Kbira
30000 Fez •
telephone: +212.35.741 839 •
facsimile: +212.35.741 6873 •
email: resa@maisonbleue.com •
website: www.maisonbleue.com

century building was once home to another prominent resident of Fez who was also a judge and a professor of theology. In addition, from the 1920s onward, the riad was the birthplace and home of Aziz Lahbabi, noted poet and philosopher.

Boasting 13 guestrooms—of which 11 are deluxe and two standard—arranged around three interlinked courtyard patios, the Riad Maison Bleue rivals the very best in terms of luxury and majesty. All throughout, an Arabic-Andalusian architectural style captures the imagination, while gracious touches like a welcome snack of orange-blossom milk and stuffed dates will impress even the most jaded traveller. The Riad Maison Bleue's central courtyard features a pool, and guests

may be interested to know that all three wings have rooftop terraces that showcase markedly different views of the medina.

The advanced TechnoGym at the Maison Bleue Spa also overlooks the city rooftops, giving guests an incomparable sight to accompany their workouts. After a visit to the hammam or a soothing traditional body treatment using aromatic oils, a relaxation room with windows facing the Borj Nord awaits with teas and herbal infusions to complete the rejuvenation process.

Whichever property you choose, you are guaranteed a world-class boutique hotel experience. Add that to the winning charm of their classic Moroccan interiors, and the result is a stay that won't be forgotten.

riad laaroussa

THIS PAGE: The medina of Fez as viewed from the riad.

OPPOSITE (FROM TOP): The well-appointed Grey Suite exudes warmth and welcome; the Red Room's bathroom is strikingly decorated in brilliant shades of red and gold.

No visitor to the ancient city of Fez can go without spending several days exploring the depths of its colourful medina, and there are few better ways to absorb the activity and atmosphere of this UNESCO World Heritage Site than to remain squarely in the middle of it at all times.

A great base camp from which to explore the city is the magnificent Riad Laaroussa, a palace of a 17th-century structure which spans nearly 1,000 sq m (10,764 sq ft) in the heart of the old city. At one point, it was home to the Defence Minister, Mehdi Mnebhi, but it has now been reworked to a state of classical elegance that far surpasses that of any point in its storied history. The process took two long years of meticulous work by a large team of local craftsmen who used traditional restoration techniques and materials.

Privacy is one of the Laaroussa's strongest draws, with the riad enclosing a walled patio planted with orange trees. Here, in the shade of leafy branches, soothed by the sound of running water from the fountains, guests are invited to enjoy the Moroccan sun in a world that is virtually theirs alone.

The hotel's Fassi cuisine regularly takes centre stage on the patio, with the attentive staff ever-ready to set tables for an intimate meal under the stars or mid-afternoon sun. Experienced chefs prepare spectacular meals cooked in the traditional style that captures the spirit of the region, created with fresh market produce only. As an additional service, guests of the riad are welcome to learn how to reproduce their favourite meals in cooking classes conducted by the kitchen staff.

Eschewing the creation of a large multi-room hotel, the owners deliberately restricted themselves to just four suites and three rooms within the massive property. The result is a refreshingly unhurried pace of life, where each resident has as much personal space as they desire. The rooms were originally living room lounges, and their detailed floors and ceilings have been entirely retained.

rooms
3 rooms · 4 suites

food
traditional Fassi

drink
beverage list

features
rooftop terrace · spa · patio gardens · cooking classes · traditional hammam · massage area

nearby
medina · shops · Royal Golf de Fès · hot springs · horse riding · Roman ruins

contact
3 Derb Bechara
30000 Fez ·
telephone: +212.74.187 639 ·
email: contact@riad-laaroussa.com ·
website: www.riad-laaroussa.com

All accommodations take their names and design directions from colours, with red, blue and yellow influencing the three rooms. Equipped with either double beds or twin singles, these lovely rooms are fully air-conditioned and heated, and each has a spacious bathroom with tadelakt plaster walls in their theme colours. For instance, the Red Room matches red tadelakt with red brick, set off against gleaming gold fixtures for effect. Entry into these rooms is through the original doors of carved wood.

Suites feature separate living areas, and some are able to house up to four guests. The Cream Suite offers gorgeous baldaquin beds, one of which is on a separate loft level, and a fireplace in the common area. For parties of three, the Green Suite offers one double bed and an additional single bed. Furnishings throughout these rooms are elegantly simple, while intricate mosaics and Arabian-inspired motifs lend colour and character to various surfaces. Large windows ensure plenty of natural light throughout the day, and provide views of the medina by night, when it is most vibrant.

A large rooftop terrace is another ideal spot from which to take in the surrounding landscape, especially over a cup of the freely flowing Moroccan tea. Whether guests are on a short stopover or an extended vacation, the Riad Laaroussa provides the royal treatment.

riad myra

THIS PAGE: *The central courtyard in the evenings seems almost like an entirely different place.*

OPPOSITE (FROM TOP): *Lush fabrics, antique English furniture and modern amenities combine to produce comfortable havens; its style originally inspired by both Andalusian and Moorish architecture, the building's beauty has been restored.*

Any potential visitor to Fez will have heard of its Medina El-Bali, a sprawling labyrinth filled with shopping souks, mosques and donkey-pulled carriages. This UNESCO World Heritage Site is not only a tourist attraction, it is the authentic, still-beating heart of the ancient city's formidable history. Yet of all the riads in the medina, few can be said to offer a living experience that complements the old city quite as well as Riad Myra.

Any appreciation of the historic building that houses the hotel must begin from its central courtyard, with its stucco walls and azure columns clad in zellij tiles, all arranged around a star-shaped marble fountain. It is furnished with antique English tables and chairs set off against lush plants, rich carpets and immense cedar doors leading off into the guestrooms and lounges. By day, the patio is a peaceful haven where one can sip scented teas, but lit by lanterns for evening dining, it takes on a markedly different atmosphere of grandeur and romance.

In each of the 12 rooms and suites, the same attention to detail has been observed with traditional designs and handcrafted

...lit by lanterns for evening dining, it takes on a markedly different atmosphere...

rooms
12 rooms and suites

food
Al Fassia: traditional Moroccan

drink
beverage list

features
hammam • rooftop terrace • salon lounge •
wireless Internet access • concierge • library

nearby
Dar Batha Museum • Medina El-Bali • golf •
pool • tennis • Atlas Mountains

contact
13 Rue Salaj, Batha
30000 Fez •
telephone: +212.35.740 000 •
facsimile: +212.35.638 282 •
email: info@riadmyra.com •
website: www.riadmyra.com

furnishings. Beds are all very large and many are four-posters draped with enough flowing fabric to satisfy even the most demanding modern-day classicist. En suite bathrooms, too, are very generous and feature the luxury of full-sized bathtubs and bidets.

The majority of rooms at Riad Myra are configured as suites, and each has a unique feature that distinguishes it from the rest. Regardless of choice, all are guaranteed to be fine examples of Moroccan hospitality. The largest option available is suitably named Le Vizir, and it boasts a separate dressing room in addition to the usual extras.

In every room, the latest technologies have been quietly integrated for convenience. Direct telephone and fax access, satellite television, Internet connections, minibars and air-conditioning are just some of the modern comforts one can expect to find.

A number of common areas like a library and a terraced deck for sunbathing are on offer for guests who do not wish to lounge in their rooms. There is also a hammam on the premises for relaxing body treatments. The restaurant Al Fassia's name may be familiar to those who have spent time in Marrakech, and its traditional Moroccan fare can be served throughout the riad, including in the rooms.

The final detail in Riad Myra's tribute to Fez's illustrious past as a city of privilege and refinement comes in the form of the excellent service encountered throughout. All that's left for one to do is enjoy.

rabat+thecoast

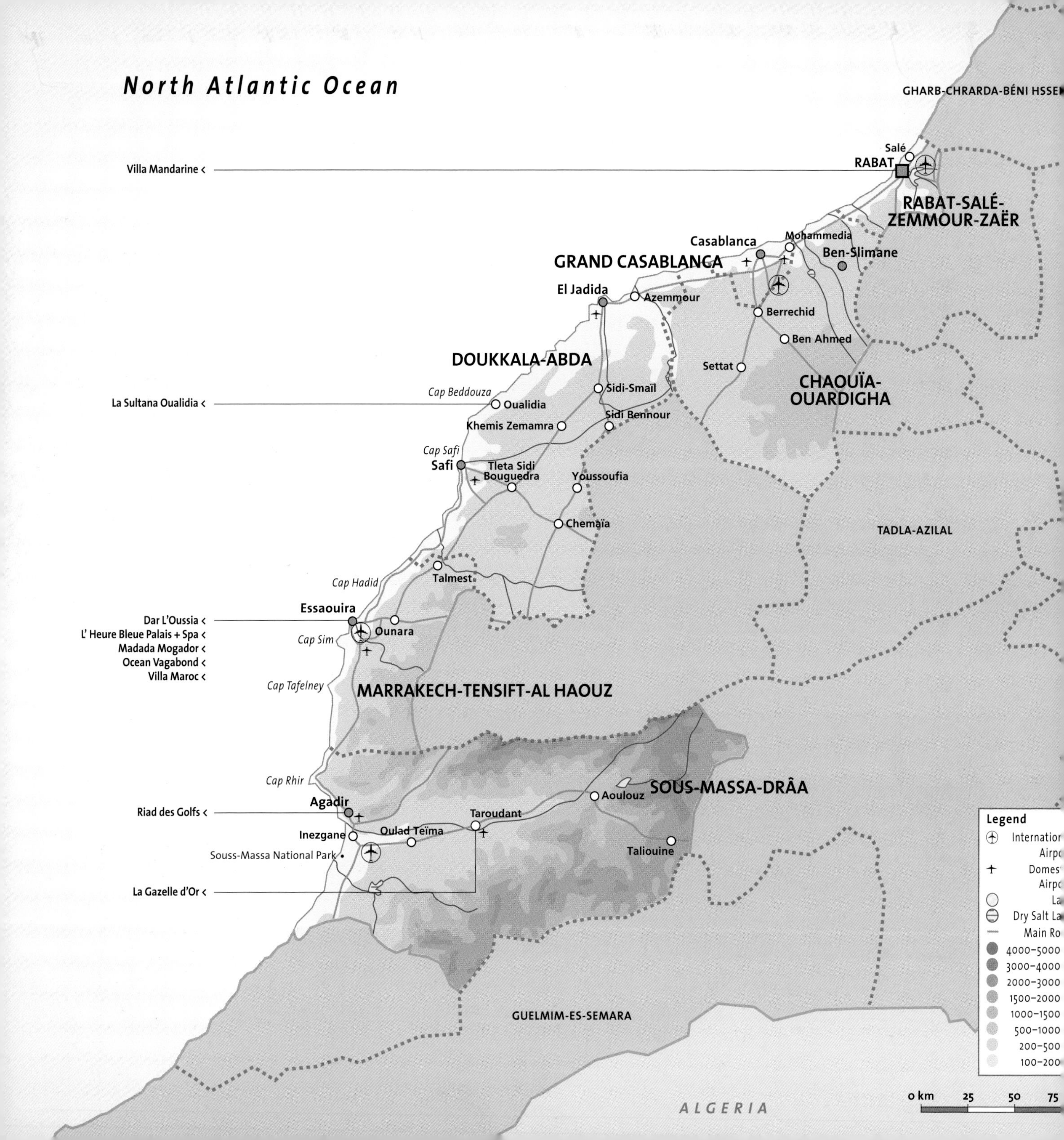

North Atlantic Ocean

GHARB-CHRARDA-BÉNI HSSE

Villa Mandarine ‹

Salé
RABAT
RABAT-SALÉ-
ZEMMOUR-ZAËR

Casablanca
Mohammedia
Ben-Slimane
GRAND CASABLANCA

El Jadida
Azemmour
Berrechid
Ben Ahmed

DOUKKALA-ABDA
Settat
CHAOUÏA-
OUARDIGHA

Cap Beddouza
La Sultana Oualidia ‹
Oualidia
Sidi-Smaïl
Khemis Zemamra
Sidi Bennour

Cap Safi
Safi
Tleta Sidi
Bouguedra
Youssoufia

TADLA-AZILAL

Chemaïa

Cap Hadid
Talmest

Dar L'Oussia ‹
Essaouira
L' Heure Bleue Palais + Spa ‹
Ounara
Madada Mogador ‹
Cap Sim
Ocean Vagabond ‹
Villa Maroc ‹

Cap Tafelney
MARRAKECH-TENSIFT-AL HAOUZ

Cap Rhir

Aoulouz
SOUS-MASSA-DRÂA
Riad des Golfs ‹
Agadir
Taroudant
Inezgane
Oulad Teïma
Souss-Massa National Park ‹
Taliouine

La Gazelle d'Or ‹

GUELMIM-ES-SEMARA

Legend
Internation
Airpo
Domes
Airpo
La
Dry Salt La
Main Ro
4000-5000
3000-4000
2000-3000
1500-2000
1000-1500
500-1000
200-500
100-200

ALGERIA

o km   25   50   75

rabat + the coast

the atlantic ports + medinas along the coast

Essaouira, Agadir, Taroudant, Rabat, Salé, Casablanca, El Jadida, Safi, Oualidia, Rabat—ports, forts, medinas, and new towns are strung out along the Atlantic coast. There is nearly 3,000 km (1,864 miles) of varied coastline—long beaches and cliffs, rocky creeks and blue lagoons, some developed, some left untouched. In places, the desert meets the sea.

Since antiquity, this coast has been a busy and bitterly fought over trade route linking Africa to the eastern Mediterranean. In the earliest makeshift landing places, along the shore, the Phoenicians established trading posts for exchanging gold, ivory, wood and other exotic goods for more essential items. These ports became favoured anchorages, access to which was much coveted by the Romans, the Carthaginians, and the King of Mauretania.

The Spaniards and the Portuguese built forts and fortresses, not so much with the aim of conquering, but rather they wanted to set up a military and commercial structure, which would enable them to trade profitably. These developed into medinas where, from time to time, pirates and buccaneers sought refuge between raids for themselves and their plunder. In the 19th century, the French created new towns and seaside resorts in the latest European style.

THIS PAGE (FROM TOP): *A marabout tomb on the beach at Essaouira, abandoned to the wind and the waves; fishing continues to be practised traditionally around Essaouira—simple wooden boats are still in use.*

PAGE 94: *With its fine seafront promenade, beaches and cafes, Agadir remains a popular seaside resort.*

essaouira

Known as Amogdoul in the Middle Ages and Mogador under the Portuguese in the 16th century, the town only took the name of Essaouira in the 18th century. Its history, however, dates back to antiquity, to the 1st century BCE, under the rule of King Juba II of Mauretania. The Phoenicians, great sea merchants, named it the 'Port of Timbuktu'. The Romans came in their galleys to the offshore Purple Islands in search of crimson, the precious dye extracted from a shell, the murex, which, once ground, was used to colour the togas so essential to the Roman aristocracy.

With its Berber population living alongside former black African slaves, Jews and Christians—leading to fruitful, if occasionally violent, exchanges—Essaouira has always been open to the outside world, adopting a variety of cultures and traditions.

the heart of the city

Essaouira was both a fishing port and a prosperous trading post when the Alaouite Sultan, Mohammed III, added the kasbah (citadel). At his request, the French architect Théodore Cornut drew up plans for the port and the kasbah. Behind the double row of ramparts, the rigorous

order of the medina is both surprising and reassuring. 'Es-Saouira' rightly signifies 'the well-designed'. From the northern to the southern bastions and from the marine gateway to the Bab Doukkala, all the streets run at right angles, converging on the main thoroughfare, which is divided into three sections: Avenue Oqba ben Nafii, Avenue de L'Istiqlal and Avenue Zerktouni. On each side are the various souks: one for fish, another for spices, others for babouches (open-backed sandals), jewellery and grain. Along the western edge of town, exposed to the full force of the Atlantic winds, the skala (kasbah) is the fragile heart of the medina. The bronze cannons facing the sea nowadays threaten nothing more menacing than seagulls. Lashed by waves and eroded by salt, the city walls are in need of restoration.

a very special place

Essaouira's townscape emerges from its pink ramparts gracefully clad in white and blue. Myriad boutiques, antique shops and art galleries line the narrow, mainly pedestrianised streets of the medina, making it an ideal place in which to wander quietly and buy presents or souvenirs. Small squares shaded by monkey-puzzle trees and surrounded by cafés invite one to linger, to watch leisurely the world pass by, observing the local women dressed modestly in their traditional white haïks (a long garment which completely covers the body).

There is a square at the entrance to the medina named after Orson Welles, the famous film director, who brought a moment of commotion to the otherwise quiet skala when he filmed his version of *Othello* there in 1952. Thereafter, throughout the 1960s and 1970s, the town was a haven for hippies, with crowds of young admirers flocking to see their idol, Jimi Hendrix. Guitarist Brian Jones and rock musician Mick Jagger, of the band Rolling Stones, also spent some time there, drawn by the Gnaoui music, whose rhythms subsequently found their way into their own music. With strong piercing rhythms, played on drums accompanied by a three-string lute, the gambri, the Gnaoua recount the story of their ancestors ripped from their birthland—not dissimilar to the gospel songs of African-American communities.

Gnaoua sometimes perform at private functions, but they mainly can be seen at festivals, which has earned them international acclaim and popularity. Every year there are more and more festivals, art exhibitions and concerts held in Essaouira, attracting ever larger crowds. The Festival of Gnaoua Music has become as famous as the Festival of Sacred Music in Fez. Won over

THIS PAGE: Clothed in ample white haïks, the women of Essaouira move through the streets as silently as shadows.

OPPOSITE (FROM TOP): A door-knocker in the shape of Fatima's hand provides good luck and protection for the household; the northern bastion of the former fortress stands with its cannons seemingly still waiting for invaders from across the water.

by the cultured atmosphere and charm of the town, an increasing number of people are buying riads and converting them into luxury guesthouses, mirroring the trend in Marrakech. Indeed, prices for these charming accommodation options in Essaouira are as high as in Marrakech.

The other great tourist attraction is the lively port, surrounded by noisy seagulls, with its constant to-ing and fro-ing of fishing boats and the mouth-watering smells of grilled fish wafting from the small open-air restaurants lining the quay. The bay itself is a paradise for surfers and has a long, idyllic, sandy beach with dunes running behind it.

thuya wood, an essaouiran tradition

An entire generation of self-taught native Moroccan artists lives and works in Essaouira, working on wood or plywood, painting in an unusual, naïve style, full of colour and rhythm, drawing inspiration from the Gnaoua and their art. Most of the woodcarvers and marquetry workers have their workshops in the former merchants' warehouses in the citadel. They usually work with Barbary thuya, which grows abundantly in the region. Its roots have a strong, sweet fragrance and beautifully flecked grain which, once sculpted, are sometimes used in combination with citrus wood, ebony, mother-of-pearl or silver to create stunning objects and pieces of polished furniture, often copies of Art Deco works.

the argan tree + its properties

The argan tree, a thorny shrub-like plant, grows only in the Essaouira region. The wood of this prolific and bountiful tree is used for heating. Its fruit, yellow when ripe, is particularly appreciated by goats who happily climb up into the trees to get to them. The fruits' seeds, once they have passed through the goats, are collected and cleaned. The women at both the Coopérative Tamounte and Tiguemine crush them by hand and grind them to extract an oil which is highly nutritive. One hundred kg (220 lb) of kernels is required to obtain 2 litres (4 pints) of oil, hence the exorbitant cost of the cosmetics, creams and essential oils made from the argan tree.

Argan oil is also used in traditional cooking. It has a strong taste of hazelnut and is often used to flavour salads and fish. It is also drizzled on a mixture of honey and grilled almonds to make the dish called amlou, a particularly energising food. Women have used the oil for their bodies, faces and hair since the beginning of time.

mogador, essaouira's star scheme

The modern seaside resort of Mogador faces the old Portuguese city once known by the same name. On a 580-hectare (1,433-acre) site, with the ocean as a backdrop, this tourist scheme will eventually contain three top-of-the-range hotels, luxury villas, guesthouse accommodation and hotel residential units spread throughout a hamlet. At the heart of the resort there will be a village with apartments, shops and a souk, a lively place for exchange and culture. Also, this kingdom of waves and trade winds will have a water sport base for water skiing and surfing. In conclusion, there will be plenty to satisfy an upmarket international clientele.

It is a bold concept, which breaks with traditional urban codes, consciously opting for a very contemporary architectural statement. Each district has been assigned to a different architect in order to create diversity. Also, a 20-hectare (49-acre) area has been left untouched at the centre of the site, and a wide strip of dunes runs along the seafront. Amid the dunes and lakes, a superb 36-hole golf course designed by Gary Player follows the terrain's topology. Artificial lakes serve as water reservoirs. In order to preserve the region's water resources, used water is taken to the purification station so that it can be reused. This is backed up by the aquatic plant filtration process, which purifies water naturally and makes use of a desalination process. With the wadi and dunes, this environment is ideal for the nest building of several species, so a 10-hectare (25-acre) ornithological area has been reserved for sea birds—harmonious cohabitation at its best.

agadir, the 'seaside resort'

Its name, in Berber, literally means 'communal granary', a recurring term in the place names of southern Morocco. Agadir was, indeed, originally a granary in the 16th century, near a protected roadstead at the start of the Souss Plain. Alongside it was the Santa Cruz Cabo de Guer Fort, belonging to Manuel I, King of Portugal, which considerably facilitated the trade of wheat, cloth, amber and gold with Sudan. A terrible earthquake in 1960 flattened the entire place, leaving no vestige of the past. Apart from the kasbah wall which was subsequently rebuilt, Agadir is a modern metropolis, created by Moroccan and French town planners and architects, including Jean-François Zevaco, Aziz Lazrati and Michel Pinceau. It is totally dedicated to seaside tourism, with luxury hotels, thalassotherapy centres and holiday resorts rivalling each other in the area between Boulevard Mohammed V and the seafront, all with their own fully-equipped beaches.

The Amazighe Heritage Museum on Boulevard Mohammed V houses the rich collection of Bert Flint, a passionate Dutchman who dedicated a large part of his life to collecting Berber tribal objects. An excellent introduction to southern Moroccan Berber culture, the permanent collection includes jewellery, rugs, clothes and agricultural tools.

taroudant, a miniature marrakech

Eighty kilometres (50 miles) inland, east of Agadir, lies Taroudant, once a hideaway and refuge for rebellious princes defying the Portuguese and other ruling powers. As the sole means of access between the Atlas and the Anti Atlas, it was an unavoidable stopover for trading caravans. Its Berber souk, at the entrance to the town, is still one of the most important markets in the south. Alternately independent under the Almohads, destroyed by the Merenids, free and then reconquered by the Saadians, Taroudant was the seat of the resistance of El Hiba, the Blue Sultan, during the period of the French Protectorate.

Although set well back from the coast, Taroudant was fortified in the 18th century: 7 km (4 miles) of remarkably well preserved ramparts and five gateways surround the town. The thick crenellated walls, shining golden in the sun, with gardens and groves of olive and pomegranate trees all around, make an extremely seductive and welcoming sight, especially when one is being driven around the town in a calèche (horse carriage) at sunset.

rabat the imperial + salé the rebel

The royal town of Rabat and the pirate city of Salé, separated from each other by the mouth of the Bou Regreg ('the river which sings'), have spent their time either eyeing each other contemptuously or being on the best of terms, depending on the hazards of history. But whether as rivals or companions, linked by two bridges and endless small boats, the one lives off the other.

THIS PAGE: Rabat by night: its skyline dominated by the Mohammed V Mausoleum and the Hassan Tower, every detail of their elegant architecture carefully picked out by a thousand lights.

OPPOSITE: Hues of ochre offset by green palm trees, the tower of Taroudant's Salam Palace rises up proudly, reminiscent of the majestic kasbah architecture further south.

One is immediately struck by the city's wide avenues, its green parks and its gardens...

Rabat, the political city, with its Royal Palace, ambassadors, top civil servants and bourgeoisie, was once, according to the reports of Léon the African, no more than 'a straggling village of a hundred houses or so'. Ribat al-Fatah, 'the Victorious Fortress', was the glorious name given to the city by the great Yacoub al-Mansour, who wished to make Rabat the equal of Alexandria, a vast and prestigious religious capital whose mosque's minaret (the Hassan Tower) would rival those of the Giralda, in Seville, and the Koutoubia, in Marrakech. In 1912, Morocco's Resident-General Maréchal Lyautey chose Rabat as the country's administrative capital. His former residence, the present Ministry of the Interior, overlooks the Oudaias Kasbah and the medina of Salé beyond—the perfect position for keeping an eye on all the comings and goings of the medinas.

It was King Hassan II and his son Mohammed VI, the present king who was born in Rabat, who definitively named Rabat a 'royal city'. One is immediately struck by the city's wide avenues, its green parks and its gardens—everything about it, including the elegant nonchalance of the place, leads one to believe one is in paradise. To prove it, both the Hassan Tower and the Mohammed V Mausoleum stand out as the most perfect examples of the pure classicism of the Almohad dynasty. The impressive Hassan Tower, the mosque's minaret, is formed with ochre stone, which rises 44 m (144 ft) above ground, each of its façades decorated with slender blind arcades and varied tracery. Of more recent vintage (completed in 1971), the Mohammed V Mausoleum represents the very finest of traditional Moroccan art. Created entirely by contemporary master craftsmen and artists, it abounds in painted wood, sculpted marble, plasterwork, engraved bronze and stained glass. At its centre, carved in onyx, lies the sarcophagus of Mohammed V, together with his two sons, Prince Moulay Abdallah and King Hassan II.

the oudaias kasbah

The Rue des Consuls, lined with stalls, leads into the large square where the wool market used to be, the Souk el-Ghezel. Opposite, the Oudaias Kasbah rises up on a rocky spur, like the prow of a ship anchored alongside the estuary. Founded in the 10th century, this fortress-like citadel rubs shoulders with its old friend and rival, the medina of Salé. In the 14th century, the kasbah served

THIS PAGE: Guards keep watch over the Mohammed V Mausoleum, a masterpiece of the utmost refinement.

OPPOSITE: The Andalusian Gardens run alongside the outer wall of the Oudaias Kasbah, offering a pleasant place to stroll.

THIS PAGE (FROM TOP): *Sweets and pastries made with honey, orange-blossom water and cinnamon are enjoyed throughout the day; pottery from Fez and Salé, and ceramic plates from Safi are displayed like paintings.*

OPPOSITE: *Casablanca, the largest city in Morocco, is home to its largest mosque, the Hassan II.*

as military barracks. Of the pirates' bastion, only the name remains now, but it was from here that pirates and buccaneers attacked and ransomed the Spanish vessels that dared to venture too close to shore. The pirates' power extended to both sides of the river, pillaging ships' cargoes and capturing their passengers to sell as slaves. Nowadays, the small white and blue houses, each with their own well and fig tree, are peacefully inhabited by fishermen and ferrymen, together with a few artists who have discretely joined them, who have been struck by the unique atmosphere and energy of the place, by its resemblance to a quaint Greek village and by the stirring view of neighbouring Salé.

The Oudaias Garden links the medina to the estuary, gently descending the slope towards the strand. Enclosed by high walls, this peaceful haven resembles a Hispano-Moorish convent garden, with paths of flowering queen's wreath (Petrea volubilis) and daturas bordering the rectangular gardens, walls lined with cypresses, lemon trees, oleanders and water flowing in channels. Gentle and inviting, it's a perfect spot for a lovers' stroll. The Café Maure is a favourite meeting place for the young, who sip mint tea while watching the spectacular sunsets.

what to visit

Salé's medina, dating from 12th century, is older than Rabat's, and is a masterpiece of Merenid art. The best view of Rabat is found here—from the city walls running alongside the river, with the cemetery in the foreground, spreading out to the sea and the white shrine of Sidi Abdallah ben Hassoun, the patron saint of Salé. Eleven kilometres (7 miles) of ramparts with eight gateways lead to the lattice of lanes within, criss-crossing that of the Grand Mosque, and all through the different souks (for jewellery, for embroidery, for silk, for wool) before eventually reaching the Fondouk Askour (the former hospital) on the other side of the medina.

Not to be missed is the old potters' district. The clay in Salé is particularly pure and is mostly used to make tajine dishes, fired with eucalyptus wood and glazed. The 'village' centres around a series of workshops and a long gallery of shops selling the full range of Salé's wares.

Dar Belghazi Museum, one of Africa's most well-endowed museums, 17 km (11 miles) beyond town, before the Plage des Nations, is also an excellent place to visit. It is the private collection of the Belghazi family, exhibiting beautiful examples of North African and Jewish art.

the bou regreg valley linking rabat + salé

An innovative scheme is underway on this symbolic site to bring together the twin towns of Rabat and Salé. The Bou Regreg River flowing through the valley linking Rabat to Salé is steeped in history. It meanders its way across the 6,000-hectare (14,826-acres) basin, with unspoilt countryside on either side as far as the eye can see. The vast development within the Bou Regreg scheme is based on the all-important notion of an ecological approach and improving the environment for the inhabitants of both towns. The new Moulay el-Hassan Bridge and a tramway will ensure a steady flow of traffic, while a tunnel under the Oudaias will aid the traffic circulation and keep the noise and pollution away from the delightful 12th-century kasbah. Also, the renovation of the Chellah Necropolis and the restoration of the ramparts of the Oudaias Kasbah will help to keep the memory of the place alive. Officially launched in 2006 by His Majesty the King, four of the programme's six stages should be complete around 2010.

Fifteen kilometres (9 miles) upstream a range of varied accommodation is under construction, including flats, villas, riads and penthouses. An area for community and leisure activities will complete the ensemble, with shops, theatres and cinemas. On the leisure front, public spaces, beaches, an artificial lake and hanging gardens are all due to be created, as well as a brand new university complex and a technology centre.

casablanca

If Rabat is the political capital, Casablanca is without doubt the economic centre, the great metropolis of Morocco, with over 3 million inhabitants. Casablanca is frequently left out of standard tourist circuits due to its apparent

lack of history. However, this once-small Berber settlement, Dar el-Beida ('the white house'), which Mohammed III provided with a fort, cannons and anchorage, was so feared by sailors in the past that it was nicknamed the 'ship's graveyard'. Today, the port handles the bulk of Morocco's sea traffic. Clearly, it was destined for greatness.

two towns in one

Casablanca was 'reinvented' in the early 1920s by Maréchal Lyautey, who wished to make it not only the colony's main economic area, but also a sparkling showcase of colonialism. It became a vast building site where modern architecture could express itself freely, all the while drawing upon traditional Moroccan housing styles—an exciting architectural exercise referred to as 'colonial', in keeping with Lyautey's grand ambitions. Yet again, the Resident-General of Morocco called upon the town planner Henri Prost to dream up the overall plan.

The Place de France (Place des Nations Unies), a commercial centre, was designed by Hippolyte Delaporte, as was the Hotel Excelsior, outstandingly modern for the period. The Place Administrative (Place Mohammed V), for the various civil service departments, was designed by Joseph Marrast in a functional style, but which in no way ignored comfort or pleasure.

the new hassan II mosque

Built on a 9-hectare (22-acre) site next to the sea, this grand mosque was inaugurated on 30 August 1993. Its sheer size and magnificence mark the apogee of Islamic religious architecture in the 20th century. Six years and over 35,000 craftsmen from Safi, Fez and Marrakech were required to create this gigantic work. Everything about it is superlative: a minaret 200 m (656 ft) high, 25 titanium doors, a prayer room large enough for over 25,000 faithful, and a sliding roof made in cedar weighing over 1,000 tons. The esplanade is designed to welcome 80,000 faithful. Below ground level, the hammam and ablution chambers are equally splendid. In the near future, Avenue Royale is intended to link the mosque to the centre of town.

el jadida

On the road between Casablanca and Essaouira, this former Portuguese town, surrounded by soaring walls, appears to defy the ocean. During the Protectorate period, the French attempted to develop it into a sea resort—a sort of Deauville, less than 100 km (62 miles) from Casablanca—but without experiencing any great success. Perhaps the idea was simply a little too far ahead of its time, for bathing had not yet become a summer ritual for the denizens of Casablanca then, as it has in recent times.

THIS PAGE: *The interior of the famous café-restaurant Rick's in Casablanca;*

OPPOSITE: *The fortified ramparts of the Portuguese town of El Jadida, formerly Mazagan, restored in the 19th century.*

The Portuguese discovered the place in 1505, calling it Mazagan and occupying it for two centuries. In 1769, Sultan Mohammed ben Abdallah took possession of the town and immediately renamed it El Jadida, 'The New'. With its well protected natural harbour, El Jadida might well have become the largest trading port on the Atlantic coast. This, however, was not to be, overshadowed as it was by the formidable development of Casablanca, the ultimate business centre, and the successful mining port of Safi, with its relentless export of phosphate, which is a major element of the country's economy. Although not a commercial centre, El Jadida has become more of a museum town, admired by visitors for its extremely well preserved ramparts

and fortified city, which is truly a masterpiece of 16th-century Portuguese military architecture. The bastions of the Portuguese city are still known by their original names, and the walls enclose the 17th-century Church of the Assumption, alongside the mosque's white minaret and the Chapel of the Inquisition, which stands as a reminder of the religious intolerance of the period. Of particular interest is the Portuguese cistern, originally built as a guardroom in the 16th century, but which later became a water reservoir, an amazing feat of engineering that is still functional today; its ethereal beauty continues to attract many tourists. The vast chamber is magical and somewhat unreal, with five rows of sturdy columns reflected in the water. Not surprisingly, Orson Welles chose to shoot certain scenes of his film *Othello* here.

The future looks bright in El Jadida. Under construction at the time of printing, the resort of Mazagan lies between 15 km (9 miles) of beaches and a eucalyptus forest. When the resort is completed, it will have a capacity of 3,500 beds, a golf course and water sport facilities, making it a convenient getaway for the inhabitants of Casablanca.

safi + oualidia

Safi is best known as Morocco's major port for exporting phosphate, also dubbed 'Morocco's white gold'. But besides its industrial side, it is also well known for its pottery. Encouraged by the master craftsmen of Fez, potters and wood-fired kilns have occupied the hillside opposite Bab Chaba ('the gateway to the valley') since the 16th century, where visitors can still see them at work every day. Lower down, near the medina, prime examples of their work are for sale in the shopping gallery. The National Ceramics Museum is housed in the kechla, the former fortress, with its crenellations and look-out towers.

Oualidia is a charming seaside resort, wedged like a shell between undulating dunes and surrounded by long wild beaches backed by hills. As the tide recedes, an expansive rocky lagoon emerges in front of the town, with oyster beds appearing at low tide, running as far as the eye can see. There are a few houses, an abandoned palace, two or three seaside hotels and, right at the end a restaurant, named Ostréa II, where one can sample freshly caught oysters, shellfish and spider crabs in front of the lagoon. There are a few bedrooms above the restaurant, so diners can always stay on for a day or two of sea air and escape from the hurly-burly of modern living.

THIS PAGE: El Jadida's Portuguese cistern originally held up to 3 million litres (6 million pints) of water, an amazing engineering feat.

OPPOSITE: By night, El Jadida's ramparts are bathed in soft lighting, belying the town's war-like past, the scene of many feudal confrontations.

...truly a masterpiece of 16th-century Portuguese military architecture.

dar l'oussia

THIS PAGE: *Breakfast is served on the sun-dappled terrace, but guests can also choose to savour lunch and dinner here.*

OPPOSITE (FROM TOP): *The tadelakt plaster walls and intricately tiled floors are a showcase of traditional Moroccan design; the spacious accommodations here are artfully appointed and spotlessly clean.*

For an appreciation of Moroccan style and hospitality look no further than Dar L'Oussia in Essaouira. Having recently undergone a renovation, the hotel has kept its charm with original details and a focus on traditional customs. Tadelakt plaster walls and zellij tile flooring can be found throughout the five-storey building, and the guestrooms—located around a central patio—are framed with intricate balustrades reminiscent of Berber architecture. Superbly situated, this building was once a sentry on the city's ramparts. Now its roof terrace is put to good use as a shaded dining area and as a sunny spot for some uninterrupted sunbathing, its views over the ocean and harbour the icing on the cake.

Home to 19 rooms and four suites, this riad is unique because of its size; the rooms are huge. However, they do not seem empty. Rather, they are spacious and bright, with soft furnishings and small details that add to their charm. The marble flooring and stone walls, while comfortably cool in the summer, can get chilly in the winter months, making the under-floor heating a definite plus.

In the hammam, trained therapists will perform a ritual massage that is supposed to help cleanse, calm and rebalance the soul. Use of locally produced, extremely rare argan oil in massages and body treatments makes the whole spa experience that little bit more special and authentically Moroccan.

When hunger strikes, there are options galore. The terrace, where breakfast is served, is great for dinner or a barbecue. Alternatively, the central patio is a comfortable, shady spot, with the stylish lounge furniture, plants and candles adding to the ambience. The dining room is also tempting, with its Moroccan décor, stone archways and open fireplace. In any of these venues, guests can savour delicious European or Moroccan fare; the fish is extremely fresh and seasonal vegetables come fresh from the local markets. After dinner, the little bar serves a superb mojito, or whatever else might take your fancy.

For day-time pursuits, guests can visit the nearby souks and shops or head for the beach. The staff can also organise trips such as cultural visits to the camps of Bedouin tribes. A bit nearer home, quad biking, boat trips, windsurfing and camel riding will keep guests busy. Should you be here on a business trip, the fully equipped meeting room can cater for up to 30 people, and the outings and activities add some entertainment. In all, this is Moroccan hospitality at its best. It's simple, unfussy and Moroccan through and through.

rooms
19 rooms • 4 suites

food
Moroccan and European

drink
bar

features
hammam • babysitting • quad biking • massage • concierge • airport transfer • high-speed Internet access

nearby
Iles Purpuraires • Borj El Berod • beach • Essaouira harbour • sand dunes • desert

contact
4 Rue Mohamed ben Messaoud 44000 Essaouira •
telephone: +212.24.783 756 •
facsmile: +212.24.472 777 •
email: loussia@menara.ma •
website: www.dar-loussia.net

l'heure bleue palais + spa

THIS PAGE (FROM TOP): *The central courtyard is a great place to relax with a glass of mint tea; the rooftop offers a lovely view of the medina.*

OPPOSITE (FROM TOP): *Take in the stunning view from the spa; unwind in the traditional marble-clad hammam.*

Situated at the edge of the medina in coastal Essaouira, L'Heure Bleue Palais & Spa was originally built in the 19th century. It has since been carefully restored by regional artisans, using some of the finest materials from all over Morocco, to create an elegant mix of chic European style and colonial charm. This palatial riad, which is a member of the Relais & Châteux group, is now recognised as one of the most prestigious hotels in Essaouira.

Framed by blue and white houses, the quiet, sleepy town of Essaouira (meaning 'beautifully designed') is a tourist favourite. This old walled town offers a laid-back atmosphere where a visitor can stroll through colourful streets steeped in the town's history while admiring the eclectic mix of French and Portuguese architecture. The labyrinth of alleyways is lined by market stalls selling clothes, food, arts and crafts and Berber jewellery. Watch fishermen bring in the catch of the day or while away the hours watching surfers and kite-runners traipse along the beautiful white sands of the beach.

In recent years, Essaouira has found fame as a film set—most recently in Ridley Scott's *Kingdom of Heaven* in 2005 but perhaps more notably as the backdrop to Orson Welles' adaptation of Shakespeare's *Othello*. The film was re-released in 1992 to great acclaim and Essaouira held a screening to mark this event. The square along the seafront was then renamed Place Orson Welles in his honour.

L'Heure Bleue Palais & Spa was designed to bring together Morocco's many cultural influences. Guests are welcomed to the riad with an impressive English lounge that is adorned with hunting trophies. With a grand piano tucked into the corner and soft lounge chairs surrounding a fireplace, it makes any traveller feel at home. The rooms here are individually designed in North African, classic English, Portuguese and Oriental styles, with a variety of rustic colours, tasteful zebra prints, elegant silk fabrics and mahogany woods. Guests can fully immerse themselves in the impressive selection of literature and DVDs in the library or engage in some light recreational activity in the billiards room. For movie-lovers, an intimate home-cinema room is available, where films can be thoroughly enjoyed from a comfortable armchair. If the

rooms
16 rooms • 19 suites

food
gastronomic French-Moroccan fusion •
pool terrace: light meals • room service

drink
English lounge

features
pool • rooftop terrace • hammam • library •
billiard room • cinema • Internet access •
conference room • lounges • fitness room •
Zen Rituals Spa • boutique

nearby
bay • beach • port • city ramparts

contact
2 Rue Ibn Batouta, Bab Marrakech
44000 Essaouira •
telephone: +212.24.783 434 •
facsimile: +212.24.474 222 •
email: info@heure-bleue.com •
website: www.heure-bleue.com

draw of sun is just too irresistible, guests can bask by the pool on the rooftop, with fresh sea air and blue skies all about, and unwind while taking in the panoramic view.

The hotel's restaurant serves a fusion of French and Moroccan cuisine, and the open courtyard, with its bright, airy atmosphere, provides a relaxed setting for every meal. For a light afternoon snack, enjoy distinctive cultural favourites such as pigeon pie with almonds; guests can also dine by firelight in the evening. Typical dishes served at L'Heure Bleue Palais & Spa include vegetable or lobster tajine, for those who prefer more traditional fare, and some of Essaouira's finest

seafood. Other guests may find a tender shoulder of Haddra lamb or the tantalising seasonal spider crab to be more to their taste.

Guests can recharge both spiritually and physically in the Zen Rituals Spa, where privacy, ambience and respect for tradition are held as paramount. Detoxify in the hammam and indulge in a body scrub or wrap. Allow time for experienced masseurs to work their magic with organic argan oil, renowned in North Africa for its healing properties, and relieve yourself of all tension.

With the many luxuries offered at L'Heure Bleue Palais & Spa, this laid-back seaside town makes an ideal holiday getaway location.

madada mogador

THIS PAGE: On the rooftop terrace, guests can savour a leisurely breakfast accompanied by sweeping views of the ocean.

OPPOSITE (FROM TOP): The hotel's two suites are not only spacious and comfortable, they also come with private terraces that overlook the ocean; Moroccan antique brass basins go surprisingly well with a modern Asian design.

Two and a half hours from Marrakech may feel like a long trek, but few would deny that a trip to Essaouira is well worth it; and it's made even more worth it if you are staying at Madada Mogador. Loved for its special, homey boutique style that can't be found anywhere else, the hotel's impeccable service begins with the airport pick-up by a friendly driver. When you arrive, the entrance is quite misleading; tucked behind the ramparts and up a flight of communal stairs, it's not until you are inside the hotel that it bares all of its true beauty and style.

Upon arrival a warm welcome will ensue, most probably accompanied with a cup of mint tea, and you will be shown up to your room. If you have booked well then the room will open out onto the city ramparts, with a stunning view of the port beyond. If not onto the ramparts, all but two guestrooms have a terrace boasting views of the ocean. The vast roof terrace is available to all guests so no one misses out on the stunning 360° views.

What makes this particular hotel so refreshing is that, while it is deep within a traditional medina, its décor has moved away from the ubiquitous Moroccan style and branched out with an Asian Zen feel. In the seven guestrooms, beige, sand, deep reds and dark woods blend easily with the more local details such as the tadelakt plaster baths and antique brass basins. Detailing in each room has been carefully thought out and the end result is something homey yet uncluttered, with fresh flowers and open fireplaces that only add to the hotel's charm.

Of note, one of the two suites features a mezzanine floor for twin beds, making it ideal for family holidays. The terraces, whether private or on the communal rooftop, are all kitted out with stylish and comfortable lounge and dining furniture, a move which shows great forethought as guests are sure to want to sit outside as much as possible.

For breakfast, the terraces are perfect, with beautiful views to accompany the first meal of the day, or guests can choose to be

rooms
5 rooms • 2 suites

food
After Five: Moroccan and French fusion

drink
roof terrace

features
airport transfer • alcohol licence • solarium • high-speed Internet access • babysitting • library and board games • massages • organisation of sports activities

nearby
sand dunes • desert • town centre • beach • quad biking • camel and horse riding

contact
5 Rue Youssef el Fassi
44000 Essaouira •
telephone: +212.24.475 512 •
facsimile: +212.24. 475 512 •
email: info@madada.com •
website: www.madada.com

served inside their rooms (it does rain in Essaouira sometimes). The fare itself is well-balanced and fresh, for example, pancakes with strawberries, and yoghurt with local honey. In the afternoon the snack bar serves paninis, sandwiches and salads, and for evening drinks, the rooftop terrace offers music and a great ambience, to say nothing of the fantastic view.

On the subject of dinner, the hotel owns the restaurant housed downstairs, After Five. Also decked in a more Asian than Moroccan design, the feel is relaxed and uncontrived, the stone arches reminding you that you are in a Moroccan medina despite the deviation from traditional Moroccan design style. The cuisine served here is a tasty fusion of Moroccan and French and is appealing in its modern approach to food.

The helpful and friendly staff are very knowledgeable about the area and are able to assist to organise a variety of activities for all guests. For a more relaxed excursion ask about the thalassotherapy centre, or the best local hammam and the nearest pool. If guests prefer something a bit more active, quad biking or cycling can be arranged as well as riding—camel or horse. Lastly, as you're on the coast, windsurfing, sailing or kitesurfing can round up your holiday nicely.

ocean vagabond

Locals in Essaouira are proud of their claim to fame that Jimi Hendrix wrote 'Castles in the Sand' while visiting this seaside town. Whether this is actually true, no one knows. However, it is utterly believable that a rock and roll icon came here in search of inspiration. Essaouira is an enchanting place; it takes on the winds of the Atlantic Ocean and has stood firm. Home to castles, palaces, ramparts, forts and other historical buildings, its architectural heritage gives it some

touristic weight and, while the charm of the harbour and the seaside ambience is another pull, Essaouira is off the beaten track enough to dodge the terror of mass tourism. It is no surprise then that world travellers Marie and Sébastien Deflandre decided to settle here in this picturesque town and open their beautiful guesthouse, Ocean Vagabond.

Located just 200 m (656 ft) from the walled city, the distance is small enough to appreciate the pulse of the medina but large enough to escape the bustle if necessary. Just as important on a trip to Essaouira is the beach, and that is just 100 m (328 ft) from the hotel. Furthermore, Ocean Vagabond has its very own Nautical Base with private beach, restaurant and watersport facility. You can learn to surf, windsurf and even kitesurf while the kids play safely on the shore under the watchful eyes of the staff. The beach restaurant, Joint, is decked in the colours of the Caribbean and serves fresh juices, salads, sandwiches and snacks from its summer kitchen. Back at the hotel, the garden restaurant serves local and Mediterranean specialities with light lunches available for a spot of poolside dining, where guests can drink in amazing views of the medina.

For a more indoor pursuit, the in-house spa therapist, Karima, can smooth out all the kinks in one's body with a superb massage or iron out any wrinkles with a facial treatment. If you prefer to unwind first, the hammam offers release in its steamy environment.

rooms
11 rooms · 3 suites

food
Moroccan and Mediterranean ·
Joint: light snacks and breakfast

drink
bar · Joint

features
watersport facility · excursion planning · spa ·
hammam · pool · wireless Internet access ·
garden · library · private beach

nearby
medina · shops · beach · ruins

contact
4 Boulevard Lalla Aïcha
Angle Rue Moukawama
44100 Essaouira ·
telephone: +212.24.449 222 ·
facsimile: +212.24.474 285 ·
email: hotel@oceanvagabond.com ·
website: www.oceanvagabond.com

Elsewhere in the hotel is a living room and library, perfect for an après spa recovery; guests can relax with a book or watch a DVD, or head to the well-stocked bar for a drink.

The 14 rooms are all unique and inspired by regions of the world that Marie and Sébastien have travelled through. Indian, African, Southeast Asian and South American styles are all evident in the impeccably prepared rooms. Each room has a private terrace with views of the medina, square of Bab Marrakech or, best of all, breathtaking views of the ocean. The bathrooms are all kitted out with tadelakt plaster baths, bringing the Moroccan element, and some rooms connect with one another, making it ideal for families or groups.

Overall, the hotel is trendy and spacious, with a relaxed atmosphere. The cheerful staff show real passion for giving guests a great holiday. Each one is knowledgeable about the area and can help you find exactly what you want, from the best craftsmen in the medina to the best seafood on the harbour, from kitesurfing teachers to quad biking hire kiosks. This little gem of a hotel, with its unique charm, will make Essaouira a destination of choice for a long time to come.

villa maroc

In the charming coastal town of Essaouira is an ancient walled quarter. Here, as in the medinas of many Moroccan cities, narrow streets snake past century-old riads that sit side by side with artisans' workshops and craft shops. A series of four riads has been converted into Villa Maroc. Spotted by enterprising couple Cornelia Hendry and Abderrahim Ezzaher, these riads were mostly former residences of wealthy merchants, although one was purportedly a house of pleasure. Cornelia and Abderrahim created a maison d'hôtes so intimate and cosy that visitors feel like they are guests in a family home rather than a hotel.

Essaouira is an artist's town, and the décor and ambience of Villa Maroc echo this free-spiritedness. Vibrant blue and white paintwork adorns the walls, in keeping with the Arab-Andalusian style that typifies Essaouira. Furniture and ornaments are a mix of antiques and local artisans' products. Art pieces by both local and international artists are scattered throughout the hotel. Each of the villa's 21 rooms is individually decorated. The emphasis at Villa Maroc is on originality, uniqueness and elegance.

Meals here are a worthy subject unto themselves. The cuisine combines the best of traditional Moroccan fare with European refinement. For the freshest ingredients, kitchen staff press olive oil, grow organic vegetables, preserve jams and ferment yoghurt. Chefs whip up delicacies such as tajine of baby goat, rabbit baked with preserved lemon, or vermicelli madfoun with shredded chicken. So confident were Cornelia and Abderrahim of the quality of their hotel's cuisine that they published the *Villa Maroc Cookbook*, which reveals the secrets behind their delectable, ingenious recipes and also features mouth-watering photography.

The most recent addition to Villa Maroc is its hammam and Oriental spa. A special ingredient in the spa's treatments is argan oil, an oil extracted from the kernel of the argan fruit. Besides treatments using argan oil, the spa also offers popular indulgences such as shiatsu and reflexology.

The emphasis at Villa Maroc is on originality, uniqueness and elegance.

rooms
13 rooms • 8 suites

food
private kitchen: Essaouiran home cooking

drink
beverage list

features
lounges • open-air rooftop terrace • hammam • Oriental spa

nearby
historic ruins • bay • port • city ramparts

contact
10 Rue Abdellah ben Yassine
44000 Essaouira
telephone: +212.24.473 147 or +212.24.476 147 •
facsimile: +212.24.475 806 •
email: hotel@villa-maroc.com •
website: www.villa-maroc.com

riad des golfs

THIS PAGE: The riad's comfortable daybeds by the sprawling pool invite guests to lounge in the warm Moroccan sunlight.

OPPOSITE (FROM TOP): The patio's central fountain is Moroccan style through and through, yet it goes well with the Oriental influences and modern lines of the rest of the décor here; guests can wine and dine in style in one of the riad's two well-appointed dining rooms.

Imagine teeing off on undulating green hills punctuated by eucalyptus trees and quiet pools of water. Imagine a mild climate which makes this possible all year round and top-notch facilities that ensure a sublime golf experience. This can all be found in Agadir, a coastal holiday town which is fast gaining repute as a premier golf destination. On its fringes is Riad des Golfs, an elegant hotel that is walking distance from two of the area's finest courses—Club Méditerranée Dunes Golf Course and Golf du Soleil.

Nestled between these two famed golf courses, Riad des Golfs has been designed in an elegant, refined and warm style. As comfortable and opulent as any large luxury hotel, some of the riad's rooms overlook a verdant garden and the hotel's large pool, around which breakfast is served. The main patio, decorated with a tasteful mixture of Oriental architecture, contemporary colours and clean, refined lines, can either be a pleasant lounge or a stylish dining room that features three impressive fireplaces.

While breakfast may be savoured on the pool terrace, lunch and dinner may be taken in one of the two dining rooms. Prepared by proprietors Paule and Bernard Brilhault using fresh local ingredients, the cuisine is marked by a strong regional emphasis.

Accommodation comes in the form of eight junior suites with private terraces, two of which also have small gardens. In each suite stands a large double bed which is convertible into twin beds, and a sitting area that can take a third bed should one be needed. Bathrooms have spacious baths, freestanding washbasins and separate toilets and bidets. In addition, moden amenities such as satellite television, minibars and Internet access are installed in every suite.

The quality of golf here is superb. Dunes Golf Course is a world-class course designed by golf legend Cabell Robinson, with three nine-hole courses on its grounds that will pose a challenge to even the most seasoned golfer. Golf du Soleil is probably less daunting, if only marginally so. Now a 36-hole course, it comprises formidable greens surrounded by some of the most beautiful landscaping to be found in Morocco, complemented by the natural, gentle contours of the terrain.

rooms
8 junior suites

food
private kitchen: Moroccan and Mediterranean

drink
beverage list

features
heated pool • private gardens • lounges • hammam • massage • Internet access

nearby
Golf du Soleil • camel and horse riding • town centre • beaches • Club Méditerranée Dunes Golf Course

contact
Chemin des Français
Aghrod, Ben Sergao
80000 Agadir •
telephone: +212.28.337 033 or +212.528.337 033 •
facsimile: +212.28.335 455 or +212.528.335 455 •
email: riadgolf@menara.ma •
website: www.riaddesgolfs.com

la gazelle d'or

Arriving at La Gazelle d'Or is like reaching the end of a pilgrimage: after driving through arid countryside, you turn off the road into the nave of a Norman cathedral, formed with a vaulting of green bamboo instead of grey stone. Once through the gate, you are at last in the sanctuary of La Gazelle d'Or.

La Gazelle d'Or was acquired by the present owners in 1981, when they saw its potential as an exotic country retreat. Since then, they have worked tirelessly for more than 25 years to preserve and enhance the original magic and charm of the property.

The property is large, with 30 stone cottages spread over 9 hectares (22 acres) of lush gardens and a park. Orange groves and a farm also flourish on the grounds.

The farm is certified 100 per cent organic and biodynamic, with regular checks carried out by European organisations such as Demeter and Ecocert. As a result, all produce delivered daily to the hotel is healthy and wholesome, including vegetables, fruit, herbs, spices, lamb, chicken, eggs, milk, yoghurt, cheese and even relatively rare organic items such as duck and guinea fowl.

As such, eating at La Gazelle d'Or is a delicious, healthy and memorable experience. Breakfast is delivered to your room at whatever time you wish, while lunch is usually served as an extensive buffet with salads, hot and cold dishes and fresh desserts beside the pool. Dinner is slightly more formal, and is served either in the dining room, with its tented ceiling incorporating Berber motifs, or outside on the cool terrace twinkling with a myriad of candles in glass lanterns. Guests are given a choice of tasty traditional Moroccan fare or equally delicious international dishes for dinner.

After all this eating, salve your conscience with some exercise: play some tennis, swim a little or polish up your golf. In addition, guests can ride the horses in the stables and make use of the fitness centre with its state-of-the-art equipment. Even just walking around the grounds is good for the constitution, and excursions into the town, the surrounding area and into the mountains can be arranged upon request for more vigorous walks.

For guests who prefer more sedate activities, there's always a steamy session in the hammam to fall back on, with a clay body mask and exfoliation followed by a powerful massage or some soothing aromatherapy. A whole range of other beauty treatments using organic products are also available.

The suites are housed in stone cottages, and every suite is individually decorated in a blend of Moroccan, Berber and European styles. Each has a large private terrace that is perfect for sunbathing, an en suite bathroom, a direct-dial telephone, an open fireplace and central heating and air-conditioning. They also showcase views of the gardens and the snow-capped High Atlas Mountains beyond.

rooms
30 cottages

food
Moroccan and international

drink
bar · lounges

features
heated pool · 2 tennis courts · horse riding · hammam · massage · golf · fitness room · aromatherapy and beauty treatments · excursions off the property

nearby
souks · ramparts · Agadir Royal Golf Club · Tioute Kasbah · Tizi n'Test Pass

contact
BP 260
73000 Taroudant ·
telephone: +212.28.852 039 or +212.28.852 048 ·
facsimile: +212.28.852 737 ·
e-mail: reservations@gazelledor.com ·
website: www.gazelledor.com

villa mandarine

Located in the distinguished ambassadors' district of Souissi in Rabat, Villa Mandarine is a lush garden paradise set in the middle of a verdant 2.4-hectare (6-acre) orange grove. Surrounding this beautiful maison d'hôtes is a rambling garden with peaceful pockets for guests to spend quiet time revelling in the magnificence of the Moroccan outdoors.

The villa, with its dazzling mosaic tiling and impressive arabesques, was once the home of the owner Claudy Imbert's father. An avid art historian and a lover of Islamic arts, Claudy Imbert transformed her family holiday home with the help of an accomplished Moroccan architect and turned it into the beautifully unique guesthouse that it is today. The addition of modern amenities like air-conditioning and heating, personal digital safes and minibars, which guests have come to expect in every hotel and guesthouse, has not compromised the authentic splendour of the place. The original ochre walls still remain, as do the vibrant red communal spaces which are a joy to explore. A vividly blue tiled patio overflows with bougainvillea that tumble in rich hues of fuchsia, coral and pink over wrought-iron trellises and terracotta pots.

Villa Mandarine's guests are made to feel like they are the only honoured visitors to a sumptuous family home. Imbert's personal collection of art—from Moroccan landscapes to modern abstract works—adorns the walls of the villa, and a serene library, open to guests and stocked with a myriad of books,

keeps book-lovers occupied while others take the chance to immerse themselves in the culturally-enriched environment at the villa.

Avid golfers will be glad to know that some of Morocco's best golf courses are located in the area. Just 10 minutes away is the Royal Golf Dar Es Salam, one of the best known and most challenging golf courses in the world. Indeed, it is host to the annual Hassan II Trophy.

For a more historical experience, explore Rabat's royal city on foot and witness the monumental fortified walls that surround the capital and gave the city its name. Horse riding, fishing, surfing or simply sunbathing on the nearby sandy beaches of the Atlantic

THIS PAGE (FROM TOP): Villa Mandarine's central patio; rich greenery abounds throughout the property.

OPPOSITE (FROM TOP): The villa tries to provide a home away from home for its guests; indulge in a refreshing glass of juice while drinking in the natural beauty of the gardens.

rooms
31 rooms • 5 suites

food
Moroccan and French

drink
beverage list

features
spa • sauna • jacuzzi • pool • hammam • courtyard • garden • library

nearby
Royal Golf Dar Es Salam • Casablanca • Ben Slimane Golf Course • Bou Regreg • Mohammédia Golf Course

contact
19 Rue Ouled Bousbaa, Souissi 10000 Rabat •
telephone: +212.37.752 077 •
facsimile: +212.37.632 309 •
email: reservation@villamandarine.com •
website: www.villamandarine.com

coast are also some of the many recreational activities that Villa Mandarine's staff are happy to arrange for its guests.

Set around the luxuriant garden filled with bougainvillea, fragrant roses and orange trees are 36 well-appointed rooms and suites, each clad in a tasteful combination of colours. Brightly coloured lamps and pretty ethnic rugs add vibrant accents to the rooms, and some of the accommodations even come with private terraces that overlook the carefully tended garden.

When hunger pangs strike, be sure to dine at Villa Mandarine's highly acclaimed restaurant, where the head chef Wolfgang Grobauer—with one Michelin star to his name—serves a menu of both classic French and Moroccan cuisine. Needless to say, he uses only the freshest produce in his culinary creations and supplements them with herbs plucked directly from the villa's own gardens.

Before dinner, a quick dip in the sapphire-tiled pool is a great way to wind down from a fun day on the beach or a tiring trek through town. It will also whet your appetite in preparation for the delicious meal to come.

Villa Mandarine's beautiful surroundings and impeccable facilities allow guests to live like dignitaries, as befits its location in the great imperial capital of Morocco.

la sultana oualidia

For three whole years, an artisanal assembly of Morocco's finest architects, designers and builders worked tirelessly on an untouched coastal site in the secluded town of Oualidia to produce an astonishing work of art from scratch. The result of their efforts is La Sultana Oualidia, an exclusive five-star hotel resort and spa housed in an incredible, historically-inspired castle structure that appears to be anything but a 21st-century creation.

Located on the Atlantic coast, it overlooks a private beach and a peaceful lagoon whose inviting waters are sheltered by two promontories and a range of cliffs, creating a paradisal enclave bordered by green pastures and natural saltwater marshes. Guests can venture closer to the water on a landing platform, or simply enjoy the beach from under one of its thatched straw parasols. Stretching up high above the water level, the hotel's walls offer many vantage points where visitors can get better views of the bay and horizon. Up several flights of stairs lies a series of terraces which provide private spots from which the vast scope of the land can be best appreciated. Here, one also finds a 40-m (131-ft) infinity-edge pool surrounded by thatched huts and peaceful seating areas.

The hotel's collection of paintings by Régis Delène-Barthodi—descendant of the renowned Frédéric-Auguste Barthodi who created the Statue of Liberty—are displayed throughout the guestrooms to great effect. Amongst the standard comforts you will find in these accommodations, there are extra features such as soundproofed walls, plasma screen televisions with satellite channels, CD and DVD players, Internet access and complimentary non-alcoholic minibars.

Every one of La Sultana's luxurious rooms and suites also provides a towering vantage point overlooking the lagoon or surrounding countryside. Bright and airy, the rooms are decorated in a pleasing colour palette that recalls the golden sand of the beach and the rich blue of the sea and sky. Cool marble floors and tadelakt plaster-coated stone walls give the rooms a natural vibrancy, complementing the movement of water from the irrigation channel water features and private jacuzzis that can be found in each room.

rooms
4 rooms • 7 suites

food
La Lagune: fresh seafood

drink
The Lounge

features
spa • outdoor pool • jacuzzi • hammam • library • private beach • Internet access • meeting facilities • hairdresser

nearby
water sports • bird watching • golf • fishing • marketplace • Safi • El Jadida • Boulaouane Castle

contact
Parc á Huîtres N°3
24000 Oualidia •
telephone: +212.23.366 595 •
facsimile: +212.23.366 594 •
email: reservation@lasultanahotels.com •
website: www.lasultanaoualidia.com

The sound of water from the heated indoor pool in the hotel's vast cavernous centre echoes throughout the complex. Built from carved stone, the high-ceilinged vault serves as the hotel's spa. Equipped with hammams, steam rooms, jet showers, saunas and a gymnasium, the spa offers everything a body could need, from hair styling and beauty treatments to a wide menu of massage therapies. The spa employs a philosophy that combines Eastern and Western techniques, with carefully matched colours, scents and music to put every guest's mind and body into a Zen-like state of relaxation.

La Sultana's location also finds it first in line to some of the freshest seafood and produce in Morocco, which are put to excellent use throughout three dining areas. On the beach, guests may enjoy lobster and oysters at La Lagune restaurant and the Boat House, while up on the park level, the aptly-named White Awnings is ideal for scenic afternoon lunches.

Few coastal resorts offer the serenity of Oualidia and its quiet cove, and fewer still allow the setting and view to be fully appreciated in as many ways as the La Sultana Oualidia hotel and spa.

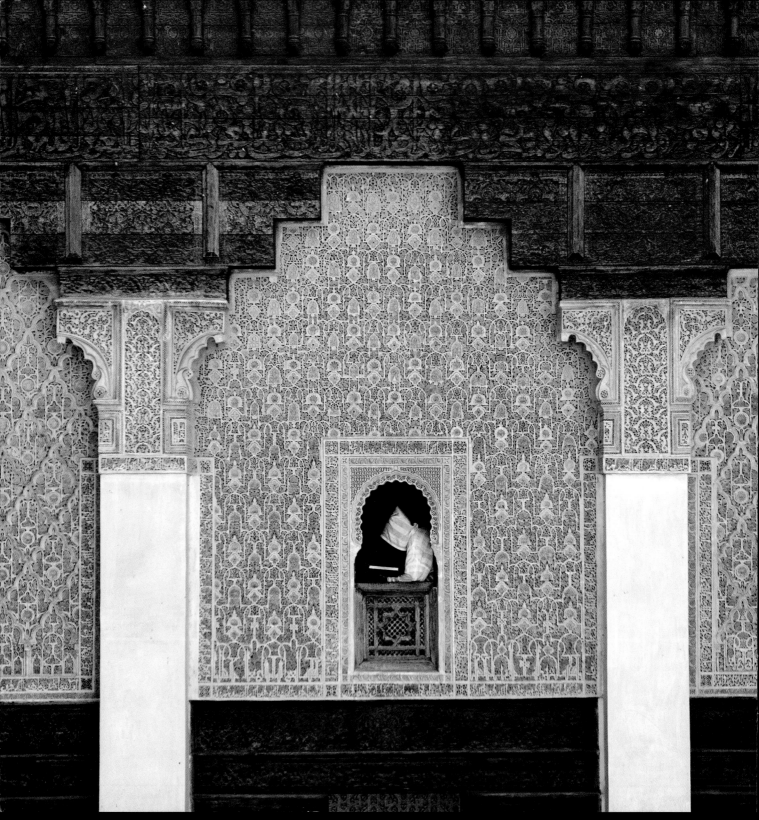

marrakech

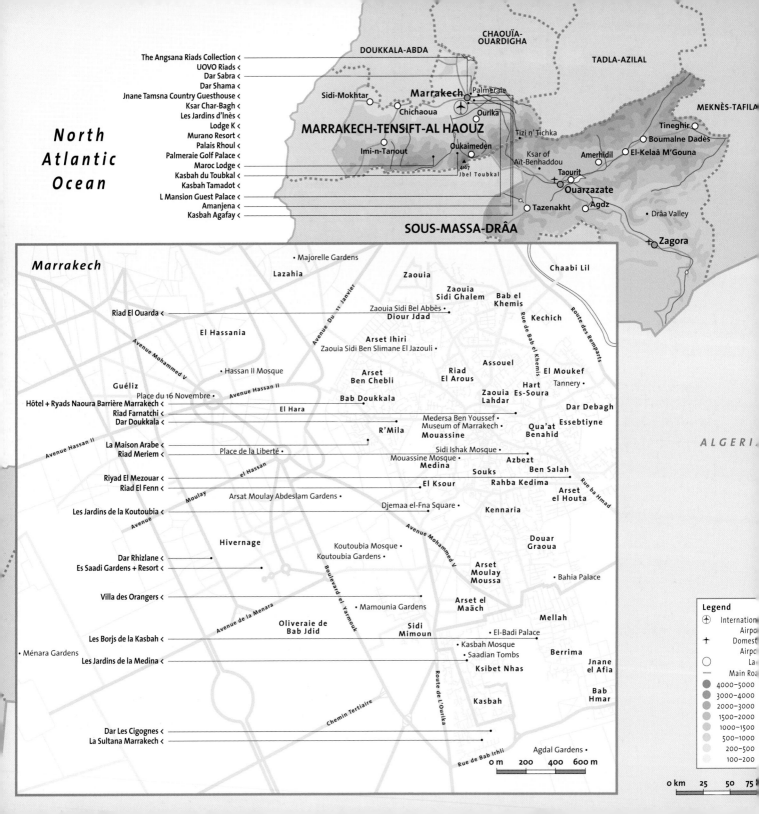

marrakech

ever-beguiling marrakech

Against the spectacular backdrop of the snow-capped Atlas Mountains hovering above the Haouz Plain, Marrakech voluptuously unfurls her crenellated ramparts, 19 km (12 miles) of reddish-ochre and orange hues, depending on the time of day. Before becoming an imperial capital, Marrakech was a Berber metropolis and its name literally meant 'don't stop here, pass through quickly'—ironic given its popularity today!

Built by the Almoravids in the 11th century, in the vernacular style of the time, the city's mud walls and palaces rise up out of the dust in perfect symbiosis, fragile yet enduring masterpieces. It was later, during the Almohad dynasty, that the city's finest monuments were erected, including the famous Koutoubia Mosque, the most perfect example of Hispano-Moorish art. There are seven gateways, seven saints, seven tombs still venerated today and it is said that the city only reveals a seventh of itself to laymen—a sacred number!

a place of words

Hungover from the night before, the city gradually awakens from her amnesic slumber, bathes in the first rays of sunlight and is revived by dawn's light. She powders herself pink, pampers herself, decks herself out in all her finery, lifts back her veil and, amid the ever-growing noises and smells, prepares herself for the daily spectacle of life. Marrakech, conjuror of time and space, continues to enchant us with a combination of timelessness and perpetual renewal.

djemaa el-fna square

A place of transformation, of fable, of make-believe, and of non-stop energy, Djemaa el-Fna Square is the focal point of the city onto which everything converges, where all journeys start and end. Although its origins remain uncertain—'Square of Oblivion' or 'Meeting Place of the Deceased' are some of its evocative epithets—this barren hectare of dusty tarmac, in all its splendour and misery, is unmistakably the 'Square of Words', and that of laughter, of forgetfulness and of fleeting chance encounters.

Every morning, the same magic is released anew. As if by a set order, the vendors of oranges, watermelons and roasted almonds appear and set up their trestle-tables; then the blind man, the man with an incurable limp and the beggar soon take up their own posts. They are followed by the snake charmers, the Gnaoua musicians, the acrobats and the fire-eaters, all seeming to arrive from nowhere. Only later do the taxis and calèches (horse carriages) disgorge the flow of tourists. Tight circles form around storytellers whose tales, recounted in the local Arab dialect, are accompanied by masks of horror or joy and the dry scraping sound of the gambri. From these

THIS PAGE: Shrouded in a halo of golden light, the minaret of the Koutoubia Mosque looks over the bustling market in Djemaa el-Fna Square.

PAGE 128: The exquisite, delicate stucco and carved wood décor of the Medersa Ben Youssef, a Koranic school, is the perfect setting for peaceful study.

parables, fables and metaphors, notes of truth sometimes emerge. Words of honey, words of venom, all for the delight of the Marrakchis.

When the sun disappears from the medina (old town), Djemaa el-Fna Square empties, and the entertainers collect any remaining scraps of words before disappearing and leaving the night to the djinn (spirits) and to that other world which emerges from the shadows and finds its way towards the golden lights of the Koutoubia Gardens, the Café de France and the Mamounia Hotel in search of some more refined pleasures and stylish entertainment. Marrakech certainly lives by day, but even more so by night. No excuse is needed for whiling away an entire evening with one's friends on the candlelit terrace of a riad or in the brightly lit courtyard of a Moroccan restaurant. Fusion food is the latest trend in the many fashionable restaurants of the Guéliz district. Luxurious private palaces are the settings for strange and eccentric evenings orchestrated for socialites, celebrities and their galaxies of acolytes, a fashionable nightly ritual that varies with the hour before finally drawing to a close at the coming of dawn.

a way of life

Many of Marrakech's districts—the medina, the Palmeraie, Hivernage or Guéliz—have their own separate rules and ways of life, reflected in the wide range of accommodation options available, varying in atmosphere from the laid-back to the frenetic, depending on one's taste.

the medina, riads and refinement

The ancient gateways in the city walls, Bab Doukkala, Bab Agnaou, Bab el-Jdid and Bab Ighli, are tollgates, passages into the seething den of the working classes, Marrakech's other face, made up of hard labour, daily grind, noise, laughter and shouting, contrasts of light and shadow. A sort of forbidden city, in perpetual movement, which transports one into an exciting and foreign land.

THIS PAGE: Relaxing on a rooftop in Marrakech at dusk is the ideal way to drink in the unique atmosphere of the city.

OPPOSITE (FROM TOP): Rose petals are poetically arranged at the edge of a marble fountain in Hotel La Mamounia; stylish, contemporary touches in hues of reds and pinks are set against the Hispano-Moorish architecture of the courtyard in a riad.

The warren of narrow streets are flanked by high walls and heavy metal-studded doors, firmly shut, concealing private houses known as riads. These vast homes, with their courtyards, fountains, archways, passages, terraces and living rooms, traditionally face inwards to allow nothing of their splendour to be discerned from the outside. Many of these riads have been bought, restored and transformed into small luxury hotels providing that 'shared intimacy' so sought after by foreigners. What was once hearsay or wildly extravagant has become a trend! Staying in a riad is a must for any self-respecting aesthete, with its pronounced Oriental atmosphere and touches of Western décor. By choosing this once forbidden way of life, until now reserved for Marrakchis, it is as if one is transgressing a taboo.

Of course, one has to be prepared to walk a bit, to have one's wits about to avoid being pestered and to find one's bearings while tracing the way back through the myriad of narrow alleyways, the derb. After the suffocating heat and deafening throng of the derb, the enclosed garden and the gentle trickle of the courtyard fountain are pure bliss. After the overwhelming smells, the sweet fragrance of a bowl of rose petals is particularly heady. Returning to the luxury of the hammam, the bedroom bedecked in striped sabra (Moroccan silk), the sofas plump with silk cushions, the light filtered by veils of linen, is pure heaven.

palm trees, palaces... for a thousand + one nights

On the edge of town, the Palmeraie is Marrakech's last remaining oasis and its lungs: 13,000 hectares (32,124 acres) of land punctuated by more than 100,000 palm trees, irrigated by an extensive, deep network of channels—a symbolic balance between water and trees, sources of life. Created during the Almoravid dynasty, the extraordinary irrigation complex now carries a mere dribble of water, overstrained as the water supply is by the local population. Vegetables, however, still ripen happily, shaded by clusters of palm trees, leaves rustling in the wind. Figs and cacti also thrive, thrusting their roots deep into the ground. Daub walls, dilapidated over time, still attempt to mark out boundaries. Douars (villages) with farm buildings of mud and their roaming herds of goats conjure up a scene of rural existence which is fast disappearing.

from the middle ages to the 21st century

Reclaimed, encroached upon and divided up, the Palmeraie is no longer its former self. Hit by development fever, the Palmeraie unashamedly trades its farmland for real estate. All that space is a real luxury, an opportunity for constructing vast palaces, sprawling villas, hotel complexes, holiday homes and golf courses. Dirt tracks are tarmacked over, tidied up, illuminated, to lead the way to fenced-off private properties. Villas, fuelling Western dreams of a fantasy Morocco, have

sprung up all over the place, almost outnumbering the ever-decreasing palm trees; they have become refuges, private gardens of Babylon, for the international jet set. The architectural styles vary according to the tastes and backgrounds of the villas' owners: sumptuous, Moorish, Andalusian or Hollywood, rivalling each other in pure luxury and comfort.

Protected from prying eyes by high walls, fertile gardens full of citrus fruit and exotic trees are impeccably maintained, with lawns and pools, patches of blue in a sea of green. On the other side of those walls, not too far away but not too close either, are all the authentic smells and colours necessary to complete that sense of being somewhere foreign.

Anxious to preserve the building style of southern Morocco to which the Palmeraie belongs, architects such as Elie Mouyal, Aziz Lamghari and Charles Boccara have created homes which are as beautiful as they are traditional, and they are designed for ease of living as well as ease of entertaining. Their houses are built with thick walls of unfired mud bricks, diagonal ribs and vaults, cupolas lit by colourful stained glass, ceilings of plaited thuya wood, painted walls and glazed tiles. Bunches of orange-coloured bougainvillea are trained across the entire length of terraces shaded by coarse, unbleached linen. Fresh water flows freely in channels winding through Cordoban-style gardens. The shady bower of climbing roses and queen's wreath (Petrea volubilis) protects one from the heat of the day. In the evening, when everything has calmed down, flickering night-lights illuminate open-air receptions under a star-studded sky. This is the next page from the *One Thousand and One Nights*.

saving the palmeraie

According to legend, Marrakech's Palmeraie grew out of thousands of date stones discarded by Almoravid soldiers. The palm trees were originally irrigated by an entire underground network of khetarras (underground cisterns), a remarkable engineering feat. Most of these no longer exist, having been destroyed to make way for the real estate that is now the primary role of the Palmeraie. Not surprisingly, the last remaining khetarra, that of Aïn Tahir, 660 m (2,165 ft) in length, is the focus of much attention.

The Palmeraie is an area of tall palm trees interspersed with a number of adobe settlements and food crops, a symbolic, natural legacy dating back to the Almoravid Era (1061-1147). Greatly coveted by visitors, tourists and property developers alike, the combination of rapid demographic expansion, urbanisation and drought have weakened this remarkable ecosystem to the nth degree, leaving it utterly exhausted and fragile.

Something had to be done, and urgently. In 2007, under the presidency of Her Royal Highness Princess Lalla Hasnaa, a rescue programme was drawn up to save the Palmeraie, involving several simultaneous plans of action. First and foremost, 450,000 palm trees are to be planted over a six-year period. The city of Marrakech and its partners have already planted 55,000 palm trees in a 3,000-hectare (7,413-acre) area. To ensure continuity, this action is backed up by the creation of a nursery intended to produce nearly 80,000 palm trees a year and a water purification station, which will provide water for irrigation.

A number of different direct operations have been carried out to clean up and maintain the Palmeraie. The Association de l'Observatoire de la Palmeraie, for instance, organised a competition for young school children to collect all the plastic bags and refuse in the settlements of Tamsna and Sidi Ghanem. Similarly, information panels have been put up within the Palmeraie itself, to help increase the public's awareness of the environmental issues at stake. Social operations have also been undertaken in favour of the women in the settlements in the Palmeraie, especially those in Tamsna and Abbiad.

THIS PAGE: Outside of the medina, hotels like the Amanjena have the space to spread out and create oases of luxury.

OPPOSITE (FROM TOP): What finer gift of welcome than a dish of figs; full of promise: a date palm weighed down by its fruit.

...ideal for those seeking peace and comfort—a real luxury.

An international programme for environmental education, Eco-Schools, has been drawn up focusing on several priority themes: water and energy conservation and refuse disposal and reduction. An innovative pilot project, the Oases Living Museum, is in the process of being created with the help of the Mohammed VI Foundation for the Protection of the Environment. In regards to the Palmeraie, the scheme involves the foundation of an Eco-Museum, a botanical garden, to be named the 'Jnan Oasis of 7 Flavours', and a permanent centre for oasis environmental education. A remarkable initiative combining ethics and sustainable development, this project plans to aid the oasis-dwelling traditions by offering information on water conservation and methods for building adobe architecture, techniques which will hopefully be passed down to future generations.

the hivernage—homes designed for an everlasting summer

Compared to the confusing warren of the medina, the orderly topography of the Hivernage, the most accessible and comprehensible district of the city, is striking. Henri Prost, Maréchal Lyautey's appointed town planner, was responsible for creating it in the 1930s, with the intention of making 'a city-garden for tourists'. Fleeing the severity of their own cold winters, Europe's aristocracy and burgeoning middle classes took up quarters here 'to winter' (hiverner) in the mild Moroccan climate, hence the district's name.

Bordered on three sides by the long Avenue de la Menara, Avenue Hassan II and Avenue de France, this elegant district, with its alleys lined with jacaranda trees and large, palm-fronted gardens, has been the favoured area for luxury hotels and residential homes since the 1970s. Some are veritable Gardens of Eden, like the Es Saadi Gardens & Resort, set in 8 hectares (20 acres) of private grounds, with its own casino and theatre. Just a short distance from Guéliz, and not that far from the medina, the historic centre and Menara Airport, the Hivernage is ideal for those seeking peace and comfort—a real luxury.

guéliz, heading west

Running from the old town, in the north, to the new town, in the west, is the 2-km (1.2-mile) Avenue Mohammed V, which links Koutoubia to the Guéliz district. The Avenue is the backbone of the city and its principal artery, punctuated by three vast circles known as the Place de la Liberté, the Place du 16 Novembre and the so-called 'Café-Circle'. The never-ending flow of traffic is very heavy and chaotic: pedestrians, cars, taxis, calèches and motorbikes negotiate around each other in a terrifying, whirring spectacle, a cacophony of blasting horns, in which right of way is a seemingly random concept.

OPPOSITE: *With the Atlas Mountains for a backdrop, the architecture of the crenellated ramparts, crowned with palm trees, creates a memorable image of the city.*

THIS PAGE: *The sumptuous villas of Es Saadi Gardens & Resort in the heart of the Hivernage district are like small palaces.*

Guéliz, which gets its name from a rockface situated to the west of Marrakech, has been well worn by time, offering all the antiquated and old-fashioned charm of the colonial years. Both the Gidel and Société Générale buildings, as well as the Café de la Renaissance, are fine examples of an architectural style which spanned Art Deco through to the 1950s. Vinyl, neon, flecked tiles, brass plaques and lifts all denote the functional modernism of the 1970s. Café terraces spread themselves comfortably in between office buildings, banks, agencies and shops, their clients, for the most part masculine, wandering from one to the other, following the shade. Elsewhere, the faded red and ochre façades of smaller buildings are covered with jacaranda and orange blossoms, their balconies nurturing miniature gardens.

At the centre of Guéliz lies the covered market, 'the small market', where everyone and everything meets. Sadly, its presence is threatened by developers wishing to create a commercial centre in its place. For the time being, however, it is still there, overgrown as it is with thuya trees and invaded by cats. Every morning, the locals meet in front of the main entrance with baskets in hand, there to buy flowers, fruit, bread and vegetables. Well-informed tourists also sometimes find their way here to shop for simple souvenirs, wooden objects, ceramic bowls and dishes, or that last little gift, all at very moderate prices.

The surrounding streets, such as Rue de la Liberté and Rue Sourya, contain the most fashionable boutiques, interior decorators, antiquarians and designers. Aimed at an international clientele, these talented designers creatively reinterpret traditional Moroccan art forms, crossing them with those of Asia and Africa. North African leather with an Italian design, djellabas (hooded robes) made from Indian silk, cedarwood tables in Art Deco style, Berber rugs and nickel silver trays, all of which would not look out of place in London or Paris.

green space + fresh air

Marrakech is rich in green spaces and gardens, 950 hectares (2,3478 acres) in total—not bad for a city on the edge of the Sahara! A stroll around the city's gardens takes one from the little-known Arsat Moulay Absalam Gardens; to the star-status Majorelle Gardens, owned by the late Yves Saint Laurent; via the enchanting Agdal Gardens, which date back to the 12th century, the time of the Almohads; to the Andalusian-inspired Ménara Gardens, with their groves of lemon, orange, olive and pomegranate trees irrigated by water basins; through the recently restored Koutoubia Gardens surrounding the famous minaret; to the Mamounia Gardens, 15 hectares (37 acres) of orchards for those lucky enough to live there; and finally to the gardens of the Bahia Palace, an outstanding 8-hectare (20-acre) haven of peace within the medina. There are also two nurseries, one in town which cultivates the precious palm trees, and the other within the Palmeraie, which has the capacity to produce thousands of plants, including Aleppo pines, carob trees, acacias and eucalyptus.

the majorelle gardens + the ménara

The Majorelle Gardens were created by the artist Jacques Majorelle in the 1920s. Arriving in Morocco in 1917 to convalesce from tuberculosis, Majorelle was totally won over by the country and set to work creating a haven of freshness and calm as if it were a canvas onto which he could transcribe his emotions. This magical oasis in the heart of the city perpetuates a taste for Oriental gardens, with water flowing gently through channels and water lily-laden pools. Amid lush vegetation— bamboo, cacti and palms—the multitude of greens contrasts with the intense blue (the famous Majorelle blue) of pergolas and kiosks. Magnificent bougainvillea perfume the entire property. 'Morocco has arrived with its colours: those of the earth and sand, but also those of the street, women's kaftans in turquoise, mauve and every imaginable colour.

OPPOSITE: The Guéliz district is where everybody tends to congregate. Lively cafés, fashionable boutiques and trendy restaurants and galleries jostle for space along the Avenues Mohammed V and Nations Unies and the Rue de la Liberté.

THIS PAGE: The Majorelle Gardens are a dazzling vision of greens and blues, where cacti, bamboo, tall palm trees and a thousand essences provide a heady mix for those visiting this haven of calm.

THIS PAGE (FROM TOP): *The High Atlas is just outside the city; the pavilion in the Ménara Gardens is an ideal spot for taking photos.*
OPPOSITE: *Jbel Toubkal and the Oukaimeden Ski Resort cater for all kinds of snow sports.*

Until now, I only used dark shades,' said the famous couturier, Yves St Laurent, on discovering Marrakech in 1967. Together with Pierre Bergé, he bought and restored the villa and its gardens, which had lain abandoned since Majorelle's death in 1962. The studio has since been transformed into a museum of Islamic art, displaying some of Majorelle's works.

With the snowy peaks of the Atlas Mountains as a backdrop, and far from the bustle of the medina, Ménara is one of the most picturesque spots in the entire city, together with the Koutoubia Mosque and Djemaa el-Fna Square. It is also one of the most spectacular: a 900,000-sq-m- (1 million-sq-yd-) domain protected by 4 km (2.5 miles) of earthen walls. During the reign of the Almohads in the 12th century, water was elevated to the status of an art; a large central pond, 200 m (656 ft) long and 150 m (492 ft) wide, was constructed to irrigate the gardens via an extremely elaborate system of underground conduits. In the 19th century, this extraordinary cistern acquired an elegant pavilion with a pyramidal roof from where one can admire the setting sun. Surrounded by olive groves, it is a marvellous place to relax, much appreciated back in the time of the sultans and still one of the favourite spots for Marrakchi families.

getting away: oukaimeden

Seventy kilometres (43 miles) south of Marrakech, the massif rises to over 3,000 m (9,843 ft). From December to April, the pastures are covered in snow, providing the best skiing in Africa, based at Oukaimeden Ski Resort, some 2,600 m (8,530 ft) high. The ski lift rises to the summit, at 3,273 m (10,738 ft), from where, in good weather, there is a breathtaking view of Jbel (mountain) Toubkal and the Marrakech Valley. In summer, while it is a sweltering 40°C down on the Haouz Plain, Oukaimeden is a haven of freshness, providing plentiful pasture for animals, hence the azib (shepherds' huts) dotted around the place. At the entrance to the resort, several red sandstone rocks bear engravings from the Bronze Age, which are identical to representations discovered in Europe.

At Jbel Yagour, a national park featuring a collection of prehistoric rock engravings, was founded in 1994, according to the wishes of travel writer Théodore Monod. More than 3,500 of these works, dating from prehistoric times, have been identified, depicting weapons, animals and humans.

From December to April, the pastures are covered in snow, providing the best skiing in Africa...

the ourika valley

Beyond Marrakech and the Haouz Plain, the Ourika Valley slowly winds its way up through the lower foothills of the High Atlas Mountains, amid terraced plots of land planted with cereal crops and alfalfa. This tranquil landscape is dotted with small villages of daub houses, some scattered among orchards and groves of walnuts and olives, others clinging to the mountainsides. Beyond the abandoned village of Aghmat, which still retains the Mausoleum of Moatamid ben Abbad, the early 20th-century Andalusian poet-prince, a path leads to Dar Caïd Ouriki, where the valley's most popular market takes place on Mondays.

The road goes as far as the village of Setti Fatma, to a height of 1,500 m (4,921 ft), the lofty domain of the Haouara Berbers (who founded the small village of Rhmate), and of plentiful wild boars. Cars do not get beyond this point, but the physically fit can walk up to the seven waterfalls

or hike along the mule paths towards Jbel Yagour or the Toubkal massif. Next, the Neltner Refuge, 3,200 m (10,499 ft) high, is the last stop before embarking on the 5-hour ascent to Jbel Toubkal, the highest summit in the Atlas chain, standing at 4,167 m (13,671 ft) in height.

once upon a time in the deep south

The road from Marrakech to Ouarzazate follows the old caravan route and is spectacularly beautiful. As it crosses the High Atlas region, one starts to feel the pull of Morocco's Grand Sud (Deep South), while getting a glimpse of the nomadic tribes and the legendary Berber culture. The road twists and climbs, ever more stunning, through a strange, chaotic universe, almost another planet.

Sometime during the upheaval that created these mountains, the quartz rocks burst open and turned violet. On the horizon, the wine-coloured, pleated mountains unfold like a fan. Rounding another sheer drop and bend in the road, great faults appear with Aleppo pines and eucalyptus clinging to their sides, forming wide gorges with terraces of greenery in their depths far below. In between walnut and almond groves, some rudimentary stone dwellings huddle together, well camouflaged against the mountainside. There is sometimes snow on the Col du Tichka, which looms above at 2,260 m (7,415 ft); the passes at higher elevations are sometimes blocked in the winter. On the southern slopes, the scenery changes from plant to mineral, and becomes softer and flatter. Rich in copper and manganese, the valleys flush pink and green. Finally, the plain stretches out, stony and milky white in hue.

At Telouet, once an obligatory stopping point on the caravan route, the first kasbah looms into sight. It was the feudal stronghold and domain of the Glaoui, the overlords of the region, who imposed a levy on everything that passed through. Dilapidated and yet still majestic, it is a prelude to the ksar (villages) of the Draâ Valley.

on the desert's doorstep

Ouarzazate was built by the French in 1928 as a Foreign Legion lookout post at the edge of the great unknown. This former small garrison at the end of the Tichka Road is now the administrative centre of the Draâ region and a necessary stopover en route to assuaging one's craving for the desert. Beyond this modern town lies the legendary route of a thousand kasbahs, the Zagora Oasis and the Merzouga Dunes.

THIS PAGE: *Colourful rugs and hand-made Berber products from southern Morocco are often sought after by tourists.*
OPPOSITE: *Shepherds bring their flocks to graze in the Ourika Valley, surrounded by the snow-capped peaks of the High Atlas Mountains.*

a mirage, an image

Boulevard Mohammed V divides Ouarzazate across the middle, from east to west, like a wide furrow. On either side, the bazaars are hung with warm-coloured Berber rugs with geometric patterns. The most prized are those made by the women of the Ouzguita tribe. Further on are veritable Ali Baba Caves where, just occasionally, some pieces of fine old ethnic jewellery in heavy silver can still be found, hidden among the mountains of bric-a-brac. Modern hotel complexes are springing up all around. Only the saffron-coloured high walls of the Taourirt Kasbah remind visitors of the purity of the architecture that was. Once the residence of the powerful Thami el-Glaoui, the Pacha of Marrakech, it has been transformed into a museum. The banquet room and the 'chamber of the favourite one' are both remarkably well preserved.

architectural treasures

Ksar and kasbahs are an architectural heritage to be saved. These fortresses served as residences for the nobility, as well as places to store the harvests and as refuge for oases-dwellers against pillage. This extraordinary adobe architecture forms the cornerstone of the Ouarzazate region's heritage, and conservation programmes are now helping to preserve its villages and settlements. The Ksar Aït-Benhaddou (a UNESCO site) and Taourirt Kasbah are prime candidates for this programme, launched by the Ministry of Culture with the assistance of international bodies like the Organisation Mondiale du Tourisme (OMT) and, of course, UNESCO.

The Taourirt Kasbah was one of Pacha el-Glaoui's most extravagant residences. Situated in the middle of the town of Ouarzazate (itself a museum nowadays), the kasbah is undergoing extensive renovation and conversion into a luxury guesthouse.

an oasis transformed by the cinema

Ouarzazate certainly owes much of its rapid expansion to tourism—but even more so to the film industry. The change is striking. Since 1984, the quality of light, the blue sky, the ksar, the colourful valleys and the sand dunes have been appropriated as scenery or as open-air studios by two film production companies, Atlas Corporation and Aster Production. This 'land of contrasts' offers everything these producers ever dreamed of, with no shortage of enthusiastic extras. The list of major feature films shot in Ouarzazate includes *Harem* by Arthur Joffe, *Il tè nel deserto* (*The Sheltering Sky*) by Bertolucci and *Kundun* by Martin Scorsese. A few kilometres from the town, alongside the dried up Ounila riverbed, the Ksar Aït-Benhaddou and its stunning architecture has become a film director's favourite star. Films such as *Lawrence of Arabia*, *Sodom and Gomorrah*, *Jesus of Nazareth* and especially *The Jewel of the Nile*, have exploited its photogenic qualities in varying scenes and guises. As one's dazzled eyes get used to the bright light, one can gradually make out the silhouette of the fortified village, perched on a hillock, extraordinarily poetic, ochre against ochre, in perfect harmony with the earth. The jagged, crumbling crenellations of the towers meld with the kasbahs and agadirs (granaries).

THIS PAGE: Set alongside a dried up wadi in a fairytale landscape, 30 km (19 miles) northwest of Ouarzazate, lies the Ksar Aït-Benhaddou, a remarkable ochre-coloured fortress, which has been featured in many a film.

OPPOSITE: Morocco's Deep South is dotted with ksar (villages), kasbahs and oases. Taourirt Kasbah at Ouarzazate is a ksar in itself. It was the Glaoui's principal residence, and has been restored and transformed into a museum which is open to visitors.

an introduction to the desert

Skoura, Zagora and Merzouga—they could be three sisters, but they are in fact three landmarks, places to stop while travelling through the Dadès and Draâ Valleys. Whether nestled in a palm grove beside an oasis or in the hollow of a dune, they provide the perfect bases from which to embark on an exploration of the great pre-Saharan regions.

skoura

It is the palm grove and the magnificent kasbahs that surround this modest village, a douar, that make this place so remarkable. Large palm trees offer shade all along the Skoura and Amerhidil Oueds (Valleys). Figs, pomegranates, apricots and almonds grow in abundance, as well as roses whose petals are picked to make rosewater.

Out of the lush palm grove emerge the imposing ruins of proud and melancholy kasbahs. Vestiges of a glorious past, works of earthly art, both eternal and ephemeral, kasbahs only come to life when they are inhabited and maintained. Abandoned, they quickly return from whence they came. The Kasbah ben Moro has been saved and converted into a hotel; the Amerhidil Kasbah is the most impressive and best preserved. Others await new masters with sufficient taste and funds to restore them. Also, there are now several comfortable campsites, equipped with Berber tents, on the banks of the Skoura, where one can spend a few days enjoying the calm and beauty of the place.

zagora, in the draâ valley

'Timbuktu, 52 days camel ride'. After this famous signpost on the edge of town—as much a warning as it is a piece of information—there is nothing, or almost: just the loneliness of the hamadas (desert lands), with the first sand dunes 30 km (19 miles) away—guaranteed to disorientate! Zagora is the southernmost stopover point. Descendants of the Harratines—a tribe whose presence dates back to the cave paintings at Tassili, approximately 5,000 BCE—still inhabit this territory. These lords of the desert were the progenitors of the Berber dynasty. Semi-sedentary, they move from one watering place to another with their families and herds. These 'blue men' continue to feed our dreams of childhood adventure.

erfoud, in the dadès valley

Erfoud, lying dormant on the edge of the Ziz Oued is another garrison town built during the French Protectorate period to keep an eye on the tribes of the Tafilalt Valley. Little of the colonial era remains other than the peeling pink arcades and rows of tamarisks. Beneath the scorching sun, a group of haughtily dozing camels watch the latest 'motorised meharis' pass by. Hot competition!

the dunes of merzouga

About 50 km (31 miles) down the track that peters out along the Algerian border, the Erg Chebbi appears—a plateau where the waters of the flood still appear to shimmer on the surface. In fact, it is the reflection from the silvery salt crust covering the Dayet Srji, an ancient dried-up lake. On this desolate ground, tufts of vegetation grow persistantly, while mis-informed flamingoes and other avian waders continue to believe in the convincing mirage.

Beyond, suddenly, voluptuous and vertiginous, in successive waves of whites, pinks, rubies and blood reds, according to the time of day, the Merzouga Dunes loom. The tallest among them culminates at around 150 m (492 ft), a breathtaking sight both at sunrise and sunset, for those prepared to sleep roughing it in a tent. These dunes are one of Morocco's genuine Saharan ergs, and seeing them is an unforgettable experience.

richly varied yet simple food

Moroccan cuisine makes the most of colours, smells and flavours. Its preparation is the exclusive domain of women who, from mother to daughter, hand down their secret know-how—a subtle alchemy of spices, sugar and salt. Coming from the East, saffron, cumin, cardamom, turmeric, nutmeg and plenty of other spices add a little heat to the meat. 'Ras el-hanout' is a mixture of

THIS PAGE: Couscous, a symbolic dish, is for sharing with friends. Eating it correctly, using your right hand to serve yourself straight from the dish, requires a certain amount of practice!

OPPOSITE: The vast desert is not far away! A replica of an ancient signpost has been erected on the edge of Zagora, informing caravans of how many days are needed to cross the desert. Today wheels have replaced the camel caravans, and the first dunes are just a stone's throw away.

20 or so ingredients, including rosebuds, cinnamon, root ginger and monk's pepper, which is used to add zest to most dishes. Harira and chorba, fortifying soups, are served accompanied by dates during the Muslim month of Ramadan.

Based on Andalusian and Judeo-Christian cooking, tajines (meat-based stews) have the sweetness of honey, the delicacy of olive oil and the smoothness of quince or pear, combined with dried beans, marrow, cardoons or artichokes—plenty of scope for the imagination. Presented in the shape of a cone, couscous grains are topped with pieces of chicken, mutton or lamb, covered with vegetables and moistened with the cooking juices—the ultimate in culinary art. However, these main dishes shouldn't hog all of the spotlight. Make sure to try the small salads served as starters and the desserts: slices of orange with cinnamon, bastela ktefa, layered crispy pastries with milk and sugar fillings, briouat and pastilla, small honey-flavoured cakes. The regions in the Deep South in particular are known for sumptuous and flavourful food, which is made to be enjoyed and shared among friends.

hospitality: the ritual of mint tea

Saying, 'Salam 'lekum... 'lekum salam...', as a piping hot glass of mint tea is handed to strangers is a traditional gesture of welcome. Whether in a souk bargaining for a handmade carpet or a piece of pottery, or lost in a village in the Tafraout, or even in the home of a caïd (a patriarch), taking a sip of green tea with a sprig of fresh mint in it is to partake in a sign of courtesy, a friendly preamble to any negotiation or discussion.

More than in any other part of Morocco, the southern regions, the land of the Berbers, are renowned for their tradition of hospitality. Depending on the season, visitors are also likely to be offered something small to eat, such as oranges, a handful of almonds or walnuts plucked straight off the tree, or perhaps even some sweetmeats.

the charm of henna

Berber women have never hidden their faces. On the contrary, unveiled, they show off their wild beauty and freedom. For feast days, weddings and births, the women deck themselves out in colourful finery, shimmering materials and flamboyant jewellery.

They use makeup and skilfully paint tattoos on their bodies with henna. Black khol underlines their dark eyes and, at the same time, protects them from the dust. Carmine-red cheeks mask the shyness of young girls. Hands and feet are embroidered in beautiful, complicated geometric patterns by the mekacha (the tattoo artist) with henna, which, once dry, form a beautiful work of art that resembles delicate black lace.

THIS PAGE (FROM TOP): Whether in a market stall or a friends' house being offered a glass of steaming hot mint tea is a sign of welcome; traditionally, women decorate their hands with henna for weddings or feast days, only removing it on their next visit to the hammam.

OPPOSITE: Erfoud was once the point of departure for caravans setting out for the Merzouga Dunes and beyond. Today, the Tuaregs are becoming mostly sedentary, but a long expedition across the desert with camels is still an iconic image of Morocco.

...the southern regions, the land of the Berbers, are renowned for their tradition of hospitality.

dar doukkala

It would be inaccurate to group Dar Doukkala with the many riads scattered throughout Marrakech's ancient medina, for it is more of a guest palace than a guesthouse. Where others merely fall back on traditional forms, Dar Doukkala has chosen to innovate within the boundaries of its ancient mansion walls, incorporating the romance and intrigue of the 1930s. Art Deco flourishes throughout the enormous property recall the mood of European-influenced Casablanca, as do a number of design and décor choices.

These small additional touches coexist surprisingly well with the interior design's local elements and the 19th-century building's formal architecture. The designer brought the two styles together into a harmonious whole and restored the riad's features to their former glory. The central courtyard is rich in details like stone pillars and wrought-iron work and overflowing with lush tropical greenery. Interiors comprise intricate zellij tile and stucco walls, accented by carved wood panels, painted cedar ceilings and original oak doors. The Grand Salon on the ground floor is the best example of this, offering an intimate atmosphere around a crackling fireplace. Furnishings defy the minimalist aesthetic of so many trendy lodgings with a mix of antique Arabic and Art Deco pieces.

THIS PAGE (FROM TOP): The décor is a delicate blend of traditional Moroccan and Art Deco styles; Room #5 is ornamented with intricate detailing that gives the room depth and character.

OPPOSITE (FROM TOP): Sip mint tea in peace on the rooftop terrace while relaxing in the shade; tall, sculpted pillars decorate the central courtyard, which is filled with verdant foliage.

rooms
4 rooms · 2 suites

food
European and Mediterranean

drink
beverage list

features
hammam · massage room · rooftop terraces · pool · salon lounge · TV room

nearby
souk shopping · Djemaa el-Fna Square · Koutoubia Mosque · museums

contact
83 Rue de Bab Doukkala, Dar el Bacha
40000 Marrakech ·
telephone: +212.24.383 444 ·
facsimile: +212.24.383 445 ·
email: riaddoukkala@yahoo.fr ·
website: www.dardoukkala.com

Now and again, one may catch a glimpse of some retro-modern article like Philippe Starck's neo-Baroque Ghost chair.

The opulent décor extends to each of the four guestrooms and two suites, which are in some instances twice the size of standard riad accommodations. All feature period fireplaces with Art Deco ornamentation and intricate attention to detail. Some rooms are enhanced with ornate stained-glass windows, but all are nonetheless airy and well-lit. Spacious bathroom facilities are always a pleasure, and Dar Doukkala has some of the best in town with their sumptuous claw-foot tubs and tadelakt plaster or mosaicked walls.

Room #3 is a suite with a private loggia, romantically decorated with fiery red feature walls, red bed linens and stylish red furniture.

Room #5 invites guests to relax for hours on end, either admiring the ornate ceiling from bed, or in the traditional-style tiled bathtub. For larger groups or families desiring the comforts of a private residence, Room #6 is ideal. In addition to a peaceful balcony area, it opens out onto an exclusive roof terrace.

It is common in most riads to place the pool in the courtyard, but Dar Doukkala's expansive grounds allow for its heated pool to be placed on a separate tiled terrace with lots of sunlight. This not only affords guests greater privacy and reduces the disturbance to rooms around the courtyard, but also enables poolside views over the medina that stretch all the way to the Atlas Mountains. When choosing a riad stay that over-delivers on character and comfort, Dar Doukkala is a well-suited candidate.

dar les cigognes

THIS PAGE: *Multilingual staff are meticulous and attend quickly to guests' every request.*
OPPOSITE: *A well-furnished room at Dar Les Cigognes.*

Set in the lively medina of old downtown Marrakech, this 'House of Storks' was named for the birds that could often be seen on the ramparts of the Royal Palace just across the street. Restored to a state of classic grandeur by architect Charles Boccara in association with its owners, the main riad of the boutique hotel was originally home to a wealthy merchant, with history stretching as far back as the 17th century. Over 50 local craftsmen and artists were involved in the redecoration, with long-faded details meticulously reworked and repainted over a period of two years.

Now joined with a second historic property by way of a bridge that crosses one of the medina's many colourful alleyways, Dar Les Cigognes is a masterpiece of luxury in the heart of the city. Its proximity to the Royal Palace means that no cultural or commercial landmark in the medina is ever far away, and indeed the famous Djemaa el-Fna Square is only a short walk from the hotel's front steps.

As is true of all Moroccan riads, Dar Les Cigognes' buildings were designed to be privately contained spheres of serenity and comfort. There are majestic public spaces, with solid columns that rise above to join with dark cedar balustrades and carved stucco arches under open sky. As lounges, these areas are suited for leisurely reading or conversation over drinks. In the heat of summer, the thick walls and lush vegetation contribute a cool atmosphere. Guests who prefer to avoid direct sunlight may choose one of the four bhou seating areas, which are elegant couched salons recessed into the walls of the courtyard. These feature the beautiful hand-carved ceilings that are a hallmark of Moroccan architecture.

Surrounding the open courtyards are a number of exceptional social areas, including an African Living Room designed around the history of the region's link to ancient Saharan trade. Warmed by a fireplace and decorated with period furniture, maps and other artefacts, this salon transports guests to a time when Morocco lay at the centre of the world's most important trade routes.

Travellers wishing to learn more about Moroccan history may want to spend an evening in the hotel's evocatively furnished library. With books covering all subjects from the ancient arts to modern society, there are few questions that cannot be answered from the comfort of one of the many comfortable seats lining the space. For sheer indulgence, fine cigars, whiskeys and traditional Arabian nargileh water pipes are available to pass many pleasurable hours with.

Meals from the hotel's Moroccan and Mediterranean restaurant and bar can be enjoyed in any of the public spaces around the property, or in the privacy of guestrooms. All food is freshly prepared from local ingredients in the regional style. Not to be missed is the traditional breakfast that consists of a variety of breads and pastries served with honey and homemade jams.

Throughout the hotel, many Moorish and Berber design conventions can be seen, from the use of fresco-like paintings in some corridors, to traditional motifs and the choice of materials used. Most guests will encounter these delightful touches in some form in one of the property's 11 rooms. All rooms have their own unique designs, and are readied for comfort before the arrival of guests with complimentary fruit platters, bottles of still

water, and either duvets or summer blankets depending on the season. Air-conditioning as well as safes and telephones are standard.

Well-suited for first-time visitors, three superior rooms feature generous floorplans and bathrooms with shower-equipped baths. The Zouak Room has an incredible hand-painted ceiling, achieved using the fine-brushed Zouak technique perfected in Marrakech. It is a lavish visual feast that can be found in palaces throughout the kingdom; its high labour requirements reserve it for

only the finest of lodgings. Here, its intricacies grace not only the ceiling, but also the closet doors, bed and select pieces of furniture.

Dar Les Cigognes' deluxe rooms, of which there are seven, are even more impressive with separate sitting areas. Six of them even enjoy their own fireplaces. The Silver Room, which does not, makes up for it with loads of sumptuous style and views of the Royal Palace and the interior courtyard. The walls in the bedroom and bathroom are made of silver-coloured tadelakt plaster, and the mirror and sink are fashioned from hammered silver.

Another deluxe room pays tribute to a city that enjoyed especial prominence in the early 20th century: the Casablanca Room is entirely inspired by Art Deco, with period armchairs situated by a fireplace decorated in the iconic style of the era with a black and white mosaic pattern. Equally enchanting for couples is the Harem Room, richly draped in swathes of extravagant red velvet and gold. Furniture is alternately gold and brass, with the walls painted a deep solid red, and the floor bearing a red zellij tile border.

The Orientalist Suite is Dar Les Cigognes' largest and most opulent room. From the 2-by-2-m (7-by-7-ft) bed to the replica Jerôme painting that hangs above it, everything has been carefully considered to give the best stay possible. A swirled tadelakt chimney emerges from the fireplace in the reading area, while ornate windows offer views of the streets below. The bathroom is a grand affair with two skylights set in high vaulted ceilings, a separate shower, and on the tiled floor, a carpet that is a work of art on its own.

The riads also house a traditional marble hammam and spa which offers therapies such as the traditional beldi with Moroccan black soap. In the cavernous treatment room—boasting a 9-m (30-ft) ceiling—and under the domes and arches of the steam bath, one can soak in a jacuzzi or enjoy an invigorating shiatsu massage.

What stands out most about Dar Les Cigognes is the way it feels like an exclusive pleasure. The staff are ever-present yet out of sight, and there's never a hurry to do something or to be anywhere else. Relaxing holidays in style should all start from a place like this.

THIS PAGE (FROM TOP): Guests may choose to take their meals in the charming dining room; the Orientalist Suite is the largest and most opulent room at Dar Les Cigognes.

OPPOSITE (FROM LEFT): The treatment room is unusual in that it has a 9-m- (30-ft-) tall ceiling; comfortable seating entices guests to stay and take in the view from the rooftop terrace.

...everything has been carefully considered to give the best stay possible.

rooms
10 rooms • 1 suite

food
traditional Moroccan and Mediterranean

drink
bar

features
library • hammam • wireless Internet access • Fassi Beauty Spa • roof gardens • gift boutique

nearby
El-Badi Palace • Bahia Palace • Agdal Gardens • medina • Djemaa el-Fna Square • kasbah

contact
108 Rue de Berima, Medina 40000 Marrakech • telephone: +212.24.382 740 • facsimile: +212.24.384 767 • email: info@lescigognes.com • website: www.lescigognes.com

dar rhizlane

THIS PAGE: *The heated outdoor pool at Dar Rhizlane.*

OPPOSITE (FROM TOP): *Rooms here are spacious and offer guests privacy and a peaceful haven in the midst of the busy city; Berber-style doorways combat the scorching heat of the day by drawing in cool breezes.*

Some cities offer natural wonders, others beautiful beaches or architectural genius. Marrakech, on the other hand, has hung onto the traditions that create the city's spectacle. Indeed, the colourful lifestyle is what makes Marrakech so attractive, so enticing and such an experience. Amid the souks, the mosques and the burgeoning crowds a certain buzz is apparent, one that can leave you wanting more one minute, or needing a good sit down with a cup of mint tea the next. And that is where Dar Rhizlane comes in.

While living the Moroccan dream is an endless adventure that hits the senses at their very core, a bit of tranquillity will not go amiss. The staff at Dar Rhizlane are well aware of this and have set up their palatial hideaway just a few steps from the Djemaa el-Fna Square and the medina. This establishment, a perfect mix between boutique hotel and luxury guesthouse, is an old palace clad in striking Berber décor. Tall and imposing walls hide the peaceful gardens and courtyards within, and immense internal structures keep the whole property both cool and intimate.

Once ensconced in the quiet space of the hotel, the stunning garden with its orange trees, jasmine, rose bushes, palm trees and bougainvillea plants is just the ticket for unwinding. The pool is just as good to look at

rooms
16 rooms • 3 suites

food
gastronomic Moroccan fusion

drink
Majorelle Pool Bar

features
in-room spa and beauty treatments •
outdoor heated pool

nearby
medina • Djemaa el-Fna Square

contact
Rue Jnane el Harti, Hivernage
40000 Marrakech •
telephone: +212.24.421 303 •
facsimile: +212.24.447 900 •
email: contact@darrhizlane.ma •
website: www.dar-rhizlane.com

as it is to swim in and the Majorelle Pool Bar serves refreshing poolside drinks. If it is too hot outside, the common spaces have Berber-style arched doorways and windows that draw in a welcome breeze.

The colour scheme and overall style is Berber through and through. Dusky oranges and reds are splashed on the walls, run rampant among the plush cushions and cover the bedspreads. The mirrors, the chandeliers, the rugs, the mosaics—they are the real thing. This guesthouse has been decorated with an explicit understanding of the Berber aesthetic.

Dar Rhizlane offers its guests a variety of accommodation in two different buildings. The Menzeh is the citadel-like structure that houses rooms and suites ranging from one to three bedrooms, some with Moroccan sitting rooms. The other building, Villa Rayane, has one suite and two bedrooms, each with a private terrace. The variety means this little gem is equally ideal for singletons, couples and families, and the spacious rooms and huge beds, as well as the privacy of each room, make it an even more obvious choice.

If it seems too difficult to go outside and forage for food, stay in and have breakfast by the pool. The restaurant is one of the best in the city for modern Moroccan cuisine, so savour a scrumptious dinner in an intimate setting that opens into the garden. Here, as in the rest of the hotel, the service is impeccable. The staff's meticulous care and their attention to junior—and his parents—mean everyone will have a good time.

hôtel + ryads naoura barrière marrakech

In the heart of the old town lies Hôtel & Ryads Naoura Barrière Marrakech. This serene oasis lies behind unobtrusive doors and high walls, shutting out the activity of the medina, which is only moments away. Already a cult address in Marrakech, guests here can be sure that they will be pampered with nothing less than the Naoura Barrière brand of luxury.

Set in the hotel's 2 hectares (5 acres) are 85 suites with expansive living spaces. Each features a large dressing room and a private terrace that faces the pool. Despite being surrounded by touches of classic Moroccan décor, there is nothing vintage about the amenities or the service provided.

Each room is equipped with high-speed Internet access, video on-demand as well as a home-cinema sound system that makes it no hardship at all for guests to remain inside their rooms. Private butler services are available for every room, ensuring that each guest's needs are efficiently tended to.

Guests can also choose to reside in any one of the property's 26 individual riads if the suites are not to their taste. These exclusive villas offer a plethora of luxury services, accompanied by personal pools surrounded by ornate flowers, where guests can relax or exercise in complete privacy.

The facilities and services provided here complement the property's fine lodgings perfectly. With the renowned Djemaa el-Fna Square located just a stone's throw away, guests can head to the medina for a taste of

Marrakech at its best; the knowledgeable concierge is always willing to share his or her expertise and provide information to guests who wish to explore the city and view its popular attractions. Guests can also be assured that the staff are competent and efficient when assisting with the logistics of such trips.

For some tranquillity after the excitement of exploring the city, there is always the U Spa. Featuring two traditional hammams, a unique aquatic well-being course and a large state-of-the-art gym, sports and health lovers alike can be assured that their needs will be met. With the fully equipped private meeting rooms, even if work intrudes while a guest is vacationing at Hôtel & Ryads Naoura Barrière Marrakech, they will not want for the appropriate facilities.

THIS PAGE (FROM TOP): An elegant tiled fountain welcomes guests to the spa, where a host of treatments are offered; vibrant red furnishings exude decadence which matches the fine fare served at Fouquet's.

OPPOSITE (FROM TOP): Private sitting rooms in the riads are sleek, elegantly decorated settings for guests to entertain visitors; creams and browns create a restful environment that offers guests a break from the excitement of Marrakech.

rooms
85 suites • 26 riads

food
Fouquet's: traditional French and Moroccan •
The Wardya: Moroccan with a twist

drink
The Nuphar Bar: cocktails and vintages

features
spa • Diwi Club • aquatic well-being course •
well-equipped gym

nearby
Djemaa el-Fna Square

contact
Rue Djebel Alakhdar, Bab Doukkala
40000 Marrakech •
telephone: +212.24.459 000 •
email: resanaoura@lucienbarriere.com •
website: www.naoura-barriere.com

Adults who wish to have a little time to themselves can safely leave the tykes at the Diwi Club. Created just for children to have a special holiday of their own, the Diwi Club has activities, workshops and even a special menu to enhance their Moroccan experience.

For a sense of how the different cultures in Morocco mix, visitors have to experience each of them at their best; and how else to embrace a culture but through food? Fouquet's, with outlets in Paris, Cannes and Toulouse, now serves traditional Parisian brasserie meals and local cuisine here at Hôtel & Ryads Naoura Barrière Marrakech. Alternatively, guests who wish to experience an adventure for the senses can visit The Wardya to indulge in Moroccan fare with a twist, to be enjoyed in the shade of fragrant flowers near the pool, under the open sky.

End the day by enjoying original cocktails and rare vintages in the idyllic atmosphere of The Nuphar Bar while contemplating the next stop on the itinerary. After all, checking into Hôtel & Ryads Naoura Barrière Marrakech is just the beginning of experiencing the warm hospitality of Morocco.

la maison arabe

La Maison Arabe is a classically styled riad hotel with all the ingredients required for an exceptional stay in the ancient city of Marrakech. Its location is impeccable, beside major pedestrian walkways in the Bab Doukkala district, near the area's place of worship which in turn enjoys a view of the landmark Koutoubia Mosque. From the front door of the property, one is only metres away from the medina's major attractions. Getting to Djemaa el-Fna Square is just a short five-minute walk, but the busy public square's celebratory atmosphere—with its multitude of shops, open-air street food stalls and snake

charming entertainment—is kept at bay by the riad's thick walls, which maintain a peaceful silence within.

Its sense of style too, is among the best of the city's riads. Meticulously restored over a span of two years by a team of local craftsmen using age-old techniques and original materials, the traditional architecture of the voluminous house now stands in perfect condition as proof of its timeless appeal. Throughout the cosy indoor salons and lounges, to the busy corridors and galleries that border the riad's two courtyards packed with thriving plant life, murmuring fountains and magnificent olive trees, one is filled with an appreciation for the way of life that brought this extravagant residence of sensual pleasures to fruition.

In the enumeration of facilities and services, La Maison Arabe impresses the most demanding of expectations. Aside from the pleasant patios where guests may recline for hours in the shade of a tree reading or sipping mint tea, the hotel also has a pool, spa and cooking school available to occupy guests during their free time. In addition, foodies may be pleased to know that the hotel allows for exemplary dining with two restaurants and a poolside café that serves light meals.

Fine dining at the hotel's main restaurant is a fully Moroccan affair, with live Arab-Andalusian music performed on a lute and a guitar setting the scene for delicious fare from a menu of traditional favourites and

...lavish living spaces that will not easily be forgotten by any visitor.

rooms
12 rooms • 14 suites

food
Le Restaurant: traditional Moroccan •
Saveurs d'Ailleurs: Asian-inspired tapas •
Le Figuier: light meals

drink
beverage list

features
pool facility • spa • private function venues •
cooking school • wireless Internet access

nearby
Djemaa el-Fna Square • Koutoubia Mosque •
souk shopping • mosques • museums

contact
1 Derb Assehbé, Bab Doukkala
40000 Marrakech •
telephone: +212.24.387 010 •
facsimile: +212.24.387 221 •
email: reservation@lamaisonarabe.com •
website: www.lamaisonarabe.com

signature specialities. Further adding to the Moroccan experience, the cavernous dining room features a hand-painted zouaké ceiling and all its walls are clad with tadelakt plaster. The Saveurs d'Ailleurs is La Maison Arabe's second dining establishment, and it evokes the feel of the 1930s with its carved walls and artwork alluding to the exoticism of colonial Africa. The menu here embraces local flavours as well as inventive Asian-influenced tapas.

Le Figuier, the hotel's café, is located by the large 18-by-7-m (59-by-23-ft) pool in a luxuriant garden a short shuttle ride away. Use of the pool is restricted to hotel guests alone, and due to its separate location, the pool is far larger and more secluded than if it were a part of the riad. The tree-lined pool area also includes a Caïd tent and Kasbah which can be booked for private functions.

It is expected that each of the property's 12 rooms and 14 suites is tastefully furnished, comfortable and luxurious, and La Maison Arabe does not disappoint. Many of the rooms enjoy fireplaces and private terraces, while all accommodations are equipped with modern conveniences such as wireless Internet access, satellite television channels, air-conditioning and minibars. Their rich interior designs make good use of a combination of zellij tiles, fine woven fabrics and an impressive art collection to create lavish living spaces that will not easily be forgotten by any visitor.

la sultana marrakech

Located in the old imperial quarter of Marrakech, La Sultana is a sprawling complex of riads built around the Royal Palace and the lavish tomb of the Saadian kings, built in the late 16th century by Sultan Ahmed el-Mansour for himself and his descendants. This property took three years and a team of architects and master craftsmen to build. Every single detail was scrutinised and carefully worked out in consultation with the Historical Monuments Commission of Morocco; the result is an amazing example of restored traditional Moroccan architecture that has placed La Sultana as a member of such alliances as Small Luxury Hotels and Great Hotels of the World.

Every building in the medina has its own rooftop terrace. Traditionally, a rooftop terrace is used for domestic chores, but at La Sultana, these spaces have been converted into lounges, dining and open-air massage areas to take full advantage of their aerial vantage point. A rooftop of 1,800 sq m (19,375 sq ft) of garden terraces overlook the Koutoubia Mosque as well as the snowy peaks of the Atlas Mountains in the distance.

Five self-contained riads make up the entire hotel complex. Opulent Arabian décor is complemented by classic Roman columns and a subtle underlying wildlife theme. Each room or suite has a unique style and boasts fireplaces, marble or zellij-tile bathrooms, king-sized beds, sculpted ceilings and a fine collection of objets d'art. Palm and orange trees sway gently in courtyards and patios.

At the heart of the hotel is its outdoor heated pool, sunk into the ground like a hammam, or steam bath. Ritual baths are an age-old Moroccan tradition, and in keeping with this, La Sultana has created a large, unique Spa that offers guests a total cleansing and relaxation experience.

Dining at La Sultana is a real treat; the innovative and experienced chefs cook up a mixture of Mediterranean, Oriental and local cuisine using the freshest ingredients from the marketplace. Guests can choose to have their carefully-prepared meals served in the courtyard by the pool or on a rooftop terrace. They also have the option of dining in the privacy of their own rooms. During the day, the superb 400 sq m (4,306 sq ft) Spa offers the best of ritual and professional treatments. With such care and pampering, you can live like a sultan at La Sultana.

THIS PAGE (FROM TOP): *Sit by the pool and relax while getting a beautiful tan; dusk is the most romantic time of day to savour a meal on the rooftop terraces.*

OPPOSITE (FROM LEFT): *The luxurious, well-appointed junior suite; the marble bathroom of the Dromadaire Suite.*

...an amazing example of restored traditional Moroccan architecture...

rooms
13 rooms · 15 suites

food
rooftop and poolside: Mediterranean,
Moroccan and Oriental

drink
lounge bar · terrace

features
outdoor heated pool · boutique · jacuzzi ·
hammams · sauna · Spa · hairdresser · library

nearby
Royal Palace · Saadian Tombs · souks ·
3 18-hole golf courses · museums ·
High Atlas Mountains (1-hour drive)

contact
403 Rue de la Kasbah
40000 Marrakech ·
telephone: +212.24.388 008 ·
facsimile: +212.24.389 809 ·
email: reservation@lasultanahotels.com ·
website: www.lasultanamarrakech.com

les borjs de la kasbah

Brand new destinations in Marrakech's old town centre may sound like a contradiction in terms, but not in the manner that Les Borjs de la Kasbah does it. Building this hotel was a labour of love that took its French and British owners, a talented local architect and a team of craftsmen four long years. Using only traditional techniques and materials such as bejmat floor tiles and tadelakt wall coatings, the development exhibits the best Moroccan architectural practices: ornate decorations, cool colours and symmetry on a grand scale. Combining six townhouses and a riad, the hotel complex—with 18 guestrooms—is large and perfectly in tune with its surroundings.

Inside, four patios recreate the protected courtyards of traditional riad structures, and are havens of peace and quiet with fountains and citrus trees. Adjacent to the courtyard, there is an open Moroccan-style lounge, a bar, two sitting rooms and a meeting room, all available for guests' use.

The hotel restaurant also features its own patio space with an ornamental fountain in addition to its indoor dining room. Although its focus is on modern French cuisine, Le Jasmin incorporates some of the approaches found in local cooking as well, to the extent of offering a few signature Moroccan favourites. Head Chef Aziz Benayad draws on years of experience and French training to create delicacies such as his chicken tajine with preserved lemons and sea bass in sweetened argan oil, using only fresh local produce.

The guestrooms boast individual styling with luxurious furnishings and large beds. All 18 rooms are soundproofed and feature air-conditioning and insulation for comfort. The latest in modern amenities are also provided, with wide-screen televisions and satellite channel access, personal room safes, minibars and communication facilities.

Those travelling alone will appreciate the hotel's five single rooms, each equipped with traditionally tiled en suite bathrooms. There are also five standard double rooms and five premium double rooms that are available in twin sharing configurations. In addition, the three Suites at Les Borjs de la Kasbah, which are appointed with dark wood furnishings and draped in fine fabrics, offer loads of space to stretch out in, making excellent starting points for romantic sojourns into Marrakech.

One of the suites overlooks the new leisure area, which includes a 10-m (33-ft) pool with sunbathing terrace, and the spa. Guests enjoy exclusive privacy with the help of 7-m- (23-ft-) high walls on two sides of the pool, built to facilitate a borj or watchtower, from which the hotel takes its name. A marble-clad, domed hammam is offered as part of Le Spa, and several traditional therapies are available in two treatment rooms. Honey, natural oils, and herbs are part of every massage, while the ubiquitous black soap also appears as part of a gommage scrub.

With all the elements of a modern luxury hotel housed in the rich heritage of its lovingly restored buildings, Les Borjs de la Kasbah is a new beginning for medina properties.

rooms
15 rooms • 3 suites

food
Le Jasmin: French with Moroccan influences

drink
poolside bar • cocktail bar

features
Le Spa • outdoor pool • meeting room • sauna • hammam • gift boutique • Internet access

nearby
medina • Saadian Tombs • Royal Palace • Djemaa el-Fna Square • golf

contact
200 Rue du Méchouar, La Kasbah 40008 Marrakech • telephone: +212.24.381 101 or +212.24.381 106 • facsimile: +212.24.381 125 • email: info@lesborjsdelakasbah.com • website: www.lesborjsdelakasbah.com

les jardins de la koutoubia

THIS PAGE: *The central courtyard is a haven of peace and quiet that guests can retreat to if the bustle of the medina becomes too much.*

OPPOSITE (FROM TOP): *The main pool at Les Jardins de la Koutoubia; a variety of treatments is available in the comfort of the many rooms in the spa.*

Mere steps from the famed Djemaa el-Fna Square—the soul of Marrakech's medina, where hundreds of sellers congregate each day to sell unique handicrafts and local street food under the open sky—Les Jardins de la Koutoubia is a riad hotel with all the comforts and extravagance of a five-star hotel. Its convenient location makes it an unparalleled starting point from which to see the medina's essential sights. The landmark Koutoubia Mosque is located mere metres away, as are many other historic points of interest and bustling shopping streets.

The 18th-century property occupies the former Riad Ouarzizi, one of the largest of its kind with an inner patio surrounded by 72 well-appointed guestrooms and suites. The décor is a blend of traditional Moroccan features and modern luxury design. The main reception hall is a towering space carpeted in rich red and capped with a carved-wood ceiling. Beyond marble columns and glass doors lie the lush courtyard gardens and pool. Sheltered from the activity of the streets, the central area is a peaceful haven of deck chairs, palm trees and lounge areas.

...a riad hotel with all the comforts and extravagance of a five-star hotel.

rooms
72 rooms and suites

food
Imlil snack bar •
Restaurant Marocain: Moroccan •
Le Relais de Paris: grill and seafood •
Restaurant Koutoubia: Mediterranean •
Les Jardins de Bala: Indian and Asian

drink
Ouarzazi Piano Bar

features
patio gardens • 3 pools • fitness centre •
hammams • Clarins Spa • airport transfers •
wireless Internet access

nearby
Djemaa el-Fna Square • Koutoubia Mosque •
souk • shops • museums

contact
26 Rue de la Koutoubia
40000 Marrakech •
telephone: +212.24.388 800 •
facsimile: +212.24.442 222 •
email: hoteljardinkoutoubia@menara.ma •
website: www.lesjardinsdelakoutoubia.com

Likewise, the rooms are sanctuaries of comfort and privacy, featuring striking works of contemporary art and furniture. Each is individually designed with fine fabrics and materials like wood and marble, with distinctive touches from brass fittings and four-poster beds to gilded mirrors and fresh flower arrangements to set them apart. Some rooms also house arches, beams and other hallmarks of regional architecture.

Most rooms open to views of the patios below, while two suites enjoy private terraces overlooking the Koutoubia Mosque. The Royal Suite on the top floor is the hotel's largest and most opulent accommodation, and is well-suited to the needs of the most discerning guests. All rooms are fully air-conditioned and feature wireless Internet access and large flat-screen televisions with cable channels.

The spa offers the services of a standard Moroccan hammam and all manner of body and beauty treatments, including exclusive Clarins products. Aside from five hammams, where therapy begins with a black soap purifying scrub and Ghassoul clay wrap, the spa also boasts seven treatment rooms, a bath therapy room, a gym and an indoor pool.

The hotel features four restaurants and a snack bar that serve fresh ingredients prepared in styles spanning the globe from India to the Mediterranean. Les Jardins de Bala is set on the terrace, while diners at Le Relais de Paris enjoy the calm of the patio's gardens. Following a meal prepared in line with centuries of culinary tradition, the Ouarzazi bar with its live piano music offers an elegant way to end a night at one of the most enthralling hotels in Marrakech.

les jardins de la medina

Royal residences used to line the narrow streets of the medina, alongside the homes of merchants and Marrakech's bourgeoisie. One of these stately riads was converted into the charming Les Jardins de la Medina. Behind high walls, this hotel offers quiet seclusion while being just minutes away from the Royal Palace, the vibrant Djemaa el-Fna Square and many colourful souks. Within the hotel's grounds, a luxuriant garden thrives, with olive, jacaranda and orange trees standing proudly amongst century-old palm trees.

Like other boutique hotels in the medina, this is an intimate establishment. There are only 36 rooms available, comprising standard, superior and privilege rooms. All rooms have air-conditioning and heating, in addition to private bathrooms, satellite television and minibars, while superior and privilege rooms also come with DVD players. Some even come with a fireplace and a private terrace. In fine Moroccan tradition, each room is decorated with large windows and high ceilings for plenty of air and natural light.

A star feature of this hotel is Le Karintia, its international restaurant. Serving a blend of Moroccan, Thai and European-inspired cuisine, Le Karintia's menu is truly exotic and refreshing. Serious foodies should try the filet of duck breast and fois gras, the date purée and kumquat sauce, or a confit of choice lamb, gnocchis with pistou and mint tea. A wide-ranging dessert menu includes mouth-watering choices such as sorbet of papaya flavoured with madras curry and pear tart with roquefort cheese, fromage blanc and a blackberry coulis.

There is no shortage of amenities at this hotel. The pool, heated in winter, is great for a swim, while a hammam and spa provide body treatments. A hairdresser and beauty centre will ensure that you look your best, and a jacuzzi offers utmost relaxation. Guests who want to keep fit have access to a free fitness area with various types of exercise equipment at their disposal. For parties, the hotel has a salon that can accommodate up to 15 guests.

Practical services and facilities ensure that your stay is a breeze. Airport transfers are provided gratis, and the concierge will handle all reservations and bookings. Guests can also request that excursions and car rentals be arranged. Golf enthusiasts will be pleased to know that three stunning golf courses are located close by, and the hotel is always happy to arrange green fees and transportation.

At Les Jardins de la Medina, luxurious modern comforts coupled with an authentic historical ambience allows you to experience the best of Marrakech.

rooms
12 standard rooms · 18 superior rooms · 6 privilege rooms

food
Le Karintia: Moroccan, Thai and European

drink
beverage list

features
hammam · spa · beauty centre · hairdresser · fitness area · salon · car park · boutique · relaxation room · Internet access · pool

nearby
Royal Palace · Saadian Tombs · souks · Palmeraie Golf Club · Royal Golf d'Amelkis · Royal Golf Club de Marrakech · High Atlas Mountains

contact
21 Rue Derb Chtouka, Quartier de la Kasbah 40000 Marrakech ·
telephone: +212.24.381 851 ·
facsimile: +212.24.385 385 ·
email: info@lesjardinsdelamedina.com ·
website: www.lesjardinsdelamedina.com

riad el fenn

When one first learns of Riad El Fenn, one of two interesting facts invariably accompanies the description. It might be that the property was rescued from near ruin in 2002 and refurbished into a luxury riad hotel by Vanessa Branson, sister of billionaire Richard Branson, no stranger to five-star resorts himself. Or it might be that the name of the hotel will be explained as roughly translating to 'Fine Arts', although, interestingly enough, the modern usage of 'Fenn' is closer to 'cool' in English.

Cool it certainly is, both in construction and in the overall experience it provides. Completely restored by local craftsmen and architects, Riad El Fenn has been lavishly appointed by its owners and managers to achieve a dynamic fusion of authentic Moroccan atmosphere and modern art appeal. Traditional motifs and furnishings share both private and public spaces with unusual colours, one-of-a-kind art pieces and the highest quality creature comforts.

THIS PAGE (FROM LEFT): All rooms are equipped with private sitting areas where guests can relax at the end of a busy day; cheerful red brings warmth to this comfortable room.

OPPOSITE: High ceilings add to the sense of cavernous space in each of the riad's rooms.

The historic townhouse building the hotel occupies stands as strong as it did when built in 1825, with fortress-like walls that are at least a metre (3 ft) thick. These high walls do an excellent job of regulating the internal temperature throughout the year while also shutting out the sounds of the medina. The riad's main entrance opens out onto a small residential neighbourhood near several major attractions. The Djemaa el-Fna Square, where a great deal of shopping and street-food is available, is just a five-minute walk away. Along the way are many other sights, including the Koutoubia Gardens and several mosques. From the international airport, visitors can have their feet up in just a little over 10 minutes. Riad El Fenn also manages to straddle both the old and new towns of Marrakech; it is located close to the Bab el Ksour medina entrance gates, while a short taxi ride will bring guests to the modern conveniences of the Guéliz district.

A progressive staffing policy employs 40 local full-timers, allowing them to share their knowledge and experience with guests of the hotel and display the warm hospitality for which Morocco is famous. The hotel places social and environmental responsibility high on its list of priorities, and has implemented a number of eco-friendly practices that may interest the environmentally conscious. For instance, much of the water heating for pools and bathroom use is derived from solar panels installed on the property's rooftops.

Expansions have raised the number of guestrooms at the riad to 22, each one individually designed for comfort with artful touches and large doses of character. Most of the rooms are luxuriously open-plan with streamlined fittings and a gracious sense of flow from bedroom to bathroom—and out onto the terraces and balconies.

Charm and personality is derived from palatial spaces that feel thoroughly organic, original art from such names as Terry Frost and Bridget Riley and features that are the height of luxury. Of special note are the large soaking tubs in the bathrooms, custom-made to be deeper than most, supplemented with rich scented bath oils and equipped with refreshing power showers.

The guestrooms at Riad El Fenn offer up to 95 sq m (1,022 sq ft) of space, but even the smallest rooms come with cosy sitting areas, en suite bathrooms and massive 2-m- (6-ft-) wide feather-soft beds made with fine linens. The minimalist décor only adds to the sense of openness and peace. Upon close inspection, many details can be found in the carved wooden doors, traditional rugs and camel leather tiling, rewarding those with a keen eye for artisanal workmanship. Some rooms have built-in fireplaces, while all enjoy modern amenities such as wireless Internet access and satellite televisions.

Room 6, or the Douiria Suite, is a split-level affair that has its own heated pool and a generous 65-sq-m (700-sq-ft) private terrace with superb views. Some rooms surround the central courtyard, which is a quiet, calm space with ornamental water features and lush vegetation, while others have views of the spa courtyard, pool, rose garden and colonnades.

Welcoming and intimate public spaces are a highlight feature at Riad El Fenn, with many cosy corners and daybed lounges just waiting to be discovered. Those seeking the sun will find the terrace's plunge pool a draw, as well as the 20-m (66-ft) putting green. Situated at a vantage point above the city's rooftops, the terrace is an ideal place from which to observe everything from life in the

rooms
22 rooms and suites

food
modern Mediterranean

drink
bar

features
spa · hammam · pools · courtyard gardens · roof terrace · library · screening room · lift · wireless Internet access

nearby
Djemaa el-Fna Square · Bab el Ksour · Guéliz · Royal Palace · souks · golf · cycling · tennis

contact
2 Derb Moullay Abdullah ben Hezzian
Bab el Ksour, Medina
40000 Marrakech ·
telephone: +212.24.441 210 or +212.24.441 220 ·
facsimile: +212.24.441 211 ·
email: riadelfenn@menara.ma ·
website: www.riadelfenn.com

medina, to the movement of clouds against the Atlas Mountains. At night, it transforms into a popular dinner spot, with tasty meals served from the hotel's kitchen.

Numerous locations for the enjoyment of meals exist apart from Riad El Fenn's newly completed dining room. Guests are welcome to dine in the privacy of their rooms, in the shade of the courtyard's trees or up on the rooftops. The fare is modern Moroccan, with an emphasis on quality and freshness. Much of the produce used in the kitchen comes from an exclusive organic garden established by the hotel at the base of the Atlas Mountains, which accounts for a selection of herbs, spices, seasonal vegetables and fruit. Various meats and other culinary necessities

are purchased on a daily basis from the local markets according to availability; this means a few limitations in variety, but the reward is superior cuisine. The only imported items are truffles from France and fine wines, which join a number of Moroccan wines on the menu.

In between meals, guests may enjoy the services of the riad's two resident therapists, who perform near-miracles in the hammam and treatment rooms. Soothing massages, manicures and a range of beauty-enhancing procedures are all part of the full-service spa. If a workout is preferred, yoga classes and two large marble pools featuring counter-current water jets are also available. Other leisure activities include private film screenings in a mini theatre with a 2.4-m (8-ft) screen.

riad el ouarda

Simple elegance is the hallmark of Riad El Ouarda. This exquisitely restored 17th-century riad is situated in Bab Taghzout, one of the oldest sections of Marrakech's medina, beside grand palaces and mansions. While secluded from the modern city by the gates of the medina, it is still easily accessible by car.

The riad displays a sensitive rendering of traditional Moroccan architectural and design features, while still incorporating sleek, contemporary lines. The original stucco ceiling of the riad was uncovered during restoration and, though not part of the hotel's initial design plans, was preserved. It is now a major highlight of the rooms. In the main courtyard, a classic, intricate mosaic floor is accompanied by the generous use of wood, with a pond and a fountain serving as the focal point. These water features also serve to bring some respite from the heat.

Renovated in 2007, Riad El Ouarda now boasts several new additions: its own pool, two patios and modern furnishings specially designed for the hotel. Guests can now bask on the main patio by the poolside, or sit indoors and luxuriate in the relaxed atmosphere carefully wrought by a combination of lush materials, custom-made furniture and eye-catching accessories.

Rooms are spacious and airy, lined with tall, graceful wooden shutters over large windows. The bathrooms are decorated in tadelakt plaster and copper. Housed in an annex to the main building are three suites.

THIS PAGE (FROM TOP): The terrace is ideal for relaxation while appreciating the breeze; the suites feature clean lines and a modern design style.

OPPOSITE (FROM TOP): The poolside is quiet and calm by night; meals are served on the patio by the pool in summer.

rooms
4 guestrooms · 5 suites

food
private kitchen: Moroccan

drink
salon

features
courtyards · rooftop terrace · pool · library · Internet access · parking

nearby
Djemaa el-Fna Square · golf course · souks · Palmeraie · Koutoubia Mosque · museums

contact
5 Derb Taht Sour Lakbir, Zaouia el-Abbasia 40000 Marrakech ·
telephone: +212.24.385 714 ·
facsimile: +212.24.385 710 ·
email: elouarda@yahoo.fr ·
website: www.riadelouarda.com

Designed in a similar style to the courtyard rooms, but larger and more sophisticated, the suites combine opulence with an absence of excess; clean, modern lines dominate. Two of the annex suites are open plan and share a courtyard, while the third is split-level, with fantastic views of the medina and the Atlas Mountains in the distance.

Breathtaking views can also be enjoyed from the hotel's rooftop terrace. Staggered to provide maximum elevation, the terrace is best appreciated while savouring one of the hotel's fine Moroccan meals and watching the sunset. Traditional dishes are whipped up by local chefs who use only the freshest ingredients from the market.

One can expect to be warmly welcomed to the hotel by Brigitte, and the owner often takes the time to interact with hotel guests. He is very much involved in the day-to-day running of the hotel, and lends his natural charm to the atmosphere. Together with his excellent team, he extends his special brand of meticulous attention and caring personal service to every one of his guests. At Riad El Ouarda, you will surely feel at home.

riad farnatchi

It is not difficult to fall in love with Riad Farnatchi. This exquisite property is one of the most stylish in Marrakech's medina. It stands out because of its modern feel, which strikes a contrast to the ancient exoticism of the medina. Here, European design is married with traditional Moroccan forms and motifs to create unique spaces and furniture that is both beautiful to look at and comfortable to use. To achieve this, every piece of furniture was custom-designed for the hotel. All this is executed within an intimate space of nine suites spread out over five small riads.

The layout of the hotel was specially conceived to allow for both privacy and socialising. A collection of covered sitting areas that open into a courtyard and lounges in classical Moroccan proportions provide places for groups to gather or for individuals to relax in. Each suite also has a sitting area for private gatherings.

Dining options are equally varied. There is a candlelit dining room that can seat 16, a formal dining room that can seat 12, and a rooftop terrace that can also accommodate about a dozen people comfortably. A barbecue stands ready for pleasant Moroccan evenings, and guests dine by candlelight.

At the end of the day, guests have wonderfully comfortable suites to retire to. Stunningly decorated, each suite boasts a handmade bed made up with fine Egyptian cotton linen that you can almost melt into. In addition, the rooms are equipped with a host of modern conveniences for those who need to stay in touch with the outside world. Each luxurious suite is unique, and all are well-lit, spacious and elegant.

Riad Farnatchi also offers a range of facilities and services. A 7-m- (23-ft-) long heated indoor pool provides an opportunity for relaxation or a few invigorating laps. In a second courtyard nearby is a white marble hammam, where a resident therapist offers a variety of massages and spa treatments. The therapist specialises in gommage, a type of treatment in which hydrating creams are applied in long, massage-like strokes.

Then there are the little touches that make this riad so charming. Fruit and pastries are laid out during the day and homemade canapés in the evening. Moroccan robes (djellabas) and slippers (babouches) are given to all guests, offering them a chance to experience comfort in Moroccan style.

THIS PAGE (FROM TOP): A blend of European and Moroccan designs permeate the riad; the warmth of the fireplace invites guests to indulge in some leisurely quiet time.

OPPOSITE (FROM LEFT): The nine suites are all well-furnished and exceedingly comfortable; one of the en suite bathrooms.

...a chance to experience comfort in Moroccan style.

rooms
9 suites

food
private dining

drink
wine cellar

features
pool • rooftop terrace • hammam • salons

nearby
Djemaa el-Fna Square • Koutoubia Mosque • Guéliz • souks • Royal Golf Club de Marrakech • Palmeraie Golf Club • Royal Golf d'Amelkis

contact
2 Derb Farnatchi, Qua'at Benahid •
40000 Marrakech •
telephone: +212.24.384 910 or +212.24.384 912 •
facsimile: +212.24.384 913 •
email: enquiries@riadfarnatchi.com •
website: www.riadfarnatchi.com

riad meriem

The celebrated New York interior designer and photographer, Thomas Hays, is the proud creator of Riad Meriem. Located in the 11th-century heart of the medina of Marrakech, the riad is a holiday destination like none other in the city. Built in a completely restored traditional Moroccan riad, the property offers authenticity coupled with a singular artistic vision from its owner cum designer that has resulted in a spectacular homage to Arabian and Oriental traditions. In 2008, *House & Garden* featured Riad Meriem as one of the most beautifully designed hotels worldwide, while *Travel + Leisure* listed it as one of the top 30 new hotels in the world.

Throughout the luxurious property, the fine handiwork of local craftsmen is apparent in every detail, from the highly polished tiling to the use of custom-woven rugs and textiles which match Riad Meriem's unique desert-inspired colour palette. A number of open-air public spaces invite guests to indulge in intimate conversations and evening drinks by moonlight, with the inner courtyard featuring a plunge pool and bhou-style patio lounge in an Oriental design amidst bright, cheery bougainvillea flowers and lush palm trees.

Just a few steps away, indoors, a series of stylishly lit spaces evoke the feel of old Morocco. The Dining Room is perfect for a delicious dinner prepared by the riad's private chef, while the Chimney Lounge and the cosy Library serve as quiet, intimate settings for socialising or unwinding.

A large, tented outdoor terrace offers views of the medina, the Koutoubia Mosque, and the Atlas Mountains. It is planted with flowers, including the fragrant jasmine, and pomegranate bushes, making it ideal for all-day dining and quiet relaxation. Outside, the Djemaa el-Fna Square is only a few minutes away, with the souks mere metres from the entrance of the riad.

The riad's five guestrooms are individual creations; names like Star, Matisse, Aubergine, Ivory, and Red give away as much about the character of these accommodations as they do about their unique colour schemes. Three of these are suites, while the other two are rooms. Although completely furnished with traditional artefacts and regional fabrics and materials, the layouts and décor combined

THIS PAGE (FROM TOP): *Guests can enjoy sweeping views from the terrace while listening to the sounds of the city; savour a meal in an intimate setting with close friends.*

OPPOSITE (FROM TOP): *One of the riad's well-appointed rooms; soak one's stresses away in relaxing environs.*

rooms
3 suites • 2 rooms

food
Dining Room: Moroccan

drink
beverage list

features
concierge • airport transfers • plunge pool • open-air terrace • wireless Internet access • Bose sound system with Apple iPod • library

nearby
Museum of Marrakech • Djemaa el-Fna Square • Medersa Ben Youssef • souks • medina

contact
97 Derb el Cadi, Azbezt
40008 Marrakech •
telephone: +212.24.387 731 •
facsimile: +212.24.377 762 •
email: contact@riadmeriem.com •
website: www.riadmeriem.com

result in rooms that are hip and luxurious without being ostentatious. Walls, especially in the spacious bathrooms, shimmer with texture and hidden depth as a result of the lighting design and the use of special materials. The large, soft beds are crafted by hand and finished with fine Egyptian cotton sheets, and all accommodations are equipped with heating and air-conditioning for comfort regardless of season.

Above all, the one defining feature of a stay at the Riad Meriem is the personalised nature of interactions with its staff. The two on-site managers are charming Moroccan-born residents of Marrakech who know the city intimately. They are always helpful and willing to share information with curious visitors, personally facilitating everything from sightseeing arrangements to airport transfers. Overseeing other affairs in the hotel are two managers formerly from London, both of whom have permanently relocated to Marrakech from previous engagements in the hospitality industry. Together, the two teams combine the best of local and global knowledge for the benefit of guests. Perhaps the best way to describe this exceptional Morocco-by-way-of-Manhattan property is as an amalgam of traditional Moroccan and international influences.

riyad el mezouar

THIS PAGE: *Meals can be served in the intimate setting of the grand salon, located on the ground floor of the riad.*

OPPOSITE (FROM TOP): *The spacious Ambassador Junior Suite is clad in neutral tones, creating a soothing, restful sanctuary; guests are welcome to make use of the hotel's large pool.*

The 18th-century Riyad El Mezouar was owned by a branch of the Alaoui royal family until the middle of last century, and was at one point graced with the royal presence of King Mohammed V. Since then, the riad has remained in the care of noble families, including those of the Caïd of El Kelaâ des Sraghna and the Caliph of Ouarzazate. In earlier days, many of the properties in the area were home to well-regarded families from Fez, and as a result tend to be splendidly constructed, with eye-catching architectural features. Riyad El Mezouar is no different, a showcase of ancient building techniques and impressive local craftsmanship.

Guests will find a thoroughly authentic Moroccan living environment here, with generous use of tadelakt plaster and bejmat tiles in a series of completely restored rooms and public areas. Its isolated central courtyard is anchored by a beautiful pool bordered by hand-cut ceramic tiles and a tranquil marble fountain. The surrounding area is shaded by fruit trees, and aromatic plants like jasmine and lavender scent the air. On all four sides of this scene are flawless two-storey high white walls with columned galleries and arcades in the traditional proportions of Arab-Andalusian architecture—a feature not seen in many of the medina's remaining riads. The interior is decorated with objets d'art collected by the owners from their travels far afield in Africa, Europe and the Orient. Gaudy ostentation is eschewed for a more refined atmosphere created by fine silks, antique furnishings and subtle colours.

The riad's five rooms each offer tasteful comfort enhanced with modern amenities such as wireless Internet access and safe deposit boxes. Toiletries by Nectarôme in the en suite bathrooms make bathing a pleasure. Two rooms are located on the ground floor for convenient access to the courtyard, while the remaining three are blessed with lofty views over the patio and grounds below.

The majority of the accommodations here are luxurious junior suites appointed with period furnishings and traditional touches such as hammam-style bathrooms with tadelakt plaster walls. Two stylish double rooms are an attractive alternative, featuring detachable king-sized beds which can be

arranged to create a twin sharing room. The riad has a large rooftop terrace with unobstructed views of the medina all the way to the Atlas Mountains. Here, guests may sunbathe or savour the cuisine from the hotel's kitchen, staffed by a veteran chef who was formerly in the service of King Hassan II's family. The fare is a creative fusion of local ingredients and customs with influences from French and Asian cooking and may also be served in the grand salon or the courtyard.

Current owner Michel Durand-Meyrier is an interior designer by trade, and his careful, reverent touch is evident throughout the entire property in its winning combination of inviting luxury and Moroccan flair.

rooms
2 rooms • 3 junior suites

food
Moroccan and fusion

drink
beverage list

features
pool • rooftop terrace • salon with fireplace • wireless Internet access • airport transfers

nearby
souks • Djemaa el-Fna Square • museums • Museum of Marrakech • Medersa Ben Youssef

contact
28 Derb el Hamman, Issebtinne 40000 Marrakech • telephone: +212.24.380 949 • facsimile: +212.24.380 943 • email: info@mezouar.com • website: www.mezouar.com

the angsana riads collection

The revival of the Moroccan riad is one of the most interesting stories behind the country's rise as a modern day Mecca for international style seekers. Traditionally built as residential homes, these structures sometimes approach the size of palaces, and are marked by sheltered courtyards and gardens bordered by tall clay buildings or mud brick walls. They were designed to protect their inhabitants from harsh climatic conditions and exterior noise, creating peaceful havens in Marrakech and many of Morocco's busiest cities.

Recognising the value of these structures, the world-renowned Angsana group has converted eight riads into highly exclusive hotel, dining and spa experiences to rival those of any five-star resort. The Angsana Riads Collection features the casual, relaxed atmosphere and stellar service long affiliated with the Angsana name, presented in several exquisite locations, each one bearing fine, meticulous craftsmanship and painstakingly restored Moroccan architecture.

Six of the riads in the collection can be found in Marrakech, with five centred around the bustling medina in the heart of the old city. The remaining riad sits just a 10-minute walk from the others, and is appropriately named for a hand-built Moorish house: the Angsana Riad Lydines, which means 'hands'.

Angsana Riad Si Said has six suites and one deluxe room; one of the former is a two-bed suite meant to house a family or group. Décor in the bedrooms epitomises Moroccan luxury, with accents of gold and rich, flowing fabric. Visitors to this riad will be happy to know that it is located particularly close to the Djemaa el-Fna Square. The Angsana Riad Blanc offers a relatively more contemporary interior design, yet still retains a number of classic features for atmosphere. Four superior rooms and two deluxe rooms, as well as two suites, make this a suitable getaway for groups of various sizes.

The remaining riads focus on different facets of the holiday experience. The Angsana Riad Tiwaline is hidden away in a 14th-century alleyway, and opens up to reveal a fountain beneath cedar beams and Berber motifs. Warm and intimate, it invites guests to pass hours in the library or by the fireplace. In contrast, Angsana Riad Aida is vibrant and colourful, with a rooftop terrace perfect for

catching romantic sunset views. Last but not least, the Angsana Riad Bab Firdaus ('Gateway to Heaven') is dedicated to the senses with a very large therapy room, jet pool and rooftop restaurant available to guests.

Dining in any of the Angsana Collection is an authentic and also very healthy pleasure, with menus catering to a wide variety of needs and tastes, bridging East and West with creativity and skill.

That same fusion of cultures and talent goes into the award-winning spa therapies offered at five of the largest riads, which are open to all guests of the Angsana Collection. A unique Angsana Spa like no other, the originally Asian ingredients and techniques are reinvented here to produce a thoroughly Moroccan identity to match the character of these newly reborn accommodations.

rooms
6 riads, each with 5 to 8 rooms

food
traditional Moroccan · Thai

drink
beverage list

features
Angsana Spa · jet pools · rooftop terraces · lounges with fireplaces · hammams · libraries

nearby
Marrakech: Djemaa el-Fna Square · medina · mosques · palaces · souks

contact
telephone: +212.24.421 979 ·
facsimile: +212.24.421 372 ·
email: reservations-marrakech@angsana.com ·
website: www.angsana.com

uovo riads

Created by its Italian owner, the UOVO group's collection of three Marrakech medina properties are most highly regarded for bringing a distinctive sense of style into the riad hotel category. Scattered towards the northern edge of the medina between the Bab Doukkala, Dar el Bacha and Bab el Khemis districts, the three riads are tucked away off the streets and offer easy walking access to some of the area's most popular attractions.

Riad 72 is an intimate property of just four rooms including a deluxe Karma Suite, which features an ornate carved wood ceiling and elements of traditional décor. Its tadelakt plaster bathroom features a large square tub, almost Japanese in inspiration, set in the middle of its spacious wet area. The rest of the suite's roomy, minimalist composition complements the bathroom perfectly; a contemporary aesthetic both announces itself and eludes description—the same can be said for the other individually designed rooms on the property.

The windows look inward to the centre of the riad and its luxuriantly green courtyard. A rooftop terrace above offers wider views of the medina. There, one will also find a solarium, while a hammam and bookshop below round up the facilities.

As with all UOVO properties, dining at the Riad 72 is an authentic Moroccan experience. Each riad employs a team of experienced, well-trained local chefs who not only have close relationships with the tastes of the land but also the suppliers at nearby markets. This allows them to put together incredible meals from fresh, seasonal produce purchased just hours before mealtime each day.

Riad 12 is even more exclusive with just three double rooms, each about 30 sq m (323 sq ft) in size, with very large comfortable four-poster beds. Stylistically, its interiors maintain the design-oriented approach of its sister property, preferring understatement to excess. En suite bathrooms are clad in red and grey marble, in contrast to the Moroccan character of the rooms, with the Camellia Room enjoying the largest of the baths.

Of the three hotels, Riad Due is perhaps the most forward-looking in terms of art direction, furnished throughout with a smart, Italian approach of clean modernism. Its four rooms still manage to incorporate a number of traditional Moroccan features, however, and the Junior Suite Samir and Kamal Room even have fireplaces. The Zan and Abdel Suites are the largest accommodations at 55 sq m (592 sq ft), with luxuries like copper bathtubs and separate dressing rooms, respectively.

Both Riad 12 and Riad Due are equipped with plunge pools in their walled-off courtyard areas, beside which are placed a few comfortable tables where complimentary afternoon mint tea puts the finishing touch on an irresistible proposition. At their very reasonable rates, the UOVO riads are hard-to-beat private boutique hotels in the loveliest parts of old Marrakech.

...the UOVO riads are hard-to-beat private boutique hotels in the loveliest parts of old Marrakech.

rooms
Riad 72: 4 rooms · Riad 12: 3 rooms ·
Riad Due: 4 rooms

food
traditional Moroccan

drink
honour bars

features
bookstore (Riad 72) · hammam · pools ·
rooftop terraces · courtyard gardens ·
solariums · room service · Internet access

nearby
Koutoubia Mosque · Djemaa el-Fna Square·
museums · souks

contact
Riad 72: 72 Arset Awsel, Bab Doukkala
40000 Marrakech ·

Riad 12: 12 Derb Sraghnas, Dar el Bacha
40000 Marrakech ·

Riad Due: 2 Derb Chentouf, Riad Laarousse,
Medina
40000 Marrakech ·

telephone: +212.24.387 629 ·
facsimile: +212.24.384 718 ·
email: info@uovo.com ·
website: www.uovo.com

villa des orangers

THIS PAGE (FROM TOP): *The central patio of Villa des Orangers; guests staying in the junior suites can entertain visitors in the privacy of their lounges.*

OPPOSITE (FROM TOP): *Chat over tasty fare in the intimate atmosphere of the restaurant; a comfortable, well-furnished suite at the Villa.*

A visit to Marrakech's old fortified medina quarter is sure to inspire a love for the city's rich history. From the narrow winding alleys that suddenly open out into large, sprawling souks, to Djemaa el-Fna Square, one of the most vibrant public squares in all of Morocco, the medina is Marrakech's source. In the past, choosing to stay in the heart of the action meant compromising luxury for authenticity. This is no longer the case.

Villa des Orangers is a luxury boutique hotel housed in a riad, a traditional Moroccan townhouse, which has successfully combined comfort and class for discerning travellers. It is conveniently located down the street from the famed Koutoubia Mosque, whose minaret towers over the medina, making it easy to find one's bearings from any location, and the bustle of Djemaa el-Fna Square is a short 10 minutes away on foot.

Like most riads, which were designed to be sanctums of tranquillity, the original 1930s residence consisted of a courtyard garden surrounded by rooms and double-storey walls. Today, after a series of expansions and renovations performed by local artisans, the hotel boasts 27 rooms and suites arranged around four lovely courtyard patios.

Three pools that range from 5 m (16 ft) to 16 m (52 ft) in length offer respite from the summer heat; one is situated on a rooftop with views of the mosque and nearby Atlas

Mountains, while the other two are set in gardens. All things considered, this riad is one of the largest of its kind in Marrakech, a fact attested to by its three spacious lounges which are warmed by fireplaces, two dining rooms, hammam and massage cabin, beauty centre, fitness club and gift boutique.

Six deluxe rooms are available on both the first and second storeys, with two of them enjoying private rooftop terraces that can be reached via an indoor staircase. Guests can see the medina and mountains from these terraces, while the other rooms overlook the Villa's courtyards. Furnished in the Moroccan style, all rooms come with expected modern conveniences such as direct dial telephones, in-room safes and air-conditioning.

The remainder of the accommodations are suites of various sizes, some with private terraces overlooking the mosque. Three Grand Suites are the largest on offer, featuring 100 sq m (1,076 sq ft) of luxury over two levels. The ground floors hold lounges with fireplaces, while the upstairs bedrooms have access to a balcony overlooking one of the pools and the gardens. The bathrooms each have twin sinks, separate baths, and walk-in showers like most rooms, but are larger and have dressing areas.

Meals from the restaurant can be served anywhere, be it in the garden or in your room. Possessing a private riad as a summer home was once a privilege few could claim, but the Villa replicates that prestige with service that makes you feel at the centre of attention.

rooms
6 rooms • 21 suites

food
Mediterranean and traditional Moroccan

drink
beverage list

features
massage cabin • fitness club • 3 pools • hammam • 24-hour non-alcoholic open bar • wireless Internet access

nearby
medina • mosques • palaces • souks • museums • Djemaa el-Fna Square • Koutoubia Mosque

contact
6 Rue Sidi Mimoun •
40000 Marrakech •
telephone: +212.24.384 638 •
facsimile: +212.24.385 123 •
email: message@villadesorangers.com •
website: www.villadesorangers.com

es saadi gardens + resort

and highly meticulous family-run Moroccan experience, as recommended in publications from *Elle* and *Marie-Claire* to *Le Point*, *Figaro* and *Travel Luxury Magazine*.

Es Saadi's first-class hotel and themed villas occupy a palatial 8 hectares (20 acres) and the property is situated in a pocket of peace and quiet mere minutes from the bustle of the medina, where colourful souks and Djemaa el-Fna Square are to be found. In its cool, lush gardens, palm, banana and olive trees grow tall alongside the renowned miniature roses of Marrakech.

Luxurious without being ostentatious, traditional and homey yet modern, the hotel is the epitome of French-inspired elegance, housing 150 charming air-conditioned rooms and suites. Offering up to 85 sq m (915 sq ft) of privacy, the accommodations boast private balconies and every conceivable comfort.

That one in three guests is a regular of the hotel testifies to the quality of its rooms and the calibre of its staff. Immaculately attired, discreet and friendly, Es Saadi's staff members represent the epitome of Moroccan hospitality, offering a warm and genuine welcome to every guest.

As Es Saadi's reputation and stature have grown, so have the ambitions of Elisabeth Bauchet, the daughter of Es Saadi's creator who runs the property, and her talented team. The recent addition of The Oriental Spa, the Palace's exclusive suites and 10 themed villas highlight this evolution perfectly.

THIS PAGE: Order a refreshing cool drink from the Island Bar after some light exercise in the pool.

OPPOSITE (FROM TOP): Expect top-notch service here at Es Saadi; one of the well-appointed and highly comfortable executive suites on offer in the Palace.

Es Saadi Gardens & Resort is an icon at the heart of Marrakech's rich architectural and socio-cultural tapestry. Home to the Casino de Marrakech, Es Saadi also boasts a world-class spa, a nightclub cum bar known as Le ThéâtrO and a variety of accommodations for the discerning traveller. Despite globalisation and the homogenising pressures of hospitality's giants, Es Saadi—following an impressive 21st-century facelift and grand reopening in 2005—continues to offer visitors an original

With its evocative lines and Oriental design style, the sumptuous Palace is entirely in keeping with Es Saadi's original ethos. Artistic direction from local master craftsmen has resulted in classic Eastern charm and style that permeates every facet of the Palace.

The 92 spacious suites available in the Palace infuse the essence of the Orient into contemporary décor. The rooms are appointed with fine Moroccan textiles, bejmat terracotta flooring and traditionally carved furnishings, with large bathtubs and double marble sinks in each bathroom. With plush areas in which to relax and balconies offering astounding views of the Atlas Mountains, evenings spent unwinding in your rooms or lounging around the tempting pool are no hardship at all.

Nestled in their own gardens, the 10 themed villas are arguably Es Saadi's post-Millennial pièce de résistance. Designed by home-grown architect Aziz Lamghari, each draws on a different Oriental influence for its architectural inspiration. The 1001 Nights, Art Deco and Sultan's Villas in particular seem to be immensely popular. From silk-draped four-poster beds and intricate mosaics and inlaid

conditioned hideaways are ideal choices for honeymooning couples or those in search of some privacy and serenity.

Es Saadi is the brainchild of Jean Bauchet, who fell in 'love at first sight' with the area in 1951. Former owner of the celebrated Moulin Rouge and the Casino de Paris, Jean snapped up this premium pocket of real estate. He opened the Casino de Marrakech in 1952, catapulting it to worldwide fame by the end of the 1950s. The Casino now enters its second halcyon era, equipped with cutting-edge machines, gaming tables, courteous croupiers and exquisite dining venues in the form of L'Epicurien and L'Estrade Gourmande.

To discover a true culinary institution, as described by French *Marie Claire* as 'one of the best tables in Marrakech', visit the hotel's Le Restaurant Gastronomique. Run by Sébastien Bontour and former Michelin-starred chef Emile Tabourdiau, the restaurant has an open-air terrace that offers a romantic setting for meals and a menu that changes with the seasons. Fresh produce from a nearby organic familial property is served within hours of being picked. House specialities include tasty local dishes, Mediterranean fare and fine French cuisine. Guests can also head for any of the other dining establishments for a good meal.

After a Moroccan dinner show featuring more than 50 cabaret performers, the trendy nightclub venue of Le ThéâtrO is next on a reveler's itinerary. It is decorated in the style of an old-fashioned theatre and has attracted

THIS PAGE: Savour La Cour des Lions' fantastic Moroccan fare in its elegant dining room.

OPPOSITE (FROM TOP): Indulge in a rejuvenating massage in either of the two spas; the 1001 Nights Villa is one of the most sought after of the accommodations at Es Saadi.

tabletops to the relatively stark beauty of the Berber suite, these accommodations offer pampered indulgence at every turn. Artisanal techniques including tadelakt—a process that layers chalk with natural pigments to give interior walls and columns incredible depth and sheen—are showcased in the villas. With luxuries such as a personal butler and an exclusive plunge pool per villa that is heated in winter, it is clear that these air-

stars from Maurice Chevalier to Josephine Baker. Today, it hosts world-class DJs and musicians who entertain hotel guests and sleek fashionistas late into the night.

To balance out the sensuous offerings of Es Saadi's restaurants, the excitement of Le ThéâtrO and the Casino and the rigour of bargaining at the souks, take advantage of the resort's two spas and its wellness centre. From aromatherapy baths to exercise and slimming programmes, a traditional tiled hammam to treatments in the open air accompanied by the heady scents of Es Saadi's fragrant gardens, the spas are ideal for either unwinding after a busy day of sightseeing or keeping your body in tip-top condition.

With this constantly evolving resort, Elisabeth strives to produce 'a 21st-century oasis for holidays of another kind'. Offering a gastronomic and vacation experience like no other in Morocco, she has hit the mark with Es Saadi Gardens & Resort.

rooms
150 rooms and suites in the Hotel •
92 suites in the Palace • 10 villas

food
Le Restaurant Gastronomique: French •
Autour de la Piscine: snacks • L'Epicurien: bistro •
Jardin d'Hiver: buffet breakfast •
Lagon & Jardin: Mediterranean •
La Cour des Lions: Moroccan •
L'Estrade Gourmande: French

drink
Le ThéâtrO nightclub • Piano Bar • Island Bar •
Salon Egyptien Bar: lounge bar with live music •
L'Epicurien: cocktails

features
Casino • heated pools • The Oriental Spas (Hotel & Palace) • sauna • hammam • babysitting • tennis court • fitness centre • high-speed Internet access • in-room massage

nearby
Essaouira • central Marrakech sights • golf • Atlas Mountains • bicycle hire • horse riding • hunting • hiking trails

contact
Rue Hibrahim el Mazini, Hivernage 40000 Marrakech •
telephone: +212.24.448 811 or +212.24.447 010 •
facsimile: +212.24.447 644 •
email: info@essaadi.com •
website: www.essaadi.com

amanjena

Amanjena, the first African resort in the Aman group's global portfolio of spectacular getaways, is an impressive accomplishment in no uncertain terms. From the outside, one is met by the sight of vast gardens teeming with olive trees, towering palms, and fiery hibiscus, bougainvillea and pomegranate blossoms. This profusion of life is made possible by water channelled from a large 'bassin', or irrigation pool, at the centre of the compound. Access to the central plaza is gained through an entrance colonnade that cuts through a courtyard decorated with green marble fountains, and a 9-m- (29.5-ft-) tall promenade space enclosed by oak doors handcarved and decorated in Agadir.

All 39 private pavilions and houses are arranged around the bassin, with the six closest Pavilions Bassin having views of the emerald pool. Like the 18 standard Pavilions, they are spacious air-conditioned suites that include private courtyards with a fountain and a pillared minzah gazebo in each. The bedroom spaces are capped by high, domed ceilings in Venetian plaster, under which inviting king-sized platform beds, Berber carpets, arched fireplaces, and majestic pieces of cherry-wood furniture are arranged in the style of a living room lounge. Enormous bathrooms with columned marble soaking tubs, separate showers, twin dressing areas, and tall double vanity mirrors tempt guests to spend more time on cleanliness than is strictly necessary.

Larger pavilions (Pavilions Piscine) are also available, each measuring an area of 360 sq m (3,875 sq ft) as compared to the 175 sq m (1,884 sq ft) of standard Pavilions. The larger space is used to house a 25-sq-m (269-sq-ft) heated pool and large private garden per pavilion.

THIS PAGE (FROM TOP): The Restaurant is ideal for a romantic dinner; at four of the Maisons, guests can relax by their private pool.

OPPOSITE (FROM TOP): The lush greenery outside Amanjena hints at the treasures to be found inside; one of Amanjena's luxurious, well-appointed Pavilions.

The Amanjena's appeal extends beyond its residential richness.

rooms
Al Hamra Maison · 6 double-storey maisons · 32 pavilions

food
The Restaurant: Moroccan and Continental · Pool Terrace: breakfast and lunch · The Thai Restaurant

drink
Fumoir Bar

features
health and beauty centre · gym · pool · tennis courts · library · boutique shopping · wireless Internet access

nearby
Royal Golf d'Amelkis · medina · biking · High Atlas Mountains · mosques · palaces · Menara International Airport · souks · museums

contact
Km 12, Route de Ouarzazate
40000 Marrakech
telephone: +212.24.403 353 ·
facsimile: +212.24.403 477 ·
email: amanjena@amanresorts.com ·
website: www.amanresorts.com

Families or groups may prefer one of the Amanjena's six Moroccan townhouse-styled Maisons. Two-storeys high, each Maison has a bedroom with a queen-sized bed and one with a king-sized bed, as well as en suite bathrooms, extravagant living rooms, and outdoor courtyards with minzahs. Of the six Maisons, four have their own private pools, while the other two, the Maisons Jardin, feature garden courtyards with fountains, an outdoor fireplace, and a pantry with butler service. Incredible as they may be, even these are overshadowed by the Al Hamra Maison, the hotel's finest offering. Ideal for couples, the Al Hamra is essentially two pavilions sharing a large living/dining area, and a large pool with minzahs on both ends.

The Amanjena's appeal extends beyond its residential richness. A health and beauty centre houses hammams, whirlpool baths, and spa body treatments while a timber-floored gymnasium, tennis courts, and golf at the adjacent 18-hole Amelkis course are available for more active guests.

Relaxed all-day meals can be enjoyed at The Thai Restaurant or Pool Terrace, both of which enjoy views of the Amelkis and the pool. At dinner, the superb Restaurant opens its doors, offering regional and Continental feasts in an enchanting setting. For even greater intimacy, private dinners with live music can be organised in a tent located in the middle of an olive grove. At the Amanjena, guests are fully immersed in Moroccan luxury.

l mansion guest palace

Sprawling magnificently across a whopping 5 hectares (12 acres) of parkland planted with citrus and olive trees is the guest palace known as L Mansion. This garden of paradise offers the ultimate in rest and relaxation just moments away from the hustle and bustle of Marrakech. Upon entering L Mansion, visitors are immediately greeted by an impressive cypress alley that leads to the reception area. With all this finery catching the eye, guests can be sure to expect something beyond the usual combination of luxury and tradition.

Guests can choose to stay in one of the seven splendidly appointed suites available in the Andalusian-styled guest palace, where the finest craftsmanship is showcased. For an added touch of luxury, guests can also choose to stay in the two-bedroom villa, which comes with its own private patio, terrace and garden. No matter which is chosen, guests will enter to find each room exquisitely decorated with delicately chiseled ceilings, zellij tile mosaics and intricately hand-painted wainscotings. Stained glass windows also adorn the rooms,

...expect something beyond the usual combination of luxury and tradition.

rooms
7 suites · 1 villa

food
vegetarian and organic traditional Moroccan

drink
bar: natural juices and alcoholic beverages

features
hammam · outdoor pool · gym · sauna ·
business centre · high-speed Internet access ·
spa · indoor pool · massage · cooking lessons

nearby
Palmeraie · Royal Golf Club de Marrakech ·
Royal Golf d'Amelkis · quad biking ·
helicopter tour of Marrakech

contact
Km 9, Route de Ouarzazate, BP 6131 SYBA
40000 Marrakech ·
telephone: +212.24.329 955 ·
facsimile: +212.24.329 977 ·
email: info@lmansion.com ·
website: www.lmansion.com

throwing brightly coloured sunbeams onto carefully chosen rare antique pieces that are arranged strategically throughout. Outfitted with a host of modern conveniences for those who need to stay in touch with the world outside, L Mansion Guest Palace ensures that each and every guest is well provided for.

Even though the guest palace is located on the outskirts of Marrakech, guests will definitely not find its facilities lacking. For some relaxation and rejuvenation of the mind and spirit, a visit to the traditional Moroccan hammam is a must. Here, guests can take the opportunity to indulge in Turkish baths, soothing massages and beauty treatments administered by professionals. Lounging in the indoor pool inlaid with mosaics is the perfect way to recover from an eventful day while thinking of where to venture next. For those who want more vigorous activity, the state-of-the-art, well-equipped gym is not far. Guests can also wade out into the emerald waters of the large outdoor pool, or take to the numerous sun loungers and daybeds that line its perimeter.

For a pleasant way of taking a respite from the heat, sip tea on the tea terrace, with its breathtaking views of the snow-capped Atlas Mountains looming in the distance. Food at L Mansion is always a luxurious affair. Be it a light vegetarian lunch or a traditional Moroccan feast, every meal is meticulously prepared with fresh ingredients produced on the property itself, thereby ensuring the quality of the ingredients. Meals can be served in the restaurant, by the pool or in the shade of the vine arbor. As an added bonus, the entire property can be reserved for events.

dar sabra

THIS PAGE (FROM TOP): *Dar Sabra's exterior has a distinctly Mexican influence; the salon offers a comfortable setting for conversation.*

OPPOSITE (FROM TOP): *The poolside is the perfect place to get a tan; the Moroccan Room.*

Tucked away in the Palmeraie, a thousand-year-old palm grove just outside the walls of Marrakech, is Dar Sabra, one of the city's most exclusive hideaways. Inspired by the abodes of the Mexican deserts, the villa is the ultimate treat for the senses. At the foot of its southern façade is a cactus forest conjuring the impression of an arid Mexican panorama. To the north, palm trees sway in the cool breeze as guests indulge in the comforts offered within the walls of Dar Sabra.

The premier address of Marrakech, the Palmeraie boasts a sense of luxury and exclusivity unique to itself. The rich and famous have gated homes here, close to villas that are rented by the likes of Donna Karan.

Hence, at Dar Sabra, it's easy to feel like a pampered celebrity, especially as impeccably trained butlers, chambermaids and staff tend graciously to your every need.

Each of Dar Sabra's seven rooms is appointed with its own theme. In the African Room, tribal rugs line the sand-coloured floors, providing a perfect complement to the African sculptures and artefacts that give the room its name. Ornately carved pillars and walls breathe life into the Indian Room, while stark white furnishings make the Modern Room a study in minimalist chic.

The jaw-dropping beauty of Dar Sabra extends to its salon, which subtly fuses old and new. Rich wooden furnishings are paired with stylish cream textiles and complement the finely woven rugs that line the red earth floors. Awash in natural light, this open-air living space is tranquil, inviting guests to pause for a moment and enjoy some fresh air.

The shimmering turquoise reflection of Dar Sabra's spectacular indoor pool casts an almost magical glow on the patio where guests can sit back, relax and unwind with a deliciously cold cocktail or a steaming cup of mint tea. The intimate library is another calm sanctuary, clad in soft fabrics and adorned with contemporary furnishings. Here, guests who wish to take a break from socialising can luxuriate in some peace and quiet.

Guests who prefer more invigorating activities can make use of the clay tennis court on the grounds, and if you choose to venture beyond the property, the centre of town is only a short 15-minute drive away. Also nearby is the renowned Palmeraie Golf Club, where international master Robert Trent Jones, Sr, has created a breathtaking and challenging 18-hole course.

In the evenings, enjoy gourmet meals prepared by Dar Sabra's master chef, laid out in lavish style in the elegant dining room. For the perfect close to the day, take a midnight dip in the lantern-lit pool and savour Dar Sabra's unsurpassed luxury.

rooms
7 rooms

food
1 indoor and 1 outdoor dining room: Moroccan

drink
beverage list

features
clay tennis court · indoor heated pool · library · outdoor pool · desert landscaping · salons · screening room

nearby
Palmeraie Golf Club · medina · Guéliz · Hivernage · Oukaimeden · Ouzoud Falls

contact
Douar Abbiad, La Palmeraie
40000 Marrakech ·
telephone: +212.61.133 684 or +212.24.328 569 ·
facsimile: +212.24.329 177 ·
email: reservation@darsabra.com ·
website: www.darsabra.com

dar shama

Not far from the chaos of downtown Marrakech is an oasis that feels a million miles away. The Palmeraie was planted during the Almoravides dynasty; it covers 13,000 hectares (32,123 acres) and houses more than 100,000 trees as well as a collection of luxury hotels, private homes, sports clubs and golf courses. Caught somewhere between home and hotel is Dar Shama, a tranquil hideaway perfect for unwinding either at the beginning or end of your trip—or ideally both. Hidden behind thick walls, Dar Shama opens up into lush gardens fragrant with roses, orange blossoms, lemon trees and all things Arabian. The extensive and carefully maintained lawns are scattered with sun loungers and hammocks.

Inside, Villa Shama—the first of the two villas—is a thoroughly Andalusian affair. Carefully restored by skilled artisans, the eight rooms and two suites are swathed in the rich colour scheme of traditional Andalusian style. The Suite Royale Shama is a vast space opulently decked in mosaics and tadelakt plaster; its 100 sq m (1,076 sq ft) houses double baldaquin beds, a dining area on the large terrace, a dressing room, a fireplace, a jacuzzi and a living room area.

In a different style, but no less refined, is the Kasbah Shama. Made of clay and straw mortar, the Kasbah's four suites are centred around a private pool. It can be hired out as a whole villa or by the single suite. Either way, it

Caught somewhere between home and hotel is Dar Shama, a tranquil hideaway...

rooms
Dar Shama: 8 rooms · 6 suites
Ksar Shama: 21 rooms including 4 Ksar Suites

food
Moroccan · international

drink
beverage list

features
Dar Shama:
airport transfers · babysitting · spa · golf · daily shuttle to the medina · 2 pools · tennis · horse riding · quad biking · hammam

Ksar Shama:
airport transfers · spa · 2 pools · trekking · hammam and body treatments · zeppelins

nearby
Royal Golf Club de Marrakech · Royal Golf d'Amelkis

contact
Dar Shama: Circuit de la Palmeraie, Douar Abbiad 40000 Marrakech · telephone: +212.24.311 350 · facsimile: +212.24.308 646 · email: contact@darshama.com · website: www.darshama.com

Ksar Shama:
telephone: +212.24.485 032 · facsimile: +212.24.485 040 email: contact@ksarshama.com website: www.ksarshama.com

is a very private option with its own separate access and independent garden. It also has a summer lounge, terrace and dining hall—perfect for a wedding.

Dar Shama's garden is its unique selling point, and guests are encouraged to take advantage of the grounds and have dinner just about anywhere in the hotel. The restaurant's refined Moroccan cuisine can be served in the garden or on the terrace; there is plenty of shaded space so it will not get too hot outside.

Dar Shama's sister property, Ksar Shama offers the same level of charm and service. Located just one hour south of Marrakech in the direction of Asni, at the gateway of Toubkal National Park, Ksar Shama sits in 15 hectares (37 acres) of lush grounds alive with

an olive grove, fruit trees and beautiful blooms. With 17 large rooms and four independent guest cottages which comprise the Suites Ksar, this guesthouse keeps things intimate and luxurious. The friendly staff welcome guests warmly and are respectful of every guest's wish for tranquillity and privacy. They can also arrange exploratory excursions to the nearby park at guests' behest.

At Ksar Shama guests will find a traditional hammam facility which allows guests to pamper themselves with an array of body treatments, such as massages with perfumed oil and hydrotherapy. In addition, guests can make full use of the jacuzzi. All these excellent services contribute to a calm and restful holiday in the Atlas Mountains.

jnane tamsna country guesthouse

Get to know the real Morocco at Jnane Tamsna. Created by style and hospitality entrepreneur Meryanne Loum-Martin, this elegant country guesthouse is located amidst the date palms, olive trees and grapevines of the Palmeraie. This is Loum-Martin's newest project, after her luxury villas with their stylish concept put Marrakech on the map for the rich and famous.

The property is a classic Moorish country abode, designed by Loum-Martin with the help of her American ethnobotanist husband Gary. Ten tastefully furnished double rooms are clustered around two garden courtyards, decorated with furniture also designed by Loum-Martin and complemented with tadelakt plaster walls, mother-of-pearl Syrian chests, fine Senegalese textiles and hand-hammered copper, bronze and brass sinks. In addition, 14 suites and bedrooms are housed in three other buildings on the same grounds. The whole property can be booked exclusively for weddings, reunions and such.

What makes this property unique is its close involvement with the Global Diversity Foundation. This is a non-governmental organisation based in Britain that promotes agricultural, biological and cultural diversity worldwide. Their partnership has attracted guests such as culinary groups, visitors from the American and Harvard Museums of Natural History, groups studying traditional Moroccan medicine, international health and women's issues and other interest groups.

While guests educate themselves on new perspectives of Moroccan life and culture, Jnane Tamsna takes care of their more basic needs. Several heated pools beckon, as do quiet reading nooks and a tranquil rooftop terrace. A clay tennis court is on offer for the energetic, while other guests may prefer an al fresco massage. The suites have their own pool, and share the rest of the facilities with the main house. By night, the rooftop terrace is lit by lanterns for a home-cooked dinner with vegetables from the property's garden. The food served combines Cordon Bleu fare with country cooking, and makes use of fresh produce harvested daily from the property's five organic vegetable gardens.

Owner Meryanne Loum-Martin exudes contemporary Moroccan style, is dedicated to community issues and is a charming hostess. Let her share her love for Morocco with you in a holiday experience you will never forget.

THIS PAGE (FROM TOP): Jnane Tamsna attracts discerning travellers from all over the world; all the rooms are decorated in traditional Moroccan style.

OPPOSITE (FROM LEFT): Cosy spaces entice guests to curl up with some reading material; one of the five pools available at the guesthouse.

...located amidst the date palms, olive trees and grapevines of the Palmeraie.

rooms
24 bedrooms and suites

food
private kitchen: European and Mediterranean •
restaurant: refined Moroccan

drink
poolside bar

features
9 acres of gardens • 5 pools (heated in winter) •
tennis court • cooking classes • boutique •
hammam • reflexology • courtyards • salons •
educational tours • art gallery • rooftop terrace •
nutrition weeks • yoga

nearby
Djemaa el-Fna Square • Guéliz • souks •
Koutoubia Mosque • golf • Majorelle Museum •
Ménara Gardens • Saadian Tombs

contact
Douar Abbiad, La Palmeraie
40000 Marrakech •
telephone: +212.24.328 484 •
facsimile: +212.24.329 884 •
email: meryanne@jnane.com •
website: www.jnane.com

ksar char-bagh

This magnificent Ksar, or palace, is located 20 minutes from the activity of Marrakech, in the isolation and natural beauty of the Palmeraie district where thousands of palm trees grow in defiance of the arid desert. Named after the place in the Islamic Garden of Paradise where all rivers are said to meet, Ksar Char-Bagh is an oasis of flowing streams and greenery, with an enormous outdoor pool as its impressive centrepiece.

The building, inspired by 14th-century Moorish architecture, features the signature arches, stucco work and domed ceilings of that style, but also incorporates many modern touches and a minimalist aesthetic that contributes to the sense of calm and serenity. All elements of the hotel were conceived and built by its Parisian owners, including every piece of furniture and decorative art on display in the rooms and public areas. The design process alone took three years, and construction took a team of more than 200 craftsmen about 15 months. It is apparent from the first glance that no effort was spared in the creation of this mansion.

Its vast garden grounds span 4 hectares (10 acres), giving ample room to afford its guests a most luxurious stay. Only 12 Harim Suites were built in all, along with a deluxe rooftop apartment, creating a very private getaway for no more than 26 guests at any time. Each suite is uncommonly large at a minimum of 70 sq m (753 sq ft). Living areas are painted in neutral cream tones and furnished in exquisite style with woven rugs and specially commissioned handicrafts.

Modern features have been tailored to blend into the interior design scheme without interfering, with air-conditioning units that are hidden behind walls and entertainment systems housed in period-style cabinets. Guests in the suites may also enjoy a private garden or terraced area, three with pools of their own, large dressing rooms and marble

rooms
12 suites · 1 apartment

food
French and Moroccan

drink
bar

features
hammam · spa services · pool · tennis courts ·
library · billiard room · Internet access ·
London Cab airport transfers · fumoir

nearby
Marrakech · shops · gardens · palm tree groves

contact
BP 2449, La Palmeraie
40000, Marrakech ·
telephone: +212.24.329 244 ·
facsimile: +212.24.329 214 ·
email: info@ksarcharbagh.com ·
website: www.ksarcharbagh.com

bathrooms with deep tubs, soothing bath oils and scented candles. The top-floor apartment even has its own rooftop terrace and pool.

The hotel's lounges and public areas have the intimate atmosphere of a private club, with facilities such as a billiard room, a well-stocked library and outdoor tennis courts shaded by olive trees. Drinks may be enjoyed throughout the day, and meals from the restaurant may be served virtually anywhere. Using meat and seafood procured fresh from the local market and produce and herbs harvested from the kitchen's own garden, the resident French chef serves the fine cuisines of Europe as well as Moroccan classics.

Deep below the Ksar, guests may enjoy a traditional hammam experience in a red-marble vaulted room kept at a constant 50°C (122°F). A menu of beauty treatments is also available; facials with Anne Sémonin products and relaxing massages with essential oils are popular favourites. Guests may luxuriate with these treatments in the privacy of their suite, in the hammam's treatment rooms, or in the open-air converted ruin behind the main pool.

Awarded a spot on *Condé Nast Traveller*'s 2004 Hot List and *Tatler*'s '101 Best Hotels' feature in 2007, this regal, classy hotel is a five-star retreat that will make a lasting impression on all visitors.

les jardins d'inès

THIS PAGE: *Beautiful tiled paths in the hotel's lush garden invite guests to take a brisk morning walk or an evening stroll.*

OPPOSITE (FROM TOP): *The pool is only one of the property's many luxurious facilities that are meant to pamper guests; each suite is appointed with lush fabrics and rich colours for every guest's comfort.*

Newly added to Palmeraie Hotels & Resorts, Les Jardins d'Inès is an extension of the luxury and elegance offered in the rest of the property. Situated in the heart of the famed Palmeraie, this deluxe boutique hotel also provides tranquillity away from the excitement of the main hotel complex. With top-notch facilities and dedicated service, it is no surprise that travellers are flocking here to spend their holidays in this exclusive establishment situated at the foot of the majestic snow-capped Atlas Mountains.

Guests reside in 26 traditional Moorish style suites, all tastefully decorated with a touch of authenticity. The Club Suites offer their inhabitants a large sitting room with a luxurious bathroom and wide terraces that add considerable space to the suites' area. In the Diplomatic Suites, guests are provided with two plush bedrooms, their own bar and an open fireplace to warm those chilly nights, while each Ambassador Suite, equipped with three rooms and two bathrooms, features a living room as well as a private bar area, perfect for entertaining visitors or lounging about after a long day spent indulging in the excitement offered by Marrakech.

Overlooking olive groves and palm trees, the property's restaurant, Dar Inès, is without a doubt one of the culinary treasures of the Palmeraie Golf Palace. Here, acclaimed chef Jean-Marie Gueraische invites guests to partake in the fruits of his labour, with a menu that is composed specially each day using the best local produce available. Foodies will be pleased to discover that a plethora of other food choices, including Italian and Japanese cuisine, are also available at any of the many restaurants scattered about the massive hotel complex.

Situated a mere 15 minutes away from the medina and the renowned Djemaa el-Fna Square, the hotel is not far from many popular attractions. In the event that a guest is in an adventurous mood, the highly knowledgeable concierge is always happy to assist, whether by proving information or helping to organise tours and visits or both. Guests who do not wish to venture from the property can bask in the sun by the outdoor pool or head to the fully-equipped fitness centre for a good workout. In addition, there is the traditional hammam and the well-equipped spa and sauna to turn to. Here, you can rejuvenate in the trained hands of professionals while all your worries slip away.

rooms
2 Club Suites • 18 Diplomatic Suites • 6 Ambassador Suites

food
Dar Inès

drink
bar

features
spa • hammam • fitness centre • concierge • baby-sitting service • outdoor pool • garden • terrace • games area • live entertainment

nearby
medina • Djemaa el-Fna Square

contact
BP 1488, Circuit de la Palmeraie 40000 Marrakech •
telephone: +212.24.334 200 •
facsimile: +212.24.334 201 •
email: info@lesjardinsdines.com •
website: www.palmeraie-marrakech.com

lodge k

THIS PAGE (FROM TOP): The African Lodge's earth tones and fine fabrics call to mind luxury safaris out on the savannah; the Egyptian Lodge is decked out in opulent fabrics and offers guests pure decadence.

OPPOSITE (FROM TOP): The large, fully equipped spa invites both male and female guests to enter and relax while skilled therapists work their magic; Lodge K's huge pool, with its central island, is almost a lake.

Situated 20 minutes away from the hustle and bustle of the famed Djemaa el-Fna Square, Lodge K invites travellers to enter and dwell here with the promise of tranquillity and adventure available just moments away. Built with the unique concept of lodges in Marrakech, guests can explore exotic African or Egyptian lifestyles here, for the lodges are individually designed with such themes in mind. To truly experience Moroccan culture, it is necessary to get to know each lifestyle that makes up the culture.

To this end, guests can choose to stay in the African Lodge, where earthy tones blend with subtle lighting to recreate the sense of being in the midst of a safari, albeit with modern conveniences, or in the Egyptian Lodge, where one can relive the splendour enjoyed by ancient Egyptian royalty.

Other options include the Art Deco Lodge, which showcases the elegance of the Art Deco period, and the Lord's Lodge, where guests are pampered with opulent fittings. Regardless of which lodge guests reside in, the service is always impeccable, with staff on hand around the clock. Although Lodge K re-enacts some parts of history, with its high speed Internet access, satellite televisions and large DVD library, guests can be assured that the amenities are not vintage.

Guests can visit the nearby Djemaa el-Fna Square, with its many shops and street food stalls. If guests wish to go somewhere else, the informative concierge is always happy to arrange for guided tours around the area or for hikes to more closely examine Morocco's natural beauty. Long and dreary bus or car rides to hiking destinations are not a concern here, as Lodge K provides a special transit service by helicopter to ensure a faster and more comfortable trip.

For something closer to the Lodge itself, guests can go horse riding, or jet ski in the clear waters near the Lodge. Lounging on one of the numerous daybeds that line the large outdoor pool for a long bask is another option open to guests. If relaxation is of top priority,

Lodge K's traditional hammam and beauty centre is the place to go to be pampered by the skilled hands of professionals.

The K restaurant at Lodge K serves a range of Moroccan and international cuisine. Guests can savour a romantic dinner under the stars, or indulge in the kitchen's delicious fare in the cosy, intimate atmosphere of the restaurant itself. Of course, should guests desire to bring an aspect of Moroccan culture home with them, the chefs will gladly share some of their knowledge of the skills and culinary secrets involved in creating the restaurant's Moroccan specialties.

With modern facilities partnered with such fine service at Lodge K, every stay here will surely be memorable.

rooms
4 themed lodges

food
K restaurant: Moroccan and international

drink
beverage list

features
spa • pool • fitness centre • hammam • personalised service • special transit service by helicopter to hiking destinations

nearby
Djemaa el-Fna Square

contact
Km 5, Route de Fez, Dartounsi 40000 Marrakech •
telephone: +212.24.328 645 or +212.60.153 924 or +212.61.337 499 •
facsimile: +212.60.159 264 •
email: info@lodgek.com •
website: www.lodgek.com

murano resort

THIS PAGE: *The reception area's mix of modernity and local design style is a preview to the rest of the hotel's décor.*

OPPOSITE (FROM LEFT): *Standing on the property are five riads, each with a classical central courtyard and its own pool; the rooms and suites offer guests the utmost in comfort.*

The bustling activity of Marrakech's city centre attracts many visitors each year, all keen to experience the shopping, street food and colourful atmosphere of the legendary medina. However, accommodations in the area are mostly of a traditional nature and often lack the modernity and design-centric approach favoured by a select clientele—the kind most likely to feel at home in, say, the chic Murano Resort Paris in France.

It is fortunate then, that embedded within the secluded grounds of La Palmeraie, 15 minutes from the medina and 20 minutes from Menara Airport, the creators of the Murano Resort Paris have established their latest luxury outpost. Consisting of five full-sized Moroccan riads surrounded by an estate of over 200,000 sq m (239,198 sq yd) of palm trees, Murano Resort Marrakech brings an opulent five-star sensibility to a country already known for its grand flourishes.

This branch possesses its own sense of style, but many of its sister hotel's best qualities have been transplanted for a more complete bridging of the two worlds. Each riad has its own pool and central courtyard patio, where smart, downtempo music has infused this traditionally Moroccan setting with a modern touch. The architectural style is rich in arches, wooden ceilings and regional details, having been constructed by a team of local craftsmen, but the interior designs are cutting-edge cool. Many pieces of furniture are duplicates of those in Murano Resort Paris.

The main riad serves as a reception area and also houses the hotel's restaurant, whose French and Moroccan cuisine bears the hallmark attention to detail of its elder sibling's kitchen. Only fresh, locally sourced ingredients make their way into the superb meals, which are both creatively prepared and presented. The dining room is a match for the chef's talents: a fireplace warms the high-ceilinged room, with light refracting through the facets of a large glass chandelier above.

The remaining four riads contain the 30 junior suites and suites, some with a private living room for in-room massages. Every room features a fireplace and is richly appointed. Air-conditioning and firm king-sized beds ensure physical comfort, while the interplay of designer décor and soft fabrics creates a sensual retreat. Modern conveniences are best-of-class, with wireless Internet access, LCD televisions with movies and satellite channels and even an espresso machine. Ground-floor suites have private terraces, with some opening out directly to the pools, while the top-floor suites are gifted with lovely panoramic views of the surrounding mountain landscape from their balconies.

A defining feature of the Murano Resort Marrakech is its striking, deep-red pool. A fitness centre has been added recently, and a comprehensive spa facility should be ready soon. Even without these extras, the hotel's exclusive setting and exciting design slant is reason enough to draw up travel plans.

...brings an opulent five-star sensibility to a country already known for its grand flourishes.

rooms
30 junior suites and suites

food
Moroccan and French

drink
1 indoor bar • 1 outdoor bar

features
5 pools • 24-hour room service • concierge •
airport transfers • spa • wireless Internet access

nearby
medina • Nikki Beach • airport • golf courses

contact
BP 13172, Douar Abbiad, La Palmeraie
40000 Marrakech •
telephone: +212.24.327 000 •
facsimile: +212.24.328 666 •
email: marrakech@muranoresort.com •
website: www.muranoresort.com

palais rhoul

THIS PAGE (FROM TOP): *A total of about 180 columns stand throughout the property; the décor at Palais Rhoul exhibits Roman influences.*

OPPOSITE (FROM TOP): *Feast in style at L'Abyssin restaurant; the spa and hammam offer many Arabian treatments.*

Hidden away in the fronds of the Palmeraie—a plantation of more than 100,000 palm trees just outside of the city, 15 minutes from the medina by car—is a gem of an Arabian palace that has been converted into a five-star hotel and spa. A true desert oasis, the Palais Rhoul is surrounded on all sides by 5 hectares (12 acres) of lush cultivated gardens that include scores of Mediterranean olive trees and palms. The inviting scene is strewn with placid ponds and walking paths, along with plenty of opportunities for lazing in the sun.

Inside, the hotel is centred around an extraordinary marble pool inspired by Roman architecture, complete with colonnades between which palms stretch majestically skyward. Throughout the building, Moroccan craftsmanship and interior designs meld with classical Roman influences, including the use of some 180 columns.

Of the 12 rooms and suites housed in the main complex, half of them are arranged in positions that overlook the central pool and atrium, allowing their occupants to bask in the daytime reflections of the water, or enjoy the gentle glow of evening, when the pool is surrounded by flickering candles and covered over with floating flower petals. The other six rooms face outwards into the landscaped gardens, with views over the top of palm trees all the way to the horizon.

All rooms are equipped with a host of high-quality amenities and technological essentials. Fully air-conditioned for comfort, they boast entertainment in the form of large televisions with satellite or cable channels, radios and wireless Internet access. All rooms in the main building have lovely balconies or private terraces for peaceful relaxation and sunbathing. The living areas and en suite bathrooms are also very large, and feature a number of varied decoration schemes. Ensuring that no two rooms are alike, they are each furnished with one-of-a-kind objets d'art and antiques sourced from around the globe. For example, the double La Cardinal Room exhibits a wealth of English influences that extend to its collection of 18th-century paintings. Those seeking a sense of the local will find it in several rooms, including the very large Penthouse La Chambre du Maitre, which is a two-bedroom master suite that features a bathroom with walls finished in traditional tadelakt plaster and its own exclusive massage table.

...a gem of an Arabian palace that has been converted into a five-star hotel and spa.

rooms
12 rooms and suites • 8 luxury tents

food
Moroccan Palace: traditional Moroccan •
L'Abyssin: seasonal international

drink
L'Abyssin bar

features
hammam • gardens • tennis court • pools •
Internet access • 24-hour room service • spa

nearby
balloon rides • lake with jet skiing • shops •
cultural visits with professional guides •
Palmeraie • Atlas Mountains • quad biking

contact
Route de Fes, Dartounsi
BP 522 Principal Guéliz
44000 Marrakech •
telephone: +212.24.329 494 •
facsimile: +212.24.329 496 •
email: info@palais-rhoul.com •
website: www.palais-rhoul.com

Unconventionally, the Palais Rhoul also gives guests the option of staying outdoors, in a series of eight tents pitched in the the Palace's gardens. These spacious Caïdal-style affairs are not the average outdoorsman's idea of luxury, instead recreating sumptuous suites complete with fireplaces, large soaking bathtubs and four-poster beds between their high ceilings and permanent floors. The romantically conducive L'Harem Tent, perfect for couples, even boasts its own sunken pool that comes surrounded by lanterns and adorned with rose petals.

The award-winning spa and hammam facilities match the Palais' accommodations in sheer merit, having been named one of the world's top 100 spas by *Harper*'s. Arabian treatments feature prominently on the menu, with many procedures utilising traditional black soap, orange flower water, and rose oils in combination with exfoliation and deep, powerful massages. The result of spending an afternoon being renewed and rejuvenated in the hammam, followed by a night under the stars, is profound relaxation worth travelling any distance.

palmeraie golf palace

THIS PAGE: The property has an outdoor pool for guests who wish to exercise under the open sky or pick up a tan.

THIS PAGE: The property has an outdoor pool for guests who wish to exercise under the open sky or pick up a tan.

OPPOSITE (FROM TOP): All guestrooms are decorated in traditional Moroccan design style paired with five-star opulence; the Palmeraie Golf Palace is expansive, with four large buildings that can house a few hundred guests at once.

One of the jewels of Morocco is undoubtedly the Palmeraie Golf Palace. Opened 15 years ago as Marrakech's first super-luxury hotel, the Palmeraie Golf Palace has been constantly stretching the limits of luxury and comfort to welcome even the most demanding guests.

Accommodation is an extravagant affair here at the Palmeraie Golf Palace. Guests can choose to stay in the 323 well-appointed rooms in the main complex. Alternatively, guests can also reside in any of the three new additions, namely Le Grand Pavilion with its 43 top-quality suites with unrivalled views of the Atlas Mountains, Le Palmeraie Village, which consists of 300 luxury apartments with full hotel services, and Les Jardins d'Inès, made up of 26 suites built in the caravanserai style. Particular attention has been paid to ensure that the traditional techniques and materials of Marrakech have been used to create this palace. Whichever accommodations chosen, guests can be assured that connection with the outside world will not be compromised as cinematic audiovisual fittings as well as high-speed Internet access and satellite digital television are provided to all rooms.

One of the highlights of the Palmeraie Golf Palace is its 18-hole, 72-par Robert Trent Jones golf course. Extending over 77 hectares (190 acres), golfers should not miss a chance to tee off among its unique panorama—including seven lakes with a supplementary nine-hole course—that makes it one of the most beautiful courses in Morocco.

If guests want to try out the plethora of alternate activities, be it sports, billiards or late-night clubbing, they can be sure that there is always something to occupy their time. Guests who prefer fast-paced activity can opt for the Palmeraie Riding School where coaching and riding lessons are available for all levels. Of course, with the medina and the famous Djemaa el-Fna Square just 15 minutes away, a tour there is definitely a must-do on every guest's itinerary. Those who want a slower-paced holiday can patronise the hammam and spa facility that is present in

rooms
286 rooms • 26 suites • 11 executive rooms in the Club House • 43 suites in Le Grand Pavillon

food
Dar Ennasim: gastronomic French • Tiramisu: Italian • Leroy's Kfe: international • Narjis: Moroccan • Geisha Lounge: Japanese • Nikki Beach • Legende: light refreshments

drink
Baccarat bar • Sports Bar: sporting events • Le Palace: night club

features
18-hole golf course • nine-hole course • International Conference Centre • Mini Club • traditional hammam and spa facility

nearby
international airport • medina • shopping • Djemaa el-Fna Square • souks

contact
BP 1488, Circuit de la Palmeraie
40000 Marrakech •
telephone: +212.24.301 010 •
facsimile: +212.24.309 000 •
email: sales@pgp.ma or reservation@pgp.ma •
website: www.pgpmarrakech.com

each of the new units of accommodation and in the main complex. Here, trained specialists provide the ultimate in relaxation for both mind and body with a selection of beauty and body treatments. Also, rest assured that the little ones have not been left out. Children are treated to activities and menus specially created for them at the Mini Club.

Palmeraie Golf Palace welcomes those who want to mix work and pleasure with the recently opened International Conference Centre. Along with a team of professionals on hand to help, this versatile space, which can be adapted to meet the needs of any type of event, is fully equipped with the top-of-the-range technical equipment needed to ensure that each event is a success.

The Palmeraie Golf Palace can be counted on to provide gastronomic adventures. One of the stars of the culinary scene in Morocco, Dar Ennasim, situated at Le Grand Pavilion, is helmed by two Michelin-starred chef Fabric Vulin, and serves up a scrumptious menu of gastronomic French cuisine. Other gems to be found at Palmeraie Golf Palace are Narjis, which serves authentic Moroccan food, the Japanese restaurant, the Geisha Lounge, and the unique, multi-faceted restaurant, Leroy's Kfe, opened by well-known Christopher Leroy. In addition, guests can head to one of the many bars that dot the immense property for a nightcap, after which they can hop onto the hotel's shuttle service back to their rooms for a good night's rest.

kasbah agafay

Morocco lays claim to some of the most spectacular and dramatic scenery the world has to offer. Just a 20-minute drive from the city of Marrakech are rolling hills and valleys, with the towering bulk of the High Atlas in the distance. Located in the midst of this breathtaking setting is Kasbah Agafay, a luxury hotel housed in a restored 18th-century fortress. Perched on a hilltop, the fortress overlooks Berber villages, olive plantations and the grand mountains.

Within the ramparts are 20 exquisite rooms and suites; the most amazing of these are four sprawling Caïdal tents. Each boasts a four-poster bed made from beams used in nomads' tents, sculpted mosaic baths, a sitting area and a private terrace with views

of olive groves. Air-conditioning keeps the interior of the tents cool in summer and central heating provides warmth during winter. Embellishing the tents, as well as the other rooms and suites, are carefully selected antique Moroccan textiles and artefacts.

In a corner of the grounds stands a herb and vegetable garden. The organic produce from this plot is a staple on the hotel's menu. The chefs will delight you with international and Moroccan cuisine which you can savour in the hotel's restaurant Dar Ouarda, in one of the courtyards or even up on the ramparts for an experience like none other.

Should the hotel's cooking inspire you to learn more about Moroccan cuisine, the Kasbah's very own culinary school is nestled in the herb and vegetable garden. Classes are conducted by the hotel's chefs, who are walking encyclopedias of local cuisine. Here, you can learn how to prepare Moroccan dishes such as tajine and couscous, and how to cook with a traditional oven, which lends Moroccan food its characteristic flavour. At the end of the class, sample your own cooking and get tips on accompanying wines.

A host of adventure activities is available nearby, and the concierge is happy to assist with any arrangements. Guests can go hot air ballooning, camel riding, horse riding, desert trekking and mountain biking. For some relaxation, retire to the Kasbah's landscaped open-air spa, with its meditation cave, yoga area, hammam and treatment rooms.

...a luxury hotel housed in a restored 18th-century fortress.

rooms
9 rooms • 6 junior suites • 1 suite •
2 deluxe Caïdal tents • 2 Caïdal tent suites

food
Dar Ouarda: Moroccan and international

drink
beverage list

features
culinary school • organic garden • pool •
open-air yoga studio • open-air spa •
tennis courts • boutique

nearby
Marrakech • Essaouira (two-hour drive) •
Berber villages • golf courses

contact
Km 20, Route de Guemassa
40000 Marrakech
telephone: +212.24.368 600 •
facsimile : +212.24.420 970 •
email: kasbahagafay@menara.ma •
website: www.kasbahagafay.com

kasbah du toubkal

The Kasbah du Toubkal is an extraordinary venture, the product of an imaginative European and Berber partnership, where the local Berbers run the establishment. There is a shared belief that the beauty of the Toubkal National Park should be accessible to all who respect it. To this end, the Kasbah has been renovated and transformed using traditional methods, from the home of a feudal Caïd into an unprecedented haven. As *Condé Nast Traveller* has stated, 'with the best rooftop views in North Africa... this is the country's first and foremost mountain retreat'.

Situated above the village of Imlil and in view of the highest mountain in North Africa, the setting is exceptional; Martin Scorsese used it as a set for his film on the Dalai Lama. This area used to be the preserve of the mountaineer or the intrepid traveller, but the Kasbah opens this opportunity to everyone else. The Kasbah can be reached by a short 10-minute walk (or mule ride) from Imlil, along a path through walnut groves to the main gate; there is no road access. Stairs lead up to the gardens and the Kasbah with its panoramic views and unique relaxed atmosphere.

THIS PAGE (FROM TOP): *Kasbah du Toubkal occupies a lofty perch in the High Atlas; large windows in the lounge display the scenic environs.*

OPPOSITE (FROM TOP): *Regardless of their price, the rooms at the Kasbah are all lush and comfy; a spectacular vista can be admired from every window.*

...from the home of a feudal Caïd into an unprecedented haven.

rooms
14 double rooms • 1 Garden Apartment • 1 private house • 15 beds in 3 Berber Salons

food
private dining: traditional

drink
no alcohol sold: bring your own

features
hammam • library • café • gift shop • guided treks, including ascent of Jbel Toubkal

nearby
Jbel Toubkal • farms • Aït Mizane tribal villages

contact
BP 31, Imlil, Asni, Marrakech • telephone: +212.24. 485 611 • facsimile: +212.24.485 636 • email: kasbah@discover.ltd.uk • website: www.kasbahdutoubkal.com

Regardless of your level of fitness, the gentle pace of Imlil and the Berber world is open to you. It is a special place beyond the reach of the modern world, and offers many possibilities—be it taking a leisurely mint tea with a neighbour or hiking to the top of Jbel Toubkal, which stands proudly at 4,167 m (13,671 ft). For the less energetic, relax on the roof terrace and take in the views before a rejuvenating hammam.

The accommodations are luxurious but in harmony with the surroundings. The range of options is varied, catering to guests on differing budgets. Stay in a Berber Salon suitable for families or groups, a standard or deluxe room (with a private balcony), or even the amazing Garden Apartment with its 12-m (39-ft) glass wall that looks out onto a waterfall and the mountains.

In this exceptional area inhabited by the Berbers, the original inhabitants of North Africa, the owners of Kasbah du Toubkal did not want to ignore the remarkable hospitality of the local hosts. They accordingly describe the Kasbah as a Berber Hospitality Centre.

The Kasbah is very much a part of the Imlil community and has won accolades for sustainable tourism, such as a British Airways Tourism for Tomorrow Award, 'Built Environment' Category, and a Green Globe Award. It is hard to describe the Kasbah in words—one has to experience it.

kasbah tamadot

THIS PAGE (FROM TOP): Some rooms come with terraces where guests can sit in peace and take in the scenic landscape; the outdoor infinity-edge pool in the waning light of dusk.

OPPOSITE (FROM TOP): Guests at the Kasbah will find themselves living in the lap of luxury; breakfast on the terrace is accompanied by breathtaking views of the surroundings.

The sole North African property in Sir Richard Branson's Virgin Limited Edition collection of luxury retreats, Kasbah Tamadot, located at the foot of the Atlas Mountains, is literally at the highest level of indulgence.

Discovered by the entrepreneur's parents while he prepared to embark on a hot air balloon journey, the property soon changed hands from one extraordinary owner to another. Renowned antiques collector and interior designer Luciano Tempo originally furnished the property as a home, filling it with an assortment of rare antiquities.

After the refurbishment of the building, his legacy continues to be displayed all over the hotel. The décor is a mix of contemporary design styles and traditional Moroccan art and architecture. In every room, unique features such as carved wood ceilings coexist with technology and glorious nature views.

Ten rooms, eight suites and six Berber tents with plunge pools make up the accommodations, each an individual creation. Some of these guestrooms even boast terraces that overlook the majestic forests and mountainous slopes below. A detached three-bedroom Master Suite in the rose garden is the highlight of the hotel, which itself serves as inspiration for the suite's design. A miniature replica of the Kasbah, right down to the upper level roof terrace, the Master Suite is the place to drink in 360° views of the exquisite Atlas landscape while relaxing in the warm sunlight, or in the cool recesses of their private pool.

In all of Kasbah Tamadot's rooms, guests will find a complimentary set of Moroccan slippers, or babouches, waiting when they arrive, along with luxurious robes and beds finished with soft cotton sheets. The rooms

rooms
10 rooms · 8 suites · 6 Berber tents with
individual plunge pools

food
Kanoun and Poolside Terrace: traditional
Moroccan and international

drink
Kanoun and Poolside Terrace bar

features
heated indoor and outdoor pools · gym ·
tennis courts · sauna · Asounfou Spa ·
traditional hammam · lounge library

nearby
Atlas Mountains · Asni · Tahanaoute ·
Marrakech · mule and hiking trails

contact
BP 67, 042150 Asni, Marrakech ·
telephone: +44.208.600 0430 ·
facsimile: +44.208.600 0431 ·
email: enquiries@virginlimitededition.com ·
website: www.virginlimitededition.com

are also equipped with CD players and an array of CDs. Televisions and DVD players are available to guests upon request.

The main building itself contains two pools: an indoor heated pool on the ground floor, and an outdoor infinity-edge pool that appears to hang over the incredible vista of mountain tops. All guests of Kasbah Tamadot may also make use of a traditional hammam, sauna, and the Asounfou Spa on the ground floor to relax and unwind, leaving the many stresses of everyday life behind.

Meals at Kasbah Tamadot come by way of the peerless Kanoun restaurant, named after the traditional Berber bread oven, and the Poolside Terrace, both of which serve a mix of authentic regional cuisine and international dishes with a selection of fine wines—some are even made in Morocco. In the evenings, the roof terrace is superb for romantic candlelit dinners, but couples may also arrange to dine at one of several private dining locations on the grounds.

Day trips to Marrakech, only a 40-minute drive away, are a good way to explore more of the local culture, along with guided mountain walks and mule treks to discover the region. Luxury car transfers are available to the city, the airport as well as other areas of interest nearby. Known as 'Soft Breeze' in the local language, the Kasbah Tamadot is surely one of the best hotels in all of Morocco.

maroc lodge

Just 45 minutes from Marrakech's airport, 1,000 m (3,280 ft) above sea level in the Atlas Mountains, lies a slice of Moroccan history in the form of a discreet and exclusive hideaway with an emphasis on tranquillity. Here in quiet Amizmiz, Dr Dubois-Roquebert, personal physician to King Mohammed V, decided to set up home. The doctor welcomed the King to his estate and together they put Amizmiz and this charming villa on the map. When the King was sent into exile, Dr Dubois-Roquebert continued to attend to him wherever he was. The doctor's children later converted their family home into Maroc Lodge and named the Lodge's pavilions after towns their father stayed in with the King.

The first thing that strikes you as you approach Maroc Lodge is the natural beauty surrounding the property. Not only is it at the foothills of the Atlas Mountains, it is also set in a park that is home to an olive tree grove (some of the trees are over 100 years old) and countless other plants and trees, from walnut, almond and pomegranate to carob, lemon and orange. The shady green space, at once peaceful and tranquil, is charged with the natural aromas of the Berber countryside. A small canal runs through the grounds, the water drawn from a spring further up the mountain. The property makes a good base from which to explore Morocco's countryside; equally, it is a great place to take a break from the colourful chaos of Marrakech and pick up an immunity against the stresses of daily life.

Maroc Lodge's villas are scattered about the park, and a great deal of care was taken to ensure not one branch of the long-standing olive trees was broken—the villas have simply slipped in between. Each with large bay windows and sumptuous furnishings, they have their own terraces and breathtaking views of the mountains beyond. Inside, skilled artisans have decorated each pavilion with local materials. The pale pink bejmat floor tiles and the colourful zellij tile friezes on the walls are all

rooms
4 pavilions

food
Moroccan and European

drink
Tananarive Pavilion

features
infinity-edge pool · library · shop · hammam ·
spa · concierge service · shaded poolside ·
guided sporting activities · gardens ·
picturesque foothill location

nearby
Amizmiz weekly souk · Berber villages ·
High Atlas Mountains

contact
BP 16, 42100 Amizmiz, Marrakech ·
telephone: +212.24.544 969 or +212.61.202 537 ·
facsimile: +212.37.727 179 ·
email: infos@maroc-lodge.com ·
website: www.maroc-lodge.com

made in the village, and the tadelakt-coated walls are offset with walnut woodwork. It is Berber style through and through, excluding the original owner's collection of international artefacts that add a little personal charm.

The guesthouse facilities make excellent use of the surroundings: the infinity-edge pool seems to fall into the valley below, and the property's gardens provide the restaurant kitchen—which serves authentic Moroccan and European cuisine—with its primary ingredients. The home-grown ingredients are used for such Berber specialities as barley couscous, chicken tajine with honey, tanourt bread and delicious timija mint tea. Guests

can take their meals anywhere on the grounds, from the private dining area in each pavilion to the terrace, from the poolside to the restaurant itself.

In addition, the staff can organise guided tours for guests who wish to explore the area, either on foot or on horseback, with itineraries that vary from full day treks to two-hour walks. After that, the Lodge's hammam and massage therapists will help guests unwind. Capacity is purposefully kept small in order to keep service up to scratch, and the owners' and staff's competence is easily recognisable. They offer their guests luxury in a way that is completely genuine and utterly unpretentious.

royal air maroc

THIS PAGE (FROM TOP): The airline carries travellers to Morocco from all around the globe; the flight crew ensures that every trip is enjoyable.

OPPOSITE (CLOCKWISE FROM TOP): Meals are followed by coffee and tea; experienced chefs produce the delicious food served on board; a well-furnished VIP lounge.

Despite being situated in Northern Africa, Morocco is not a difficult place to get to. Travelling there is made even easier by the flag carrier airline of Morocco, Royal Air Maroc. It doesn't matter whether you are travelling from Europe, America or the Middle East—the heart of Royal Air Maroc's extensive network, located in busy Casablanca, is truly at the crossroads of the world.

Catering to the needs of each customer, Royal Air Maroc offers travellers a unique flight experience on every trip. Flight menus are updated on a regular basis, maintaining the high standard of the food served, with close attention paid to each traveller's personal religious convictions, medical requirements and culinary preferences. Don't worry about

frustratingly long queues and complicated check-in procedures, for the attentive staff as well as the dedicated check-in counters will ensure a quick and smooth process. This, paired with the end-to-end check-in service, will deliver both passengers and their luggage safely to their destination.

Premium-class travellers are treated to an array of enhanced facilities and services. Prior to boarding, they are encouraged to make use of Royal Air Maroc's VIP lounges, which can be found in major international airports such as Casablanca, Marrakech and Paris. Business travellers especially should take the opportunity to settle into these fully fitted lounges to continue working or to rest before clinching the next deal.

On board the planes are spacious seats that are far apart enough to provide privacy and tranquillity as travellers work or rest in anticipation of the journey ahead. Passengers can delve into any of the many newspapers and magazines that are on offer to keep at the top of their game. In this manner, travellers can be sure they will never be behind the times even while flying from one destination to another. If they have any other requests, the highly qualified flight crew will attend to each and every one of them.

Premium-class travellers get a chance to savour food from all round the world, as the experienced chefs at Royal Air Maroc prepare a gastronomic treat for them. Both Moroccan and international cuisine are on

flights
73 destinations

in flight
reading material · beverage list · wine list ·
hot meals with Moroccan or French wines ·
coffee, herbal tea or Moroccan tea ·
champagne · Moroccan or international menu

ground
VIP lounges in major international airports ·
Safar Flyer programme · Inter Plus Card

contact
telephone: +212.22.489 797 ·
website: www.royalairmaroc.com

the menu, and passengers may also partake in a range of drinks that includes champagne and selections from the on-board wine list. Three delicacies, served piping hot, together with a variety of cheeses, desserts and wines allow travellers to indulge their palate. After the hearty meal, they may relax in style accompanied by a traditional digestive of coffee, herbal tea or Moroccan tea.

Known for offering comfort at reasonable prices, it is no wonder that travellers pick Royal Air Maroc to be their choice airline. In return, Royal Air Maroc presents the Safar Flyer programme, where customers are rewarded according to how much they frequent the airline and its partners.

Every trip with Royal Air Maroc or its partners enables customers to rack up miles, which can then be converted to bonus air tickets, seat upgrades or excess luggage benefits. As frequent flyers gradually move from Blue to Silver to Gold status, even more exclusive privileges become available.

The Inter Plus Card is yet another perk offered to customers, so that travellers can explore Morocco without worrying too much about the cost. Each personalised card allows customers to purchase domestic flights at half price and flexibility with pricing conditions. Should a traveller decide to extend his or her stay in a particular city or take an alternative mode of transport, there will be no additional charges for changing reservations or making cancellations.

With the meticulous care and concern provided by the highly trained staff, whether you are on a business trip or travelling for leisure, regardless of where your destination lies, Royal Air Maroc provides an excellent start to what will be a memorable journey.

index

index

index

index

picturecredits+acknowledgements

The publisher would like to thank the following for permission to reproduce their photographs:

Akbar Delights 38, 39 (bottom)

Alexander Burkatovski/Corbis 54 (top)

Alexander Hassenstein/Getty Images 32 (bottom)

Alonso Carlos Sanchez/Photolibrary 140 (top)

Alvaro Leiva/Photolibrary 54 (bottom)

Amanjena back cover (poolside pavilion), 27 (top), 135, 192–193

Andrea Pistolesi/Getty Images 6

Atlantide Phototravel/Corbis 45 (top), 138

Aurness/Corbis 72 (bottom)

Aurora/Getty Images 146

Bertrand Gardel/Getty Images 12

Brigitte Sporrer/Corbis 25 (top right)

Bruno Barbier/Getty Images 49 (bottom right)

Bruno Morandi/Getty Images front cover (cistern), 5, 42 (bottom), 46 (bottom), 49 (top), 50, 57 (bottom), 78, 108

C. Bauchet-Bouhlal/Es Saadi Gardens & Resort 30

Chris Caldicott/Getty Images 21

Christophe Boisvieux/Corbis 55

Craig Aurness/Corbis 73

Dar Al Andalous 80–81

Dar Doukkala 150–151

Dar Les Cigognes front flap (room in riad), 152–155

Dar Nilam 60–61

Dar Nour 63

Dar Rhizlane 156–157

Dar Sabra 196–197

Dar Shama 198, 199 (top)

David Sutherland/Getty Images 57 (top), 75 (top)

El Minzah Hotel 64–65

Erich Kuchling/Getty Images 42 (top)

Ethel Davies/Getty Images 18, 56

Fatima's Hand/Getty Images 99 (top)

Floris Leeuwenberg/Corbis front cover (henna-decorated hands), 72 (top), 148 (bottom)

Frans Lemmens/Getty Images 101

Frederic Leloup 180

Gabriel Martel 120–121

Galerie Tindouf 24 (top)

Gallo Images - Shaen Adey/ Getty Images 23 (bottom), 99 (bottom)

George Kavanagh/Getty Images 37 (bottom)

Getty Images 41 (top)

Golf du Soleil 36 (top)

Guy Vanderelst/Getty Images back cover (Marrakech at dusk), 13, 77, 79, 131

Hemis/Corbis 47 (middle)

Herman du Plessis/Getty Images 8–9, 16

Herve Hughes/Getty Images 98, 140 (bottom)

Hervé Miguet 31 (bottom), 209 (right)

Hotel Ksar Massa 47 (bottom)

Hotel Nord-Pinus Tanger 66–67

Hôtel & Ryads Naoura Barrière Marrakech 158–159

Ian Cumming/Getty Images 139

Image Source/Getty Images 97 (bottom)

J. Bravo/Es Saadi Gardens & Resort 191 (top)

Jacques Paul back flap (food), 110–111

Jean du Boisberranger/Getty Images 147

Jed Share/Getty Images 24 (bottom), 76 (top)

Jeremy Horner/Corbis 144

Jeremy Horner/Getty Images back cover (medersa), 128

Jnane Tamsna Country Guesthouse front cover (reading lounge), 200–201

João Delgado da Silveira Ramos 181 (left)

Joe Beynon/Getty Images 15

John and Lisa Merrill/Corbis 25 (top left)

Karen Huntt/Corbis 14 (top)

Kasbah Agafay 214–215

Kasbah du Toubkal 46 (top), 216–217

Kasbah Tamadot 35 (top left), 218–219

Ken Welsh/Photolibrary 103

Ksar Char-Bagh 41 (bottom), 202–203

Ksar Shama 199 (bottom)

L Mansion Guest Palace 194–195

L'Heure Bleue Palais & Spa 29 (top), 112–113

Madada Mogador 114–115

La Gazelle d'Or 122–123

La Maison Arabe 160–161

La Sultana Marrakech 34, 162–163

La Sultana Oualidia 126–127

Laurent Pons 208, 209 (left)

Le Blokk 32 (top)

Le Comptoir Paris Marrakech 26, 39 (top)

Lee Frost/Getty Images 1, 43 (bottom)

Les Borjs de la Kasbah 164–165

Les Jardins d'Inès 28, 204–205

Les Jardins de la Koutoubia back flap (pool at night), 166–167

Les Jardins de la Medina back cover (sitting area in riad), 168–169

Light Gallery 40 (top)

Lisa Romerein/Getty Images back cover (oysters), 27 (bottom)

Lodge K 35 (bottom), 206–207

Lottie Davies/Getty Images back cover (tea), 148 (top)

Louis Grandadam/Getty Images 23 (top)

Ludovic Maisant/Corbis 143

Majid 25 (bottom)

Marcel Jolibois/Photolibrary 132

Maroc Lodge 220–221

Martin Child/Getty Images 74, 75 (bottom)

Naturfoto Honal/Corbis 134 (bottom)

Neil Emmerson/Getty Images 49 (bottom left), 58

O. Alamany & E. Vicens/Corbis 43 (top)

Ocean Vagabond 116–117

P. Wagner/Es Saadi Gardens & Resort 31 (top), 137, 189 (bottom), 191 (bottom)

P. Wagner/J. M. Pêtan/Es Saadi Gardens & Resort 188

Palais Rhoul 210–211

Palmeraie Golf Club 36 (bottom), 212–213

Panoramic Images/Getty Images 104 (top)

Pascale Bodet 62

Patrick Bennett/Corbis 48

Paul Miles/Getty Images 133 (bottom)

Paul Panayiotou/Grand Tour/Corbis front cover (fountain), 133 (top)

Paul Quayle/Getty Images 49 (middle right)

Pere Planells 181 (right)

The Angsana Riads Collection 182–183

Philip Kramer/Getty Images 149

R. Balancourt/Es Saadi Gardens & Resort 190

Raphael Van Butsele/Getty Images front cover (city walls), 136

Raymond Patrick/Getty Images 104 (bottom)

Riad El Fenn 170–173

Riad El Ouarda 174–175

Riad Farnatchi 176–177

Riad Fes 33, 84–85

Riad Ibn Battouta 86–87

Riad La Maison Bleue 88–89

Riad Laaroussa 90–91

Riad Meriem front flap (hammam), front flap (riad corridor), 178–179

Riad Myra 92–93

Robert Van Der Hilst/Getty Images front cover (shadow on street), 2

Roger Wood/Corbis 53

Rohan/Getty Images 68

Romain Cintract/Getty Images 4

Romilly Lockyer/Getty Images back cover (circle of stones), 22, 45 (bottom)

Royal Air Maroc 37 (top), 222–223

S. Anita/Es Saadi Gardens & Resort 189 (top)

Sami Sarkis/Getty Images 17

Simon Russell/Getty Images 19, 44, 45 (middle), 97 (top)

Sofitel Palais Jamaï 82–83

Steve Lewis/Getty Images 145

Sylvain Grandadam/Getty Images 47 (top)

Ted Levine/zefa/Corbis 141

Tony Gervis/Photolibrary 105

Toshihiko Chinami/Getty Images 14 (bottom)

UOVO Riads 184–185

Villa Mandarine 29 (bottom), 124–125

Villa Maroc 118–119

Villas des Orangers 186–187

Vision/Getty Images 71

Walter Bibikow/Getty Images front cover (ornate door), back cover (babouches), 20, 76 (bottom), 94, 100, 109, 142

Walter Bibikow/JAI/Corbis 102, 107

Walter Bibikow/Photolibrary 106

Xavier Richer and Jacques Bravo 40 (bottom)

Yamini Chao/Getty Images front cover (figs), 134 (top)

Yann Arthus-Bertrand/Corbis 59

ZenShui/Laurence Mouton/Getty Images 35 (top right)

The publisher would like to thank Nejma Lasky of Royal Air Maroc; the Moroccan National Tourist Office, in particular, Nisrine Zaaraoui and Salima Haddour of the Paris office and Ali El Kasmi of the London office; Alison Li; Joanna Greenfield; Kerry O'Neill and Amy Broomfield for their help and support during the production of this book.

HOTELS

Amanjena
Km 12, Route de Ouarzazate, Marrakech
telephone: +212.24.403 353
facsimile: +212.24.403 477
amanjena@amanresorts.com
www.amanresorts.com

Dar Al Andalous
14 Derb Bennani, Douh-Batha, Medina, Fez
telephone: +212.35.740 700
or +212.35.741 082
facsimile: +212.35.740 712
dar.alandalous@menara.ma
www.dar-alandalous.com

Dar Doukkala
83 Rue de Bab Doukkala,
Dar el Bacha, Marrakech
telephone: +212.24.383 444
facsimile: +212.24.383 445
riaddoukkala@yahoo.fr
www.dardoukkala.com

Dar L'Oussia
4 Rue Mohamed ben Messaoud, Essaouira
telephone: +212.24.783 756
facsmile: +212.24.472 777
loussia@menara.ma
www.dar-loussia.net

Dar Les Cigognes
108 Rue de Berima, Medina, Marrakech
telephone: +212.24.382 740
facsimile: +212.24.384 767
info@lescigognes.com
www.lescigognes.com

Dar Nilam
BP 1262, 28 Lotissement Tingis,
Baie de Tanger, Tangier
telephone: +212.39.301 146
facsimile: +212.39.325 595
info@darnilam.com
www.darnilam.com

Dar Nour
20 Rue Gourna, Kasbah, Tangier
telephone: +212.62.112 724
contactdarnour@yahoo.fr
www.darnour.com

Dar Rhizlane
Rue Jnane el Harti, Hivernage, Marrakech
telephone: +212.24.421 303
facsimile: +212.24.447 900
contact@darrhizlane.ma
www.dar-rhizlane.com

Dar Sabra
Douar Abbiad, La Palmeraie, Marrakech
telephone: +212.61.133 684
or +212.24.328 569
reservation@darsabra.com
www.darsabra.com

Dar Shama
Circuit de la Palmeraie,
Douar Abbiad, Marrakech
telephone: +212.24.311 350
facsimile: +212.24.308 646
contact@darshama.com
www.darshama.com

El Minzah Hotel
85 Rue de la Liberté, Tangier
telephone: +212.39.333 444
facsimile: +212.39.333 999
infos@elminzah.com
www.elminzah.com

Es Saadi Gardens + Resort
Rue Hibrahim el Mazini,
Hivernage, Marrakech
telephone: +212.24.448 811
or +212.24.447 010
facsimile: +212.24.447 644
info@essaadi.com
www.essaadi.com

Hotel Nord-Pinus Tanger
11 Rue du Riad Sultan, Kasbah, Tangier
telephone: +212.61.228 140
or +212.39.336 363
info@nord-pinus-tanger.com
www.nord-pinus-tanger.com

**Hôtel + Ryads Naoura Barrière
Marrakech**
Rue Djebel Alakhdar,
Bab Doukkala, Marrakech
telephone: +212.24.459 000
resanaoura@lucienbarriere.com
www.naoura-barriere.com

Jnane Tamsna Country Guesthouse
Douar Abbiad, La Palmeraie, Marrakech
telephone: +212.24.328 484
facsimile: +212.24.329 884
meryanne@jnane.com
www.jnane.com

Kasbah Agafay
Km 20, Route de Guemassa, Marrakech
telephone: +212.24.368 600
facsimile : +212.24.420 970
kasbahagafay@menara.ma
www.kasbahagafay.com

Kasbah du Toubkal
BP 31, Imlil, Asni, Marrakech
telephone: +212.24. 485 611
facsimile: +212.24.485 636
kasbah@discover.ltd.uk
www.kasbahdutoubkal.com

Kasbah Tamadot
BP 67, 042150 Asni, Marrakech
telephone: +44.208.600 0430
facsimile: +44.208.600 0431
enquiries@virginlimitededition.com
www.virginlimitededition.com

Ksar Char-Bagh
BP 2449, La Palmeraie, Marrakech
telephone: +212.24.329 244
facsimile: +212.24.329 214
info@ksarcharbagh.com
www.ksarcharbagh.com

Ksar Shama
telephone: +212.24.485 032
facsimile: +212.24.485 040
contact@ksarshama.com
www.ksarshama.com

L Mansion Guest Palace
Km 9, Route de Ouarzazate,
BP 6131 SYBA, Marrakech
telephone: +212.24.329 955
facsimile: +212.24.329 977
info@lmansion.com
www.lmansion.com

L'Heure Bleue Palais + Spa
2 Rue Ibn Batouta,
Bab Marrakech, Essaouira
telephone: +212.24.783 434
facsimile: +212.24.474 222
info@heure-bleue.com
www.heure-bleue.com

La Gazelle d'Or
BP 260, Taroudant
telephone: +212.28.852 039
or +212.28.852 048
facsimile: +212.28.852 737
reservations@gazelledor.com
www.gazelledor.com

La Maison Arabe
1 Derb Assehbé, Bab Doukkala, Marrakech
telephone: +212.24.387 010
facsimile: +212.24.387 221
reservation@lamaisonarabe.com
www.lamaisonarabe.com

La Maison Bleue
2 Place de L'Istiqlal, Batha, Fez
telephone: +212.35.741 843
facsimile: +212.35.740 686

La Sultana Marrakech
403 Rue de la Kasbah, Marrakech
telephone: +212.24.388 008
facsimile: +212.24.389 809
reservation@lasultanahotels.com
www.lasultanamarrakech.com

La Sultana Oualidia
Parc á Huîtres N°3, Oualidia
telephone: +212.23.366 595
facsimile: +212.23.366 594
reservation@lasultanahotels.com
www.lasultanaoualidia.com

Les Borjs de la Kasbah
200 Rue du Méchouar,
La Kasbah, Marrakech
telephone: +212.24.381 101
or +212.24.381 106
facsimile: +212.24.381 125
info@lesborjsdelakasbah.com
www.lesborjsdelakasbah.com

Les Jardins d'Inès
BP 1488, Circuit de la Palmeraie,
Marrakech
+212.24.334 200
facsimile: +212.24.334 201
info@lesjardinsdines.com
www.palmeraie-marrakech.com

Les Jardins de la Koutoubia
26 Rue de la Koutoubia, Marrakech
telephone: +212.24.388 800
facsimile: +212.24.442 222
hoteljardinkoutoubia@menara.ma
www.lesjardinsdelakoutoubia.com

Les Jardins de la Medina
21 Rue Derb Chtouka, Quartier de la
Kasbah, Marrakech
telephone: +212.24.381 851
facsimile: +212.24.385 385
info@lesjardinsdelamedina.com
www.lesjardinsdelamedina.com

Lodge K
Km 5, Route de Fez, Dartounsi, Marrakech
telephone: +212.24.328 645
or +212.60.153 924 or +212.61.337 499
facsimile: +212.60.159 264
info@lodgek.com
www.lodgek.com

Madada Mogador
5 Rue Youssef el Fassi, Essaouira
telephone: +212.24.475 512
facsimile: +212.24. 475 512
info@madada.com
www.madada.com

Maroc Lodge
BP 16, 42100 Amizmiz, Marrakech
telephone: +212.24.544 969
or +212.61.202 537
facsimile: +212.37.727 179
infos@maroc-lodge.com
www.maroc-lodge.com

Murano Resort
BP 13172, Douar Abbiad,
La Palmeraie, Marrakech
telephone: +212.24.327 000
facsimile: +212.24.328 666
marrakech@muranoresort.com
www.muranoresort.com

Ocean Vagabond
4 Boulevard Lalla Aïcha,
Angle Rue Moukawama, Essaouira
telephone: +212.24.449 222
facsimile: +212.24.474 285
hotel@oceanvagabond.com
www.oceanvagabond.com

Palais Rhoul
Route de Fez, Dartounsi,
BP 522 Principal Guéliz, Marrakech
telephone: +212.24.329 494
facsimile: +212.24.329 496
info@palais-rhoul.com
www.palais-rhoul.com

Palmeraie Golf Palace
BP 1488, Circuit de la Palmeraie,
Marrakech
telephone: +212.24.301 010
facsimile: +212.24.309 000
sales@pgp.ma or reservation@pgp.ma
www.pgpmarrakech.com

Riad 12
12 Derb Sraghnas, Dar el Bacha, Marrakech

Riad 72
72 Arset Awsel, Bab Doukkala, Marrakech

Riad des Golfs
Chemin des Français, Aghrod,
Ben Sergao, Agadir
telephone: +212.28.337 033
or +212.528.337 033
facsimile: +212.28.335 455
or +212.528.335 455
riadgolf@menara.ma
www.riaddesgolfs.com

Riad Due
2 Derb Chentouf, Riad Laarousse Medina,
Marrakech

Riad El Fenn
2 Derb Moullay Abdullah ben Hezzian,
Bab el Ksour Medina, Marrakech
telephone: +212.24.441 210
or +212.24.441 220
facsimile: +212.24.441 211
riadelfenn@menara.ma
www.riadelfenn.com

Riad El Ouarda
5 Derb Taht Sour Lakbir,
Zaouia el-Abbasia, Marrakech
telephone: +212.24.385 714
facsimile: +212.24.385 710
elouarda@yahoo.fr
www.riadelouarda.com

Riad Farnatchi
2 Derb Farnatchi, Qua'at Benahid,
Marrakech
telephone: +212.24.384 910
or +212.24.384 912
facsimile: +212.24.384 913
enquiries@riadfarnatchi.com
www.riadfarnatchi.com

directory

Riad Fes
Derb Ben Slimane, Zerbtana, Fez
telephone: +212.35.947 610
or +212.35.741 206
facsimile: +212.35.741 143
contact@riadfes.com
www.riadfes.com

Riad Ibn Battouta
9 Derb Lalla Mina,
Avenue Allal el Fassi, Batha, Fez
telephone: +212.35.637 191
or +212.71.654 217
facsimile: +212.35.637 190
contact@riadibnbattouta.com
www.riadibnbattouta.com

Riad Laaroussa
3 Derb Bechara, Fez
telephone: +212.74.187 639
contact@riad-laaroussa.com
www.riad-laaroussa.com

Riad Maison Bleue
33 Derb el Mitter, Talaâ Kbira, Fez
telephone: +212.35.741 839
facsimile: +212.35.741 6873
resa@maisonbleue.com
www.maisonbleue.com

Riad Meriem
97 Derb el Cadi, Azbezt, Marrakech
telephone: +212.24.387 731
facsimile: +212.24.377 762
contact@riadmeriem.com
www.riadmeriem.com

Riad Myra
13 Rue Salaj, Batha, Fez
telephone: +212.35.740 000
facsimile: +212.35.638 282
info@riadmyra.com
www.riadmyra.com

Riyad El Mezouar
28 Derb el Hamman,
Issebtinne, Marrakech
telephone: +212.24.380 949
facsimile: +212.24.380 943
info@mezouar.com
www.mezouar.com

Sofitel Palais Jamaï
Bab Guissa, Fez
telephone: +212.35.634 331
facsimile: +212.35.635 096
H2141@accor.com
www.sofitel.com

The Angsana Riads Collection
telephone: +212.24.421 979
facsimile: +212.24.421 372
reservations-marrakech@angsana.com
www.angsana.com

UOVO Riads
telephone: +212.24.387 629
facsimile: +212.24.384 718
info@uovo.com
www.uovo.com

Villa des Orangers
6 Rue Sidi Mimoun, Marrakech
telephone: +212.24.384 638
facsimile: +212.24.385 123
message@villadesorangers.com
www.villadesorangers.com

Villa Mandarine
19 Rue Ouled Bousbaa, Souissi, Rabat
telephone: +212.37.752 077
facsimile: +212.37.632 309
reservation@villamandarine.com
www.villamandarine.com

Villa Maroc
10 Rue Abdellah ben Yassine, Essaouira
telephone: +212.24.473 147
or +212.24.476 147
facsimile: +212.24.475 806
hotel@villa-maroc.com
www.villa-maroc.com

AIRLINE

Royal Air Maroc
telephone: +212.22.489 797
www.royalairmaroc.com

MADE IN MOROCCO

Al Nafiss
Rez-de-Chaussée, Mega Mall
Km 4, 2 Avenue Imam Malik,
Route des Zaërs, Souissi, Rabat
telephone: +212.37.758 275

Amazonite
94 Boulevard el Mansour Eddahbi,
Guéliz, Marrakech
telephone: +212.44.449 926

Amentet
Rue el Khabbazine, Essaouira
telephone: +212.72.847 789
www.amentet.ma
contact@amentet.ma

Ben Rahal
28 Rue de la Liberté,
Avenue Mohammed V, Guéliz, Marrakech
telephone: +212.44.433 273
nicolemonteils@menara.ma

Bijouterie Ethnique
5 El Konouse, Essaouira
telephone: +212.24.473 920

Brigitte Perkins' Fondouk
Near Djemaa el-Fna Square, Medina,
Marrakech
telephone (by appointment only):
+212.44.377 416

Centre Artisanal de Fès
31 Avenue Allal ben Abdellah,
Ville Nouvelle, Fez
telephone: +212.55.625 654

Chama
First floor, Mega Mall
Km 4, 2 Avenue Imam Malik,
Route des Zaërs, Souissi, Rabat
telephone: +212.37.632 149
facsimile: +212.37.632 149
www.chama-boutique.com

Coopérative Artisanale des Marqueteurs
6 Rue Khalid ben Oualid, Essaouira
telephone: +212.24.475 676

Elahri
181 Souk el Gouz, Essaouira
telephone: +212.24.472 877

Galerie Aïda
2 Rue de la Skala, Essaouira
telephone: +212.04.476 290
facsimile: +212.04.476 324

Galerie Jama
22 Rue Ibnou Rochd, Essaouira
telephone: +212.44.785 897
galeriejama@hotmail.fr

Galerie la Kasbah
4 Rue de Tétouan, Essaouira
telephone: +212.44.473 682

Galerie Tindouf + Bazar Tindouf
72 Rue de la Liberté, Tangier
telephone: +212.39.938 892

IB (Ibrahim Al Qurashi)
Rez-de-Chaussée, Mega Mall
Km 4, 2 Avenue Imam Malik,
Route des Zaërs, Souissi, Rabat
telephone: +212.37.750 605
alqurashi-tanger@hotmail.com

La Cocema
Aïn Kadous, Fez
telephone: +212.35.645 125
facsimile: +212.35.645 760

Le Bois de Thuya
Centre Artisanal d'Essaouira
118 Rue Sidi Med ben Abdellah,
BP 141, Essaouira
telephone: +212.44.474 082
facsimile: +212.44.475 837
boisdethuya@hotmail.com

Le Trésor Berbère
66 Bis, Zqaq Lahjar, Talaâ Sghira, Fez
telephone: +212.55.740 153

Maison de Broderie
2 Bis, Derb Blida, Fez
telephone: +212.35.636 546

Majid
66 Rue les Almouhads, Tangier
telephone: +212.39.938 892
www.boutiquemajid.com
majid@boutiquemajid.com

Mega Mall
Km 4, 2 Avenue Imam Malik,
Route des Zaërs, Souissi, Rabat
telephone: +212.37.757 575
www.megamall.ma

Mounir's
First floor, Mega Mall
Km 4, 2 Avenue Imam Malik,
Route des Zaërs, Souissi, Rabat
telephone: +212.37.631 313
Mounirs7@yahoo.com

Mustapha Blaoui
142 Rue de Bab Doukkala, Medina,
Marrakech
telephone: +212.44.385 240
tresordesnomades@hotmail.com

Nejjarine Museum of Wood + Carpentry
Place Nejjarine, Medina, Fez
telephone: +212.55.740 580

Palais de Fès
15 Mokhfia, R'cif, Fez
telephone: +212.55.761 590
facsimile: +212.55.649 856
dartazi@menara.ma
www.palaisdefes.com

Parfumerie Madini
5 Boulevard Pasteur, Villa Nouvelle, Tangier
telephone: +212.39.934 388

14 Rue Sébou, Medina, Tangier
telephone: +212.39.375 038

Tazra
45 Rue Attarine, Essaouira
telephone: +212.44.474 920

DINING

Adamo
44 Bis, Rue Tarik idn Ziad,
Guéliz, Marrakech
telephone: +212.24.439 419
contact@traiteur-adamo.com
www.traiteur-adamo.com

Aïlen
Sofitel Essaouira Medina Beach & Spa
Avenue Mohammed V, Essaouira
telephone: +212.24.479 000
facsimile: +212.24.479 080
H2967@accor.com
www.sofitel.com

Crystal Lounge
Boulevard Mohammed VI,
Quartier de l'Agdal, Marrakech
telephone: +212.24.388 400
www.pachamarrakech.com

Dar Inès
Les Jardins d'Inès
BP 1488, Circuit de la Palmeraie,
Marrakech
telephone: +212 24 33 42 00
www.palmeraie-marrakech.com

Darna, la Maison Communautaire des Femmes
Place du Grand Socco, Tangier
telephone: +212.39.947 065

Grand Café de la Poste
Angle de Avenue Mohammed V at
Boulevard el Mansour, Guéliz, Marrakech
telephone: +212.24.433 038
facsimile: +212.24.434 224
resa@grandcafedelaposte.com
www.grandcafedelaposte.com

Hôtel Club Le Mirage
BP 2198, Les Grottes d'Hercule, Tangier
telephone: +212.39.333 332
or +212.39.333 331
facsimile: +212.39.333 492
lemirage@lemirage-tanger.com
www.lemirage-tanger.com

L'Elézir
1 Rue d'Agadir, Essaouira
telephone: +212.24.472 103

La Cour des Lions
Es Saadi Gardens & Resort
Rue Ibrahim el Mazini,
Hivernage, Marrakech
telephone: +212.24.448 811
or +212.24.337 400
facsimile: +212.24.447 644
info@essaadi.com
www.essaadi.com

La Giralda
5 Boulevard Pasteur, Ville Nouvelle, Tangier

La Maison du Gourmet
159 Rue Taha Houcine,
Gauthier, Casablanca
telephone: +212.22.484 846
facsimile: +212.22.484 845
www.lamaisondugourmet.ma

La Scala
Rue de l'Oued Souss,
Complexe Tamlelt, Agadir
telephone: +212.28.846 773
scalagadir@menara.ma

Le Comptoir Paris Marrakech
Avenue Ecchouada, Hivernage, Marrakech
telephone: +212.24.437 702
or +212.24.437 710
facsimile: +212.24.447 747

Le Grand Comptoir
279 Boulevard Mohammed V, Rabat
telephone: +212.37.201 514
facsimile: +212.37.707 322
yann@lesenfantsterribles.com
www.legrandcomptoir.ma

Le Kiotori
12 Rue Ahmed Chaouki, Fez
telephone: +212.35.651 700

Le Patio
28 Bis, Rue Moulay Rachid, Essaouira
telephone: +212.24.474 166

Le Restaurant Gastronomique
Es Saadi Gardens & Resort
Rue Ibrahim el Mazini,
Hivernage, Marrakech
telephone: +212.24.448 811
or +212.24.337 400
facsimile: +212.24.447 644
info@essaadi.com
www.essaadi.com

Le Tobsil
22 Derb Moulay Abdallah ben Hessaien,
R'mila, Bab Ksour, Medina, Marrakech
telephone: +212.24.444 052

Le Touggana
Km 9, Route de l'Ourika, Marrakech
telephone: +212.24.376 276

Mezzanine
17 Kasbat Chams, Ville Nouvelle, Fez
Telephone: +212.11.078 336

Ostréa II
Parc à Huîtres N°007, Oualidia
telephone: +212.23.366 451
ostreadirection@menara.ma
www.ilove-casablanca.com/ostrea

Pâtisserie La Española
97 Rue de la Liberté, Tangier
telephone: +212.39.340 188

Saveurs de Poissons
Rue du Portugal, Tangier
telephone: +212.39.336 326

Sens
27th floor, Kenzi Tower Hotel
Twin Center, Boulevard Zerktouni,
Casablanca
telephone: +212.22.958 989
facsimile: +212.22.958 090
www.kenzi-hotels.com

The Thai Restaurant
Amanjena
Km 12, Route de Ouarzazate, Marrakech
telephone: +212.24.403 353
facsimile: +212.24.403 477
amanjena@amanresorts.com
www.amanresorts.com

NIGHTLIFE

555
Boulevard Mohammed VI, Tangier
telephone: +212.39. 944 950

Bò-Zin
3, 5 Km Route de l'Ourika,
Douar Lahna, Marrakech
telephone: +212.24.388 012
facsimile: +212.24.388 014
contact@bo-zin.com
www.bo-zin.com

Café Clock
7 Derb el Magana, Talaâ Kbira, Fez
telephone: +212.35.637 855
or +212.61.183 264

Café du Cinema Rif
Place du 9 Avril, Grand Socco, Tangier

Café du Livre
44 Rue Tarik Ibn Ziad, Guéliz, Marrakech
telephone: +212.24.432 149
www.cafedulivre.com

Café Hafa
La Falaise, Tangier

Café M
Hotel Hyatt Regency, Casablanca
Place des Nations Unies, Casablanca
telephone: +212.22.431 234
facsimile: +212.22.431 334

Caid's Piano Bar
El Minzah Hotel
85 Rue de la Liberté, Tangier
telephone: +212.39.935 885

Couleur Pourpre
7 Rue Ibn Zeidoune, Guéliz, Marrakech
telephone: +212.61.246 260
or +212.24.437 302

Dar Soukkar
Km 3, 8 Route de l'Ourika, Marrakech
telephone: +212.24.375 535
or +212.24.375 538
facsimile: +212.24.375 536
info@darsoukkar.com
www.darsoukkar.com

Le Bistrot du Pietri
Le Pietri Urban Hotel
4 Rue Tobrouk, Rabat
telephone: +212.37.707 820
facsimile: +212.37.708 235
www.lepietri.com

Le Blokk
Route de Casablanca,
Circuit de la Palmeraie, Marrakech
contact@leblokk.com
www.leblokk.com

Le Palace
Palmeraie Golf Palace
Circuit de la Palmeraie, Marrakech
telephone: +212.24.301 010
www.pgpmarrakech.com

Le Relais Lounge
Relais de Paris
Complexe Dawliz, 42 Rue de Hollande,
Tangier
telephone: +212.39.331 819

Le ThéâtrO
Es Saadi Gardens & Resort
Rue Ibrahim el Mazini,
Hivernage, Marrakech
telephone: +212.24.448 811
or +212.24.337 400
facsimile: +212.24.447 644
info@essaadi.com
www.essaadi.com

Les Fils du Détroit
Place de la Kasbah, Tangier

Morocco Palace
Rue du Prince Moulay Abdallah, Tangier
telephone: +212.39.935 564

Pacha Marrakech
Boulevard Mohammed VI,
Quartier de l'Agdal, Marrakech
telephone: +212.24.388 400
facsimile: +212.24.375 444
www.pachamarrakech.com

SixPM
Hotel Hyatt Regency, Casablanca
Place des Nations Unies, Casablanca
telephone: +212.22.666 666

So
Hotel Sofitel Agadir
Baie des Palmiers, Commune de
Bensergao, Agadir
telephone: +212.28.820 088
www.sofitel.com

Tangerin's
1 Rue Magellan, Tangier
telephone: +212.39.935 337

HAMMAM + SPA

Cinq Mondes
18 Rue Ibrahim Ennakhai,
Maârif, Casablanca
telephone: +212.22.996 609
or +212.22.996 608
www.cinqmondes.com

Coopérative Tamounte
Village d'Imi'Tlit, Route d'Adagir, Essaouira
telephone: +212.24.476 092

Coopérative Tiguemine
Km 15, Route de Marrakech, Essaouira
telephone: +212.24.790 110

El Minzah Wellness Health Club
El Minzah Hotel
85 Rue de la Liberté, Tangier
telephone: +212.39.333 444
www.elminzah.com

Hammam Lalla Mira
Hotel Lalla Mira Essaouira
14 Rue d'Algérie, Essaouira
telephone: +212.24.475 046
facsimile: +212.24.475 850
info@lallamira.net
www.lallamira.net

Hotel Rif + Spa Tangier
152 Avenue Mohammed VI, Tangier
telephone: +212.39.349 305
www.hotelatlas.com

La Roseraie Health Centre
Domaine de la Roseraie
Km 60, Route de Taroudant, Val
d'Ouirgane, BP 769, Marrakech
telephone: +212.24.439 128
facsimile: +212.24.439 130
bookings@laroseraie.ma
www.laroseraiehotel.com

Palmeraie Spa
Palmeraie Golf Palace
BP 1488, Circuit de la Palmeraie,
Marrakech
telephone: +212.24.301 010
facsimile: +212.24.306 306
spa@pgp.ma
www.palmeraie-marrakech.com

Sens de Marrakech
18 Zone Industriel Sidi Ghanem,
Marrakech
telephone: +212.24.336 991
facsimile: +212.24.336 561
contact@lessensdemarrakech.com
www.lessensdemarrakech.com

Serenity Day Spa
Rue Adolpho Fessere, California, Tangier
telephone: +212.39.374 347
facsimile: +212.39.372 827
serenity_day_spa@yahoo.fr

Sofitel Essaouira Medina Beach + Spa
Avenue Mohammed V, Essaouira
telephone: +212.24.479 000
facsimile: +212.24.479 080
H2967@accor.com
www.sofitel.com

SPA
Sofitel Palais Jamaï
Bab Guissa, Fez
telephone: +212.35.634 331
www.sofitel.com

U Spa
Hôtel & Ryads Naoura Barrière Marrakech
Rue Djebel Alakhdar, Bab Doukkala,
Marrakech
telephone: +212.24.459 000
www.naoura-barriere.com

GOLF

Club Méditerranée Dunes Golf Course
Chemin Oued Souss, Agadir
telephone: +212.28.834 690
agacchefo4@clubmed.com

Golf du Soleil
Chemin des Dunes, Agadir
telephone: +212.28.337 329
facsimilie: +212.28.337 333
resagolf@tikidahotels.co.ma
www.golfdusoleil.com

Palmeraie Golf Club
Palmeraie Golf Palace & Resort
Les Jardins de la Palmeraie,
Circuit de la Palmeraie, Marrakech
telephone: +212.24.368 766
facsimile: +212.24.306 366
golf@pgp.ma
www.palmeraie-golf-club.com

Royal Club de Tanger
Route de Boubana, Tangier
telephone: +212.39.938 925
golftanger@menara.com

Royal Golf Club de Marrakech
Ancienne Route de Ouarzazate, Marrakech
telephone: +212.24.444 341
facsimile: +212.24.430 084
royal_golf@iam.net.ma

directory

Royal Golf d'Agadir
Km 12, Route d'Aït Melloul, Agadir
telephone: +212.48.248 551
facsimile: +212.48.234 702
royalgolfagadir@menara.ma

Royal Golf d'Amelkis
Km 12, Route de Ouarzazate, Marrakech
telephone: +212.24.449 284
facsimile: +212.24.403 046
hcoamelkis@menara.ma

Royal Golf d'Anfa
Hippodrome d'Anfa, Casablanca
telephone: +212.22.365 355
or +212.22.361 026
facsimile: +212.22.393 374
royalgolfanfa@menara.ma

Royal Golf d'El Jadida
Km 7, Route de Casablanca, El Jadida
telephone: +212.23.352 251
www.golf-maroc.com

Royal Golf Dar Es Salam
Km 9, Avenue Imam Malik, Souissi, Rabat
telephone: +212.37.755 864
or +212.37.755 865
facsimile: +212.37.757 671
golfdaressalam@menara.ma
www.royalgolfdaressalam.com

Royal Golf de Cabo Negro
BP 696 G, Tétouan
telephone: +212.39.978 305

Royal Golf de Fès
Km 17, Route d'Imouzzer, Fez
telephone: +212.35.665 210 +212.35.665 212
fesgolf@menara.ma

Royal Golf de Meknès
J'nane al Bahraouia, Ville Ancienne,
Meknès
telephone: +212.35.530 753
facsimile: +212.35.557 934
rgm@royalgolfmeknes.com
www.royalgolfmeknes.com

BOUTIQUES + GALLERIES

Akbar Delights
45 Place Bab Fteuh, Medina, Marrakech
telephone: +212.71.661 307

Akkal
322 Zone Industriel Sidi Ghanem,
Route de Safi, Marrakech
telephone: +212.24.335 938
facsimile: +212.24.335 941
akkal@menara.ma
www.akkal.net

Amira Bougies
277 Zone Industriel Sidi Ghanem,
BP 7227, Sidi Abbad, Marrakech
telephone: +212.24.336 247
facsimile: +212.24.335 601
amirabougies@menara.com
www.amirabougies.com

Angie
391 Zone Industriel Sidi Ghanem,
Route de Safi, Marrakech
telephone: +212.24.336 791
facsimile: +212.24.336 794
angielinge@yahoo.fr

Cinema Rif
Place du 9 Avril, Grand Socco, Tangier
telephone: +212.39.934 683
www.cinemathequedetanger.com

El Tapisero
61 Boulevard Yacoub el Mansour,
Charf, Tangier
telephone: +212.39.945 681
facsimile: +212.39.945 678
contact@eltapisero.com
www.eltapisero.com

Galerie d'Art Damgaard
Avenue Oqba Nafiaa, Essaouira
telephone: +212.24.784 446
facsimile: +212.24.475 857
www.galeriedamgaard.com

Galerie Dar D'Art
6 Rue Khalil Matrane, Tangier
telephone: +212.39.375 707
dardart.galerie@gmail.com

Galerie Mohammed Drissi
52 Rue d'Angleterre, Tangier
telephone: +212.39.338 436
or +212.39.331 336

Galerie Noir sur Blanc
48 Rue de Yougoslavie, Guéliz, Marrakech
telephone: +212.24.422 416
noirsurblanc@menara.ma

Galerie Photo 127
127 Avenue Mohammed V,
Guéliz, Marrakech
telephone: +212.24.432 667
facsimile: +212.24.432 464
Galerie127mohammedV@hotmail.fr

Galerie Rê
Résidence Al Andalous III,
Angle Rue de la Mosquée at
Rue Ibn Toumert, N° 3, Guéliz, Marrakech
telephone: +212.24.432 258
facsimile: +212.24.432 264
galeriere@gmail.com
www.galeriere.com

Galerie Venise Cadre
25 Boulevard Moulay Rachid, Casablanca
telephone: +212.22.366 076
venise_cadre@menara.ma

Intensité Nomade
139 Avenue Mohammed V,
Guéliz, Marrakech
telephone: +212.24.431 333
facsimile: +212.24.447 792

Le Taros
Place Moulay Hassan, Essaouira
telephone: +212.24.476 407
facsimile: +212.24.476 408
alainfillaud@yahoo.fr
www.taroscafe.com

Librairie d'Art Miloudi Nouiga
Kasbah des Oudaias, Rue Jemaa, Rabat
telephone: +212.37.201 175
www.nouigartgalerie.com

Librairie des Colonnes
54 Boulevard Pasteur,
Ville Nouvelle, Tangier
telephone: +212.39.936 955

Light Gallery
2 Derb Chtouka, Kasbah, Marrakech
telephone: +212.24.384 565

Made in M
246 Talaâ Kbira, Medina, Fez
telephone: +212.11.054 863

Matisse Art Gallery
61 Rue de Yougoslavie, N° 43 Passage
Ghandouri, Guéliz, Marrakech
telephone: +212.24.448 326
matisse_art_gall@hotmail.com or
matisse_art_gallery@menara.ma
www.matisse-art-gallery.com

Michèle Baconnier
6 Rue du Vieux Marrackhi, Guéliz,
Marrakech
+212.24.449 178
michelebaconnier@wanadoo.fr
www.ilove-marrakech.com/baconnier

Orientalist Art Gallery
35 Rue Abdelaziz Boutaleb,
Ville Nouvelle, Fez
telephone: +212.35.944 545
orientalistartgallery@yahoo.com

Scènes de Lin
70 Rue de la Liberté, Guéliz, Marrakech
telephone: +212.24.436 108
facsimile: +212.24.436 109
bleumajorelle@yahoo.fr

TM Design
Rue el Arrak, QI Menara, Marrakech
telephone: +212.24.496 593
thierrymatalon@yahoo.fr
www.thierrymatalon.com

Urban Living
Rond-Point des Sports,
Rue du Point du Jour, Casablanca
telephone: +212.22.474 933
ybconcept@hotmail.com

**Villa des Arts de Casablanca,
Fondation ONA**
30 Boulevard Brahim Roudani, Casablanca
telephone: +212.22.295 087
or +212.22.295 094
facsimile: +212.22.278 607
www.fondationona.com

Villa des Arts de Rabat, Fondation ONA
10 Rue Beni Mellal,
Angle Avenue Mohamed V, Hassan, Rabat
telephone: +212.37.668 579
or +212.37.668 582
facsimile: +212.37.766 047
www.fondationona.com

Yahya Création
61 Rue de Yougoslavie, Magazin 49–50,
Passage Ghandouri, Guéliz, Marrakech
telephone: +212.24.422 776
+212.24.431 217
www.yahyacreation.com

Youbi Design
66 Avenue Ibnou Houryia, Rue Liberia,
Zouhour, Route de Sefrou, Fez
telephone: +212.61.521 156

VIEWS

Café de France
Djemaa el-Fna Square, near Derb Zaari,
Marrakech

Domaine de la Roseraie
Km 60, Route de Taroudant,
Val d'Ouirgane, BP 769, Marrakech
telephone: +212.24.439 128
facsimile: +212.24.439 130
bookings@laroseraie.ma
www.laroseraiehotel.com

French Consulate, Morocco
1 Rue Ibn Khaldoun,
Dar Moulay Ali, Marrakech
telephone: +212.44.388 200
facsimile: +212.44.388 233
www.consulfrance-marrakech.org

Hotel Kenzi Saghro
BP 46–45, 800, Tineghir
telephone: +212.24.834 181
facsimile: +212.24.834 352
info@kenzi-hotels.com
www.kenzi-hotels.com

Ksar Massa
BP 222, Sidi, R'bat 80450, Massa
telephone: +212.61.280 319
facsimile: +212.48.255 772
ksarmassa@ksarmassa.com
www.ksarmassa.com

Les Camps Nomades
43 Bis, Kawkab Centre, Marrakech
telephone: +212.24.434 808
facsimile: +212.24.434 761
www.camps-nomades.com

Maison d'Hôtes Monique Chevassus
35 Ben Marzouk, Medina, Asilah
telephone: +212.68.598 007

Majorelle Gardens
Avenue Yacoub el Mansour,
Ville Nouvelle, Marrakech
telephone: +212.24.301 852
www.jardinmajorelle.com

Oukaimeden Ski Resort
telephone: +212.22.203 798

Ouzoud Falls
Tanaghmeilt, Azilal, 150 km (93 miles)
northeast of Marrakech

Sidi Bourhaba Lake
Natural Reserve Sidi Bou Ghaba
BP 133, Réserve de Sidi Bou Ghaba,
Mehdiya, Kénitra
telephone: +212.37.747 209
facsimile: +212.37.747 493
spana@spana.org.ma
www.spana.org.ma

UNESCO HERITAGE SITES

Bahia Palace
Rue de la Bahia, Zitoun el-Jadid,
Medina, Marrakech

Dar Jamaï Museum
Sahat el Hadim, Meknès

El-Badi Palace
Place des Ferblantiers, Marrakech

Koutoubia Mosque
Avenue Mohammed V, Marrakech

Medersa Bou Inania
Sahat el Hadim, Meknès

Qaraouiyyine Mosque
Place Seffarine, Medina, Fez

Saadian Tombs
Rue de la Kasbah, Kasbah, Marrakech